Becoming a Clinical Psychologist

Becoming a Clinical Psychologist

Personal Stories of Doctoral Training

Edited by Danielle Knafo, Robert Keisner, and Silvia Fiammenghi

ROWMAN & LITTLEFIELD
Lanham • Boulder • New York • London

Published by Rowman & Littlefield
A wholly owned subsidiary of The Rowman & Littlefield Publishing Group, Inc.
4501 Forbes Boulevard, Suite 200, Lanham, Maryland 20706
www.rowman.com

Unit A, Whitacre Mews, 26-34 Stannary Street, London SE11 4AB

British Library Cataloguing in Publication Information Available

Library of Congress Cataloging-in-Publication Data

Becoming a clinical psychologist : personal stories of doctoral training / edited by Danielle Knafo, Robert Keisner and Silvia Fiammenghi.
p.;cm.
Includes bibliographical references and index.
ISBN 978-1-4422-3992-0 (cloth : alk. paper) -- ISBN 978-1-4422-3994-4 (electronic)
[DNLM: 1. Psychology, Clinical--education--Personal Narratives. 2. Education, Graduate--Personal Narratives. WM 18]
I. Knafo, Danielle, editor. II. Keisner, Robert H., editor. III. Fiammenghi, Silvia, editor.
RC467.7
616.890071--dc23
2010037457

∞™ The paper used in this publication meets the minimum requirements of American National Standard for Information Sciences Permanence of Paper for Printed Library Materials, ANSI/NISO Z39.48-1992.

Printed in the United States of America

Contents

Acknowledgments

This book is the result of many peoples' efforts and many voices. The idea originated with Silvia's suggestion to bring together students' papers that inform us about graduate training in clinical psychology. It grew to be much more than that. We are all grateful to the students and graduates of our program for writing beautifully and passionately, allowing us to enter the space of their diverse but common journeys in becoming professional psychologists. We owe thanks to the Long Island University Research Grant for their financial support. We are especially grateful to Maryellen Lo Bosco for the long hours she put into reading and editing this book as well as her excellent suggestions.

Introduction

Danielle Knafo, Robert Keisner, and Silvia Fiammenghi

In the ancient Greek religion, Athena, the goddess of truth, sprang from the head of her father Zeus full-grown and wise. If only we could all attain wisdom so easily! In reality the road to insight is a long one, a struggle against ignorance and bias and a painful reckoning with issues of the heart. Those who are considering an investment of several years and thousands of dollars in clinical psychology doctoral training can easily find information on programs and associated costs. But all such objective information begs the most important question: What is it like to undergo the training? What does it feel like? What conflicts does it raise? How are students affected and sometimes transformed by the relationships they develop with peers, faculty, supervisors, and patients? How does graduate psychology training affect one's inner life? What does it add, and what does it take away? This book aims to answer those questions.

Clinical psychology, though a popular career choice, is a competitive and demanding field. Working in hospitals, schools, mental health clinics, correctional facilities, veterans' organizations, universities, research settings, and businesses, we clinical psychologists hold an honored and privileged place in society, and today we are needed more than ever to help people in psychic distress that is both personal and existential. We deal with pain of the most intense and private kind. Aspiring clinical psychologists hope to join this branch of psychology devoted to the understanding and treatment of mental health problems through research, clinical practice, and intervention.

Ours is a creative profession that offers multiple opportunities. While fewer than 6 percent of American adults will experience severe mental illness in a given year, more than a quarter will be diagnosed with a mental disorder in that same time period (Rosenberg, 2012). Meanwhile, according to the

DSM-5, more than half of people in the United States will experience a mental disorder in their lifetime (Rosenberg, 2012). Not surprisingly, the number of therapists has risen to meet the demand. According to the US Bureau of Labor Statistics (2012), employment of psychologists is expected to grow by 22 percent, from 174,000 in 2010 to 211,600 in 2020.

These projections should be heartening to individuals who are considering a career in clinical psychology. The more important issue, however, is whether the field is the right one for them. Aspiring psychologists come to the profession for any number of reasons, including the desire to understand human behavior, help others, and "fix" themselves or their family members. Indeed, Stevanovic and Rupert (2009) found a positive work-to-family spillover for professional psychologists, which they identify as "family enhancers." Their sample of professional psychologists reported a sense of personal accomplishment at work leading to greater family support and life satisfaction. Guy (1987) named the main satisfactions of the profession as independence, financial reward, variety, recognition and prestige, intellectual stimulation, emotional growth and satisfaction, and personal enrichment and fulfillment. Personality traits of those drawn to the profession include curiosity, empathy, a willingness to listen to others, emotional insight, altruism, and a tolerance of ambiguity, to name a few. Two of the less than stellar motivators for entering the profession, according to Guy (1987), include a need to be loved and a desire for power.

Regardless of their motivations, neophytes will experience highs and lows during their graduate training years, as they undergo significant transformations in their beliefs, values, and perspectives. These changes will affect the candidates' day-to-day relationships and activities and add additional stress to their lives as they manage multiple responsibilities during training. Given the challenges of training, many students seek their own therapy during this period. McWilliams (2004) pointed out that for psychotherapists to be "prepared" to do the work of psychotherapy, they should know what it is like to be on the other side of the therapeutic relationship. Phillips (2010), too, wrote of the important influence of a student's personal therapy on her development as a psychotherapist. Diguini, Jones, and Camic (2013) argued that,

> Since student-therapists are acquiring skills to work in clinical practice, having the opportunity to learn from an experienced therapist as a role model and gaining the experience of being in the client's chair is particularly relevant to them. Equally, because students are going through the process of becoming a therapist, having a space to reflect on the development of their professional identity appears timely. Student therapists can also benefit from using personal therapy as a means for self-care. (p. 214)

Some of the authors of these chapters write about their own wise decision to pursue therapy during training, and all offer compelling first-person narratives of their experiences as students. This volume covers three key elements of training—academic, clinical, and personal. The material is arranged thematically in three sections: (a) Beginner's Mind: First Experiences Conducting Therapy; (b) Navigating the Personal and Professional during Doctoral Training; and (c) Outside the Norm: Diversity in Training and Treatment. The personal element includes descriptions of relationships that these doctoral students shared with those both inside and outside the program and the effects of their training on self-identity and diversity awareness. *Becoming a Clinical Psychologist* includes twelve chapters, with some based on dissertation research and others focused on clinical encounters. The authors themselves reflect the diversity found in today's clinical psychology doctoral students.

The authors all attended the Clinical Psychology Doctoral Program at Long Island University's C. W. Post Campus. Our program shares the features of other APA-approved doctoral programs across the United States, but what is distinctive about our approach is a mission to train students to serve the underserved. We accomplish this mission in a variety of ways, first, by offering concentrations in serious mental illness, family violence, and applied child work. Second, we incorporate awareness of diversity (sexual and multicultural) in students' training. Finally, our program trains students in both psychodynamic and CBT approaches.

Our program also includes demanding coursework in basic knowledge areas: cognition, perception, social psychology, developmental psychology, and the biological basis of behavior. In addition, our students receive instruction in psychopathology, multicultural psychology, psychological assessment, therapeutic approaches, research and statistics, and ethics. Students also complete the requirements for a doctoral dissertation and clinical competency reviews. At the same time, they compete for practicum and internship slots while they demonstrate proficiencies as researchers, consultants, and supervisors.

The chapters in this book are very personal stories. Two of the editors (Danielle Knafo and Robert Keisner) have been involved with the authors of the chapters as instructors, clinical supervisors, dissertation chairpersons, and mentors. The third editor (Silvia Fiammenghi) is a recent graduate of the program and an author of one of the chapters. In addition to giving their own perspectives, some contributors share additional stories of doctoral candidates who were interviewed. The tales are told from the inside and offer readers a palpable sense of what it is like to begin and end the training journey. The stories recognize both individual perspectives and group identities and provide much insight into the ways students cope with the pressures of training.

Eschewing a dogmatic approach to healing, *Becoming a Clinical Psychologist* discusses psychodynamic, cognitive-behavioral, and dialectical behavioral approaches to therapy while addressing issues of race, gender, and sexual orientation. The book reflects current practice and applications, since some chapters make use of qualitative research (Wertz, 2011), while others address self-awareness, self-care (Bamonti et al., 2014), professional-identity development, and the role of multiculturalism on either side of the consulting relationship.

The authors also shed light on struggling with the "anxiety of influence" (Bloom, 1973) and the guilt that beginning therapists feel; the special relational experiences that "partnered" students have; the ways in which sexual-minority students "come out"; what it is like to be more culturally knowledgeable and sensitive than one's instructors and supervisors, and the challenges of juggling the student, therapist and partner roles while in training (Dearing, Maddux, and Tangney, 2005). Readers will discover how a Black, female student became comfortable with psychoanalytic thinking (Altman, 2004; Leary, 2012) and what a group of male students endured when they were exposed to the literature on sexual violence against women in a classroom where they were the minority.

Since first-person accounts of training are rare in psychology literature, the "heads-up" that this volume offers will be especially helpful to those who are thinking about entering the field. The material in *Becoming a Clinical Psychologist* will offer them—along with those already committed to clinical psychology training—access to common experiences, so that they can better anticipate what they might face. Those already in a doctoral program will find the book useful in helping them develop a deeper self-awareness about their own process and guide them in personal and professional decision-making. We believe the book will also be illuminating for faculty, supervisors, administrators, and program planners. Finally, seasoned clinicians will find an opportunity to reflect on the many ways in which their years of training impacted them as people and shaped them as professionals.

The first section of this volume begins with Dustin Kahoud's "Personal and Professional Integration in a Dual-Oriented Doctoral Program," which discusses how his training became a crucible in which he was finally able to fully confront his own feelings of "splitness" that haunted other parts of his life. Kahoud narrates his personal story of attempting to free himself from his dependence on his parents and tells how he came to realize a vocation in psychology after he entered therapy for the first time. Kahoud also became more aware of his own dualism in his tendency to strictly categorize the world, labeling everything as good or bad, desirable or undesirable. A key moment in his clinical training occurred when he volunteered to switch to a CBT supervisor, although he preferred to study under a psychodynamic mentor. At the same time, he began psychoanalysis with a new therapist and soon uncovered the origin of his own duality and obsession with fixed categories. Kahoud was able to use his insights to let go of the idea that he had to align himself with one "side" of therapy and was able to use an integrative approach in treating his first clients according to what they needed and what would be most helpful in their healing.

Adi Avivi's "Conducting Therapy for the First Time," which follows, addresses how it feels the first time a novice assumes the role of therapist. The author describes her clinical work during the first year of practicum training, in which she saw an eight-year-old boy diagnosed with Asperger's syndrome and a woman who had survived domestic violence. At the same time, Avivi entered psychotherapy. She speaks about "three places of therapy and learning"—two with her own clients and one in which she was the client—and how these experiences mutually influenced one another. In all three milieus, with the help of her therapist and a wise and caring supervisor, Avivi learned about herself as well as others.

The third chapter in this section, written by Benjamin Gottesman, is titled "Guilt in the Beginning Therapist: Etiology and Impact on Treatment." Clinical psychology students confront numerous personal emotions when faced with the daunting task of delivering therapy. For this author, guilt was the most powerful emotion that arose, and it was induced by a variety of fears, ranging from making an error during treatment to terminating the therapeutic relationship with a client at the end of the training year. Gottesman explains that his clients had their own reactions to his guilt. In his chapter he outlines the ideas of Freud and Klein on the origins of guilt and then applies those ideas to understanding the guilt often triggered in graduate students in clinical psychology.

In the fourth chapter in this section, "The Novice in the Therapist's Chair," Shoshana Lawrence also tackles the novice's experience of providing therapy for the first time. She compares her initial feelings about her new role to those she felt as a child, playing dress-up in her mother's closet. Her first patient had already seen a half-dozen neophyte clinicians who had moved on in their training, each after a year. The patient was twice Lawrence's age and had experienced a great deal of trauma. The intensity of these early experiences as a therapist moved Lawrence to conduct her doctoral research on novice clinicians. This essay explores how new therapists cope with narcissistic vulnerability as they navigate the arduous process of becoming a clinician and creating a therapeutic identity.

Part II of this volume, on juggling personal and professional lives, begins with "Clinical Psychology Training and Romance: For Better or for Worse?" by Silvia Fiammenghi. The author's move from Italy to the United States with her husband to pursue clinical doctoral training put a strain on her marriage. Difficult clinical placements, financial worries, demanding academic requirements, lack of leisure time, and the personal changes she experienced in training created an emotional storm in her relationship that destroyed old dynamics and created new ones. Her personal experiences inspired her to pursue a related line of inquiry for her dissertation, in which she examined the experiences of doctoral students in romantic relationships. Fiammenghi interviewed seventeen clinical psychology students for her qualitative research dissertation and found common narratives about how relationships were both enhanced and challenged by training.

In "Clinical Psychology Doctoral Students with a History of Eating Disorders," the second chapter in this section, Brianna Blake describes how she was surprised to learn that she was not the only one in the program with a history of maladaptive behavior around food. The author conducted a series of focused interviews with other students who claimed an eating-disorder history and discerned how that history affected professional development. Blake sought to learn whether the stress of training would reignite destructive behavior patterns, whether students' histories helped or hindered their ability to understand and empathize with clients, and how their experiences affected professional identity.

Matthew Liebman's chapter, "Life as a Juggler: Work, Family, and Study inside a Doctoral Psychology Program," follows. He points out the dichotomy of being immersed in a psychotherapeutic culture emphasizing the importance of self-care, in both personal and professional practice, while leading a life that undermines such efforts. Liebman worked full-time as a musician while studying in the doctoral program, planning his wedding, and embarking on a new life as a married man. Yet, he found that the complexity of his life ultimately enhanced his graduate training and contributed to his professional identity.

The fourth essay in this section, Noel Hunter's "Experiences of a 'Black Sheep' in a Clinical Psychology Doctoral Program," discusses the challenges of returning to school as a seasoned adult with specific life experiences, a strong sense of autonomy, and independently acquired knowledge. Hunter's predicament was compounded when previous experience and understanding came into conflict with new knowledge. Hunter says that the mental health field, though filled with life-changing opportunity for many distressed individuals, can also be rife with dogmatic ideology that violates human rights and dignity. She describes uncovering mental-health politics in the program and in the field at large, and how she became engaged in conflicts when she aggressively challenged the status quo. Hunter shares the lessons she learned through this process of taking on the role of dissident and struggling to find a balance between conformity and speaking her truth.

Part III, on the impact of diversity, leads off with "A Few Good Men: The Male Experience of Minority Status in a Clinical Psychology Doctoral Program." Ian Rugg shares how he and other White American men found themselves to be, for the first time, members of a minority group when they enrolled in a clinical doctoral psychology program. He tells how he felt being in "a sea of women," discussing topics such as sexual assault, sexual harassment, feminism, sexism, empathy, and gender. His dissertation on the male experience of doctoral training, based on his own history as well as that of twenty other male students, revealed that males in the minority felt simultaneously criticized, judged, enriched, marginalized, and special. Rugg contextualizes his qualitative findings within the framework of gender-role theory and the psychology of men.

"Notes from a Queer Student's Graduate Training," by Kathleen Kallstrom-Schreckengost, is the second chapter in this section. The author identifies herself as a bisexual woman engaged to another woman during the time of her training, which caused her to experience anxiety about how she would answer clients who asked her about her future husband. What she found was that her sexual identity and her stance as an openly bisexual woman permeated every aspect of training. Issues also arose with straight supervisors, who tempted her to administer some informal diversity training in response to certain comments that they made. Kallstrom-Schrenckengost additionally experienced strong countertransference reactions when she worked with clients with non-mainstream sexual identities, as well as with clients who were openly homophobic. She discusses how she handled relationships with classmates, faculty, supervisors, and patients as she found her way as a therapist who is also bisexual.

"Finding My Place in Psychoanalysis as a Black, Female Student," by Adjoa Osei, follows. The author explores her personal confrontation with psychoanalysis, which has been viewed as the prerogative of the White, the wealthy, and the educated; moreover, the psychoanalytic tradition has, to a certain extent, reinforced that stereotype. She describes how Blacks and other people of color, as well as those from the working class, mostly perceive psychoanalysis as an inaccessible realm. She argues that students across the board hold misconceptions about psychoanalysis, and that she also had her own biases, including ambivalent feelings about joining a "White" profession. Osei's essay focuses on how her misconceptions were challenged in classes with a psychodynamic orientation, and how cultural training and her own personal analysis transformed her viewpoint.

The final chapter in this section, written by Jeremy Novich, is titled "From the Closet to the Clinic: An Orthodox Jewish Man Comes Out in Training." Novich explains how those from an orthodox, religious community are indoctrinated with the view that homosexuality is a sin in the eyes of God. Homosexual behavior in such communities is forbidden, and gay members are expelled or ostracized, or they must hide their sexual orientation. Novich paradoxically also felt marginalized in the program, because he was in class with an openly gay student and, at the same time, felt others perceived him as homophobic because of his religious affiliation, which was highly visible because of the yarmulke he wore to express his Jewish identity. Novich describes his gradual "coming out" process, his treatment of a gay client with conservative religious beliefs, and the experience of writing his dissertation on the oppression of gay men in the orthodox, Jewish community.

These chapters display the authors' impressive degree of self-reflection, openness, and psychological maturity—the precise qualities we look for in clinical psychologists. We want trainees to enter their career paths with these skills, but we also wish to nourish and challenge students to demonstrate, expand, and extend these and other professional qualities in their clinical work by the time they graduate. These compelling stories tell how doctoral students who began their program mostly on faith took a long journey of acculturation, which ended in personal transformation and professional development. The narratives demonstrate the diverse nature, breadth, and depth of clinical psychology training. The privileged, "subjective knowledge" (Belenky, Clinchy, Goldberger, and Tarule, 1997) shared in these pages is based on intuition and first-hand experiences of program graduates, whose authoritative accounts provide an essential, inside look into the world of the clinical psychology educational experience.

REFERENCES

Altman, N. (2004). History repeats itself in transference-countertransference. *Psychoanalytic Dialogues,* 6, 807–16.

Bamonti, P., Keelan, C., Larson, N., Mentrikoski, J., Randall, C., Sly, S., Travers, R., and McNeil, D. (2014). Promoting ethical behavior by cultivating a culture of self-care during graduate training. *Training and Education in Professional Psychology.* Advance online publication. doi:10.1037/tep0000056

Belenky, M. F., Clinchy, B. M., Goldberger, N. R., and Tarule, J. M. (1997). *Women's ways of knowing: The development of self, voice and mind* (10th anniversary ed.). New York: Basic Books.

Bloom, H. (1973). *The anxiety of influence: A theory of poetry.* New York: Oxford University Press.

Dearing, A., Madux, J., and Tangney, J. (2005). Predictors of psychological help seeking in clinical and counseling psychology graduate students. *Professional Psychology research and practice,* 36(3): 323-329.

Diguini, M., Jones, F., and Camic. P. (2013). Perceived social stigma and attitudes towards seeking therapy in training: A cross-national study. *Psychotherapy*, 50, 213–23.

Guy, J. D. (1987). *The personal life of a psychotherapist.* New York: John Wiley & Sons.

Leary, K. (2012). Race as an adaptive challenge: Working with diversity in the clinical consulting room. *Psychoanalytic Psychology*, 29, 279–91.

McWilliams, N. (2004) *Psychoanalytic psychotherapy: A practitioner's guide.* New York: The Guilford Press.

Phillips, S. (2010). Up close and personal: A consideration of the role of personal therapy in the development of a psychotherapist. In R. Klein, H. Bernard and V. Schermer, eds., *On becoming a psychotherapist: The personal and professional journey* (pp. 144–164). New York: Oxford University Press.

Rosenberg, R. S. (2012, April 12). Abnormal is the new normal. *Slate*. Retrieved from w.slate.com/articles/health_and_science/medical_examiner/2013/04/diagnostic_and_stati stical_manual_fifth_edition_why_will_half_the_u_s_population.html

Stevanovic, P. and Rupert, P. A. (2009). Career sustaining behaviors, satisfactions and stresses of professional psychologists. *Psychotherapy: Theory, Research, Practice, Training.* 41, 301–9.

U.S. Bureau of Labor Statistics. (2012). Psychologists: Job outlook. In *Occupational outlook handbook*. Retrieved from http://www.bls.gov/ooh/LifePhysical-and-Social-Science/ Psychologists.htm#tab-6.U.S.

Wertz, F. (2011). The qualitative revolution and psychology. *The Humanistic Psychologist*, 39, 77–104.

I

Beginner's Mind:
First Experiences Conducting Therapy

Chapter One

Personal and Professional Integration in a Dual-Oriented Doctoral Program

Dustin Kahoud

Inspired by my own experiences in therapy, I knew I wanted to be a therapist long before I learned anything about clinical psychology doctoral programs or theoretical orientations. I first found myself sitting across from a therapist as a result of returning home from college to live with my parents. I had chosen a school in Rhode Island because I wanted to free myself from my dependence on my parents and make my own way in the world. Instead, I spent most of my four years in college doing whatever best helped me to forget what I had originally set out to do. Rather than finding out who I was, I was constantly looking for a place to hide from myself. I was terrified of failing and avoided opportunities for such outcomes at all costs. And while I had expected to emerge from the transformational cocoon of my undergraduate years as a vibrant, mature young adult, it might be more accurate to say that I crawled back out, dragging my unexpanded wings behind me.

Suddenly I found myself on I-95, heading south, back to Long Island. I was the same lost boy I had been when my parents dropped me off at school four years earlier. Not only had I been unable to free myself from my dependence, but I had put myself in a position of feeling even more dependent than ever. And while I had managed to pull good enough grades, job prospects were looking bleak for an English and writing major. Teaching English in public school seemed one of the few realistic job options. I had taken an elective on the *Lord of the Rings* during my senior year, and it occurred to me that, like that of the characters in Tolkien's classic, my four years of college had turned out to be an "unexpected journey" that seemed to be culminating in my own personal "Mount Doom."

When I returned home, my girlfriend, who was in a graduate program in social work, recommended that I see a therapist. After first putting up a good fight against the idea and then confirming that my parents would extend my financial dependence to include paying for therapy, I proceeded hesitantly into treatment. As it turned out, it was the best money they ever spent on me. My relationship with my first therapist was a powerful one and ultimately landed me on the path I am walking today. Even now, I can vividly recall how it felt to be driving home from my therapist's office, piecing together the insights I had uncovered during my session. I found it exhilarating each time I discovered a seemingly insignificant truth about myself that had been hidden from awareness, and later on this knowledge drastically changed how I perceived myself and the events of my life. Not only did my first therapist help me to feel less lost in the world, but he also helped me to find tremendous confidence in myself.

My first therapy experience lasted about two years, and by the time it was wrapping up, I knew I would dedicate my life to studying and practicing psychotherapy. Inspired by the personal changes I had experienced in my own therapy, I wanted to enable others to find their untapped potential. I was excited by the idea of fostering self-knowledge in others, eager to continue learning about myself in the process, and adamant about pursuing admission to a clinical psychology doctoral program. Since I had not been a psychology major in college, I first had to go back and take all of the prerequisite undergraduate courses. Without any research or clinical experience, I worked tirelessly to build up my resume. I wanted so badly to become a clinical psychologist that I willingly took the Graduate Record Exam *several* times.

In retrospect, I see that my interest in psychology was spurred by a nagging itch—the need to know more about myself. My first therapy experience had whetted my appetite, but I was not fully satiated. Yes, I had progressed to a new phase of my life. I was living on my own, found a direction I was motivated to pursue, and improved the relationship with my girlfriend. But somewhere inside me, I knew there was more to learn. I often found myself becoming angry over very small things that I didn't understand or couldn't control. I would become impatient and stubborn at times, insisting there was always a "right" or "wrong," a "good" or "bad" way to be, to act, or to think. I found myself flocking to people who I perceived as "the good ones" and avoiding those I labeled "bad." Without the eyes to see shades of gray, I was caught up in dualities and an endless stream of value judgments. For instance, liberals were "good," and conservatives were "bad"; science was "good," and religion was "bad"; Starbucks was "good," and Dunkin Donuts was "bad" . . . and the list went on.

Unconsciously I took great comfort in dividing the world into neat categories. My way of perceiving the complexities of human nature allowed me to smooth out the uncertainties of life and, at times, furnished me with a sense of great power and self-efficacy. Why else would I have been clinging to my dualities for dear life? And from what I have now learned about myself and others, these patterns of operating in the world are usually early adaptive strategies people use to cope with the complexities of existence. So while in some respects I took refuge in the subtle illusions of control these constructs offered, I was also largely unsatisfied embracing these "truths." When my dual-oriented framework of mind was called into question, the ground beneath my feet was liable to crumble. When I discovered that some aspect of my worldview was based on faulty logic, the foundations of my self-esteem were likely to tremble. I would experience myself as *either* brittle, weak, and the victim of badness, *or* powerful, aggressive, and the perpetrator of badness. There was very little room for me to experience the ambiguities of life. I was often locked in conflict—not ready to relinquish the psychological crutches I had grown so accustomed to, and yet unwilling to settle for my reductionist model of self, others, and the world. One part of me wanted to hide behind the "goods" and "bads," while another wanted more. Not surprisingly, I was drawn to psychology because it gave me brief glimpses into a more nuanced world—one that offered refreshing complexities and expanded possibilities.

Studying psychology nurtured my curiosity and served as shelter from the harsh winds of my dualistic mental framework. All along I maintained a hope that through my professional and personal pursuits in the field, the flame of my burning curiosity would become a blaze to illuminate parts of my mind still shrouded in darkness. Ironically, I found myself most drawn to a doctoral program comprising faculty members divided between psychodynamic and cognitive-behavioral approaches. For someone struggling to see that antithetical truths can and do coexist, navigating this split in theoretical training was like strolling through a minefield.

In considering the complex processes that one undergoes in choosing their theoretical orientation, many expert clinicians have described their personal journeys and theoretical transformations (Castonguay, 2006; Goldfried, 2001; Mitchell, 2004; Nuttall, 2008; Safran, 2003; Wachtel, 1977). For instance, Mitchell (2004) reflected on the tortuous path through schools of psychoanalytic thought previously deemed incompatible that culminated in his theoretical perspective as a relational psychoanalyst.

In this chapter, I will narrate how the personal and professional quandaries I faced, upon entering a dual-oriented doctoral program in psychology, served as the "perfect storm" for me—the impetus to addressing the conflicts of my own dual-oriented internal world. I will explain how the decision to enter psychoanalysis during my doctoral training provided me with a refuge and battleground upon which such inner strife could be "worked through." These experiences have come to influence my thinking and practice as a clinician. Finally, I will articulate my beliefs about how the many moving parts of my doctoral training have been essential in propelling me toward integration—both personal and professional.

A PERFECT STORM

During the period in which I was working toward applying to doctoral programs, I never thought much about my theoretical orientation. But after being accepted and immersing myself in the first year of the program, I grew increasingly conflicted about "choosing sides" and defining myself by one of two sharply distinct categories. Repeatedly I found myself walking out of class after a lecture on cognitive-behavioral therapy (CBT) or psychoanalysis with a greater appreciation for the value of each respective approach, and yet I was more confused than ever by what seemed to be paradoxical information. Since it had been my tendency to choose sides prior to entering the graduate program, I found myself wondering why it was so difficult for me to choose an orientation. By declaring myself a devotee of one orientation or the other, would I lose the support of professors from the opposing camp? I also wondered whether my attempts to remain open to both psychodynamic and CBT orientations might ultimately end up alienating me from those clinicians who were strong advocates of a pure psychodynamic or CBT perspective. I noticed that my classmates were not having much of a problem knowing which modality worked best for them. But for me, choosing was a dangerous decision that could end up determining whether I would be "good" or "bad" as a therapist.

With my first year in the program winding down, I began to prepare myself for the plunge into clinical training as a graduate student therapist. I would begin working in the program's outpatient clinic, seeing patients under the supervision of a faculty member—with either psychoanalytic or CBT orientation. I was eager to work with the psychodynamic supervisor I had been assigned. But when an administrative issue arose, three other students and I, who had been assigned to the same psychodynamic supervisor, were asked to redress the unforeseen imbalance of students to supervisors. The clinical director requested that one person volunteer to switch to a CBT supervisor, and if no one stepped up, then one of us would be reassigned.

I vividly remember the anxiety I experienced when I first heard the request. Despite a vague sense of dread that might have signaled I was making a decision that went against my interests, I suddenly felt a strong urge to volunteer. I was unable to resist the pull of this impulse and felt the need to take control of my anxiety, at whatever the cost. After little deliberation, and even less awareness of why, I volunteered. Almost instantly, I was upset with myself and the decision I had made. While one part of me said it was no big deal, that I would learn a lot from my newly assigned CBT supervisor, another part of me was disappointed in myself for giving up the position I had wanted and angered about the impulsive nature of my actions. I had allowed myself to stray from the path of what seemed best for me and my training goals—and it was not the first time I had done this. I had repeated such self-defeating behaviors again and again since grade school—knowing what I wanted and yet acting to the contrary, putting the interests and needs of others ahead of my own. It started with giving up favorite toys as a child and continued through adolescence (in one instance I gave a coveted concert ticket to a friend) and into adulthood. More than once I have shied away from talking to women whom I knew that a friend was also interested in.

While determined to make the best out of the year ahead, working with my CBT supervisor, I further ruminated on my tendency to excessively sacrifice my own needs in the interests of others. Inevitably this would lead to further struggles, both personal and professional, in my future career as a clinical psychologist. As a therapist, I would constantly run into such conflicts and knew I needed to come to a better understanding of what kept me locked in this masochistic pattern. Why did I miss opportunities due to lack of trust in my own instincts and give up what I truly wanted, only to regret it later? It was then that I decided to go back into therapy. My professor referred me to a local psychoanalytic training institute where I began psychoanalysis three times per week with a therapist in training. Thus began the last leg of my mission to the top of Mount Doom, where I hoped to toss the ring of my own conflicts into the fire.

THE JOURNEY CONTINUES

Although I felt confused and conflicted most of the time, suddenly upon meeting my analyst I found myself knowing just about everything there was to know about myself, other people, and the world. Michael was a man in his late thirties, and I immediately noticed how he towered over my five-foot-eight-inch frame as he stepped into the waiting room for the first time to introduce himself. Although unconscious to me initially, the dynamic created by our contrasting statures had far-reaching implications for how the therapy proceeded. At the time, I had no idea that something as incidental as my therapist's height would take on significant proportions in the therapeutic relationship. Almost instantly, I had enormous difficulty allowing myself to exhibit any sign of weakness in front of Michael.

Sitting across from Michael early on, with little access to my insecurities, I summarized my life in a positive light. Nothing really bad ever happened to me. I grew up in an affluent town in an intact family with my sister. My parents were alive and well. There was no divorce, no abuse, and no trauma of any kind. Keeping the focus off myself, I moved on to my mother and father, describing my parents as "good" people who tried their best in raising me. My mom was a sensitive, emotional woman who worried too much about my sister and me and was overprotective because she loved us so much. As someone who loved music, painting, and literature, she always encouraged my creativity and was proud of my love for writing and drawing. But she was also fragile and extremely vulnerable to being hurt by others. In particular, I recalled one instance where a driver gave her the middle finger in a supermarket parking lot and she began to cry.

While my dad was also a "good guy," he was the polar opposite of my mother. Since as early as I could remember, he made efforts to bond with and relate to me through the identification of the two of us as men in the household. My dad had a lot of ideas about what constituted a "real man," and I deeply internalized these ideas in formulating my own masculinity. For my father—and unlike my mother—expressing vulnerabilities was out of the realm of possibility. When my dad felt disrespected or slighted, he did what any "real man" would do—he became aggressive. His personality shifted drastically, and he went from being the good, loving, dedicated father to what I described, as a boy, as a roaring T. Rex. Although he was not physically aggressive with me or other members of the family, the mere presence of his anger in the household was frightening and felt physically threatening without any actual contact.

Not surprisingly, I quickly came up against a therapeutic wall in clearly describing my childhood, early relationships, and present life. *I got stuck.* Once I finished reciting the pat story of my life as I had come to know it, there was nothing left for me to say. As time went on, I began to feel my legs growing heavier before sessions while walking across the parking lot to the building where my therapist had his practice. A lump formed in my stomach as I climbed the stairs to the second floor where his office was located. I was dragging my feet and often dreading the encounter ahead. The silences were deafening at times. The tension I felt as I sat staring across the room at him often seemed unbearable. I tried the couch, and that helped a few times but eventually seemed to make things worse.

I began telling myself that everything was "fine," that there really wasn't any need for me to be in therapy. When looked at from the outside, my life was going very well. And yet, I was never quite able to feel satisfied with where I was in life—and was stuck in the perpetual mantra of "once (insert event here) happens, I'll be content." I often chalked up my dysthymic temperament to genetics and rationalizations about my unique sensitivity to the tragic truths of the human condition. After all, what was there to be so happy about anyway? I'd rather be in touch with reality and miserable than live in ignorant bliss. There was nothing in my past that had caused me to feel the way I was feeling . . . nothing I hadn't already talked about with my first therapist. Why repeat myself again and again, dwelling on events of my childhood and the past? After all, my problems were *nothing* compared to the traumas I was learning about in my doctoral program. And since I was so confident that there really wasn't much left for me to say, I found an easier topic to discuss with my therapist . . . *him.*

It was only a couple of months into our work together when I attempted to turn the tables on Michael. As when I first left home for college, I forgot my original reason for coming to therapy—to learn about myself. Instead, I became more interested in my therapist than my own process. Little by little, bit by bit, I pieced together what I thought I knew about him. I was gathering bits of information to create an image of the man that made sense to me. Michael freely encouraged my exploration of these fantasies. It all started with my associations to the diploma on the wall from an Ivy League university and continued further down paths I later discovered had little connection to reality.

I went on for some time building an image of Michael, based on stereotypes, generalizations, and artificial links. Little by little, Michael provided me with details that showed how wrong I was in many of my assumptions. The details he chose to disclose about himself were the type that shook the foundations of my dual-oriented world. For example, when he encouraged me to begin "freestyling"—a term he used in lieu of free associating—to help me break through this "stuck" period in the analysis, I learned that he had been a rapper in the Long Island underground scene for many years. Thus, the image I had fashioned of the Ivy League psychology student was shattered. For me he could be only a rapper *or* a scholarly student at Princeton who went on to become a psychoanalyst—he couldn't possibly be both! Such revelations were shocking enough to knock me back into a place where I was suddenly curious again about myself and my own thinking.

Around that time I had a dream about being in therapy and brought it up in my session. In the dream, I was free-associating on the couch. When I lifted my head to stand up at the end of the session, I looked back in horror to see that I had left the hair on the back of my head behind on the couch. After analyzing the dream with Michael, we talked about my fears of letting myself become vulnerable in therapy, particularly with another man. For me, losing my hair carried significant meaning about the loss of my masculinity, power, and attractiveness—all "good" attributes I associated with "real men." My fear of hair loss was associated with beliefs that without my hair I would become weak, emasculated, vulnerable, and helpless—all "bad" traits better suited to a small boy.

Further, what if I discovered in therapy that parts of myself *were* bad? Would possessing any traits of a small boy consume and destroy the "real man" in me? I was struggling in the therapy, but at the same time something was telling me not to stop. Perhaps it was the same part of my mind that wanted to become a psychologist. Perhaps, like the curiosity driving the pursuit of a career in psychology, curiosity would keep me in analysis to find out what would happen. So I stayed . . . to experience the first rupture in our therapeutic alliance.

HIDDEN DICHOTOMIES

It was sometime during my continued efforts to demonstrate how "good" I was that my therapist said something seemingly insignificant, the impact of which compounded and cascaded insights that continue to reverberate through me today. Perhaps appropriately on some level, he replied to my reports of "being good" by saying: "Good boy." But for me at that time, it sure didn't seem appropriate. Suddenly, with just two words, Michael had become "bad." He was *treating me like a child . . . condescending to me . . . disrespecting me . . . as if I were a small boy to be toyed with!* I was stung—my heart pounding and my skin growing warm with anger. I had been non-chalantly lounging on the couch when I suddenly bolted into an upright position, tense with feelings of betrayal. All of the "good" qualities I had experienced in my therapist over six or so months vanished into thin air. He was suddenly transformed from an insightful person—someone who really seemed to *get me* and who wanted to help me—into an unethical man who had only bad intentions. He no longer cared about me . . . was no longer trying to help me . . . he was just messing with me for his own amusement.

But at that moment, there was little need for words. I believe my analyst was keenly aware of the shift in my affect and seemed to be bracing for the impact as if he had ignited a bundle of firecrackers. I didn't say anything at first—I couldn't. I just sat with the sting for minutes that felt like days, unable to make eye contact for any extended period of time. Thoughts were whirring in my head. All along, Michael had been encouraging me to put my authentic experience of him into words. This was never an easy task, but finally, I was inspired to put it all out there. I told him that I thought he was talking down to me, condescending to me, and intentionally trying to pro-voke me to become angry with him. I am still not convinced that I was entirely wrong.

For his part Michael asked me about what it was like to feel so angry at him. It was not easy for me to describe beyond the rational explanations I already had provided. But it was the first time in quite a while that I had experienced such a depth of rage toward anyone. At least not since I was a boy—not since I was the "good boy" who had become the victim of his father's transformations into the roaring T. Rex, who was then transformed into a fierce T. Rex himself. I felt angry, self-righteous, and fierce. I told Michael what he had done "wrong." He was *supposed* to be all of the "good" things I had learned therapists *should* be . . . not this vicious monster who sat before me. As angry as I was, something kept me coming back to each session—continuing my three times per week schedule—through the intense resentment I was experiencing toward Michael. Perhaps my tenacity was an adaptive aspect of the typically masochistic patterns I had exhibited for so long.

As we continued to plumb the depths of this rupture, Michael communicated to me that he had been finding it difficult to breach my persistent efforts to demonstrate to him that I was not only a "good" patient but also a "real man." From the very beginning, I had been doing everything in my power to be a "good patient" but had yet to show myself to him as a real person with both good and bad parts. Michael's interpretations felt startlingly true to me, resonating with my own experience of myself. The insights came with the force of violent waves, crashing over me and sweeping me away like a surfboard in a tsunami. I became aware of all of the ways that, since the beginning of treatment, I had related to him through patterns that were laid down in my earliest relationships. For example, I recalled how when Michael initially asked me about dreams and I had none to share, I came back with a dream the next session, eager to please him and show my goodness.

On one hand, there was the "me" that related to others as I had learned to do in my relationship with my mother—the small boy who had always been praised for his creativity and sensitivity, yet was fragile, vulnerable, and easily bruised. Appropriately, I labeled this part of myself as the "good boy." But there were also some troublesome qualities that had become tightly bound up in my perception of myself as good. When operating in this mode as the caring, sensitive, creative individual, I often felt like a small boy in a dangerous world, often falling victim to the "badness" of the world—which highlighted my goodness even more.

But once Michael made the mocking "good boy" comment, I changed roles. As I took pains to put the feelings into words, I realized that I had become my father, the "real man" in response to Michael's "badness." As a "real man," I took on my father's aggressiveness when feeling wounded. I slipped into an impenetrable suit of psychological armor and felt little capacity for experiencing vulnerability. The "real man" inside me had his own version of reality, and it was in striking contrast to the view of the "good boy." This hard-shelled version of myself was highly motivated, driven toward success, and dismissive of the more vulnerable, sensitive, naïve aspects of myself. He loathed weakness, scoffed at insecurities, and was disgusted by the idea of complaining about his problems rather than "sucking it up" and "taking the bull by the horns." That part knew that I could accomplish whatever I put my mind to in life and wouldn't consider crying like a baby over the frightening prospect of failure.

As the treatment proceeded, I encountered many more situations in which these hidden, internal dichotomies were highlighted. I began to see patterns in how I related to others and noticed them more and more, as they happened again and again. I also came to notice subtle nuances in the ways these patterns were triggered by some situations but not in others. I came to realize that, in particularly intense interactions with Michael, I would slip into these more extreme versions of myself based on how I had come to relate to others in my early relationships. But it quickly grew clear to me that I was not becoming who my parents *actually* were—but rather, I was turning into the *constructed images* of them that I had internalized. My caricatures of them— *how* I came to perceive them in affectively intense moments over the course of my life—was what I was working from. The accumulated images of my parents impressed in my mind were snapshots taken during emotion-laden interactions I experienced as a child. And yet, at these moments, even twenty or so years later, I would refer back to those caricatures as the lenses through which I came to see myself, the world, and my relationships with others. Once I articulated this process, I began to see more clearly some of the ways that I unconsciously organized the people and things in the world, and the position in which I placed myself in relation to those people and things.

Prior to these realizations, I had little to no awareness of these tendencies in myself. In fact, I thought I was nothing like my parents. And in fact, this was true. I never was like my real parents. I couldn't possibly have been acting like them, because I was never acting. In many ways that were too difficult to see before these conflicts arose in my therapy, I *was* them! I naturally and unconsciously slipped in and out of the alternating relational templates constructed by my mind to represent my parents. Perhaps the biggest problem was that neither of these templates was *me*.

I related to Michael in a range of patterns, just as throughout my life I had related to my mother and father in different ways. Sometimes I was me and Michael was my mom . . . sometimes I was me and he was my dad . . . and sometimes I was my dad or my mom in relation to him. I began to see with increasing regularity and with greater awareness how these modes of behavior were not exclusive to the transference I had developed with my therapist. These oscillations in the experience of myself were prominent in all of my relationships, according to my perceptions of myself in relation to the other person. For instance, in a physical sense, Michael was "big" and in comparison I felt "small," which triggered my efforts to be the "real man" with particular fervency. But in other interactions, I was "big" and others were "small." The feelings attached to my experience of myself in relation to the other were continuing to color my patterns of interaction—whether it was toward my therapist, my professors, or the president of the United States— and it also applied to my theoretical orientation as a graduate student therapist.

AN INTEGRATED CLINICAL WORLD

After becoming aware of these disparate aspects of myself, I came to see how they were showing up in my own interests in psychotherapy integration as efforts to assert some sense of control over them. Similarly, Castonguay (2006) also described his initial pursuits of psychotherapy integration as a means to escaping a deep sense of confusion and difficulties tolerating a sense of lacking control. While attending classes taught by professors loyal to *either* psychodynamic *or* cognitive-behavioral approaches, the different elements of my divided mind began establishing alliances. When in psychoanalytic classes, the "good boy" in me took the reins. He fed off the validation he received from psychoanalytic theories and grew to dominate my internal world, exposing the "real man" for the imposter he had always been. The part of me that knew human beings suffer because of subtle aspects of experience and relationships, those that are often largely hidden from conscious awareness, received great validation. When learning about psychoanalytic theories, the good boy was suddenly not so naïve anymore. He had grown up, discovered powerful "truths," and could shatter the dismissive attitude and denial of the real man. On the other hand, the real man in me attached himself to the approaches I was learning from cognitive-behavioral theories. He wasn't going to lead clients on a fruitless pursuit to uncover the unconscious, falling down the rabbit hole in search of the insights. Real men did not get lost in analyzing the minutia of everyday interpersonal relationships. He was going to help them feel better by using techniques that were backed by robust empirical evidence . . . and *fast*!

I had not granted myself the freedom to be open to both approaches. It was all or nothing, black or white, CBT or psychodynamic. But as I became aware of the ways I was oscillating between the good-boy and the real-man versions of myself, I began revising the narrative I had developed to explain my own previous behavior. For instance, my decision to volunteer to receive the CBT supervision instead of the psychodynamic supervision I had originally desired took on a different cast. Similar to the interactions that had unfolded in my analysis, that decision now appeared to be an instance in which the sensitive, vulnerable, good boy suddenly took a back seat to the real man. Almost automatically, the real man stepped up to the plate and offered to volunteer—in an omnipotent effort to crush the insecurities of the weak, sensitive boy. By being the "bigger man," I could be the hero who was heralded for saving the day. As in my relationship with my therapist, I had been oscillating between alternate experiences of myself as good boy and the tough man in relation to my professors. The part of me that wanted to remain with my psychodynamic supervisor had been that of the sensitive boy who had always received praise for his way of relating in the world. My experience of myself in relation to the CBT supervisor had been in the mode in which I had come to relate to my father in order to feel accepted; by volunteering, I could prove to my father and to myself that I was the real man he "needed" me to be.

During my third year in the program, I began working with an integrative supervisor who is also an alumna of the same doctoral program. Through our work together, I have become more flexible about working in psychodynamic and CBT orientations, approaching each patient with a greater appreciation for his or her own unique level of readiness. I have become increasingly comfortable in integrating the disparate aspects of myself that had allied themselves with *either* psychoanalysis *or* CBT. While I have not had any formal training in integration, nor have I learned to practice from any systematic approach to psychotherapy integration, I have found that my clinical experiences reinforce my efforts to maintain a spirit of openness in using *both* CBT *and* psychodynamic approaches.

Two particular clinical cases highlight the value of learning to work from both psychodynamic and CBT approaches. First is my work with a young, male college student whom I will call PT. This client was mandated for treatment by his college as a part of a disciplinary action in response to his anger-management and substance-abuse problems. I initially found PT unwilling to share any details about himself—let alone explore his current distress or substance abuse. In our earliest sessions, I worked to demonstrate to him that it was safe to be "real" about the situation we were in together. I encouraged him to speak candidly about what it was like for him to be forced into therapy with me, his feelings about therapy itself, and his notions about what would be expected of him in treatment. I attempted to validate his experience of the circumstances that triggered his entry into treatment, as well as his experience of the mandated treatment.

PT expressed his conviction that my intentions were to use anything I learned about him against him. He spoke about the "bullshit policies" of his college for mandating therapy and coming down on him so harshly. He talked about why he did not belong in treatment and how much time he was wasting in being there. The anger in the room was palpable, and I found myself walking on eggshells at times, feeling "small" in relation to the "bigness" of his emotional presence—often feeling helpless and hopeless with regard to doing anything for this person. In supervision, I spent a lot of time trying to understand the strong countertransference I was experiencing toward PT. I felt like giving up on working with him and that it was hopeless to engage him in the treatment. I was experiencing the protective protests of the real man, who argued, "Why should I care if PT doesn't?" The more I talked about my personal reactions to this patient with my supervisor, the closer I came to understanding what it was like for him to be a person in the world. In contrast to PT, I was also seeing a patient in the session immediately before—a client who also had been mandated—but from whom I experienced a sense of warmth and appreciation in our interactions, which brought out the sensitive, attuned, good boy in me. PT was stirring up some very different feelings in me—triggering both the defensiveness and denial of the real man and the fear of the child at the mercy of his "T. Rex" father.

It was clear that I was not the only person in PT's life that had experienced his anger. So I began to wonder about what kind of experiences might have contributed to the construction of his aggressive, yet protective interpersonal dynamic. I talked at length with my supervisor about learning why or how PT had come to use this way of relating in the past as an adaptive strategy. How had this dynamic been helpful or protective, and how was it now constricting him? Eventually, PT and I reached a place in which we were able to discuss his family. He initially described his father as extremely strict. Later, he added that his father had a bad temper and had drunk too much for as long as he had known him. But revealing even these details about his father seemed extremely distressful. For PT, it was more important than anything to respect his father for all the "good things" he had done for him. Respecting him meant complete and absolute forgiveness of any wrongdoings and, more important, hiding his own feelings of rage he experienced toward the man.

Instead of acknowledging his anger toward his father, PT's anger was coming out in drunken rampages on weekend nights of binge drinking in his college dorm. Little by little, I worked to explore PT's relationship with his father and helped him acknowledge that if, in fact, he *were* to be angry at his father, his anger wouldn't make either him or his father "bad." He wouldn't be transformed into a disloyal, backstabbing son—left vulnerable to the vengeful retaliations of his father. His father wouldn't be condemned as an evil, abusive man who must be hunted down by the community and exiled from his town. I tried to help PT understand that if his father had hurt him or caused him pain growing up, acknowledging that pain did not mean he could no longer have a relationship with his dad. Both PT and his father had their own unique experiences that were the root of their anger. His father wasn't "all good" or "all bad," and neither was he.

On the other side of the theoretical coin, I began work with a patient who had been referred for addiction problems. VC was an opiate addict who was attending an intensive outpatient psychotherapy program but was referred for some extra support while on campus to attend classes. This woman was in the early stages of abstinence from addictions to prescription painkillers and heroin. At the time, she was suffering from panic attacks, feeling "out of control" and depressed, and experiencing intense urges to use. She reported that she had been relapsing and using heroin about once per month. Although I continuously recommended that she seek more intensive inpatient substance abuse treatment, VC insisted she was not willing to do so. At the same time, the stressors of her everyday life seemed intolerable for her in her current emotional state. In the short period of eight or so sessions we had together, I worked on helping her manage the intensity of her affect states by teaching relaxation techniques, offering coping strategies, and helping her to reframe some of the ways in which she had been thinking about herself and her recovery. While on one level, VC felt that inpatient treatment was necessary, she was terrified of failing her parents. She was supposed to be the "good one" of all her siblings, who were all also going through their own troubles with drugs. If her parents found out that she too was addicted to drugs and would have to take a semester off from college, it would "kill them"—In other words, she would be become "all bad" to them. My supervisor's openness to using a CBT approach in my work with VC was invaluable in helping me to better integrate the good boy and the real man of my clinical world. VC eventually ended up entering a long-term residential rehabilitation program.

CONCLUSION

Today my journey continues. The "one ring" of my conflicts has yet to be tossed into the fires of Mount Doom, and I continue to battle the urge to slip on that ring, which allows me to "part the seas" of life. Like the "one ring," these defensive modes of organizing my experience have become "precious" to me. They are deeply rooted in my earliest impressions of myself and the world and offer tantalizing illusions of control and power. Particularly in times of stress, there is great familiarity and comfort in holding the good and bad as separate in my mind. It is not difficult to reflect in a thoughtful and integrated mental state while writing at my desk, but as I face the ongoing stressors of everyday life, I continue to work to resist the natural inclination to divide and conquer the ambiguities of life in my head—not only with regard to aspects of myself and others, politics, philosophy, music, and coffee bar choices but also in my theoretical orientation as a graduate student therapist.

I continue to find it ironic that I ended up in a dual-oriented clinical psychology doctoral program. Had I chosen a strictly psychodynamic or cognitive-behavioral doctoral program, I could easily have ended up slipping into the all-too-familiar world of "us versus them." It probably would have been second nature for me to unite with a community of professionals who were all devoted to a singular model of conceptualizing psychological problems. While this could have been a soothing refuge for a young graduate student seeking a one-size-fits-all template to simplify therapy, it was exactly the environment that could have kept me trapped in my outmoded ways of thinking. As Yalom (2002) describes it, in remaining open to the strengths of varying therapeutic approaches and sacrificing the certainty that accompanies orthodoxy, young therapists "obtain something quite precious—a greater appreciation of the complexity and uncertainty underlying the therapeutic enterprise" (pp. 41–42).

Nevertheless, in the spirit of the theme of this chapter, I will emphasize that my intentions are not to proselytize for any particular way of thinking. Moreover, is not my purpose to state here that I no longer subscribe to dualities and have become a fully integrated human being. I'm not sure what that would look like—or if such a state exists. In fact, even as I write, I am aware of the deeply rooted parts of myself urging me to look for dichotomies, to separate the so-called goodness of integration from the badness of all-or-nothing binaries. Nonetheless, my process is ongoing and already has been influential in my life, both as a doctoral student in training and as a person in the world.

I have come to see a number of ways in which my journey through a dual-oriented program has served as the "perfect storm" for me in promoting both a personal and professional desire for integration. My clinical training in a dual-oriented program has offered me personal challenges beyond what I had expected upon entering graduate school. Due to the inherent nature of the program, choosing how to practice triggered the need for me to address underlying conflicts in therapy. Through these experiences, I have realized how my internal conflicts about my theoretical orientation have been less about my work as a therapist and more about my inability to see the shades of gray in myself, others, and the world. While becoming better able to hold multiple "truths" in mind—sometimes opposing and sometimes congruent— I have also become more capable of assessing which therapeutic techniques fit best for me and which fit best for the patients I am working with. In developing more of a bond with my theoretical approach than with my attunement to the individuality of each of my patients, I have come to fear that I will risk overlooking what I believe to be one of the most powerful therapeutic principles—what F. Scott Fitzgerald (1936) described as "the ability to hold two opposing ideas in mind at the same time and still retain the ability to function" (p. 69).

REFERENCES

Castonguay, L. (2006). Personal pathways in psychotherapy integration. *Journal of Psychotherapy Integration, 16*, 36–50.

Fitzgerald, F. S. (1936). The crack-up. In E. Wilson (Ed.), *The crack-up* (pp. 69–84). New York: New Directions Books.

Goldfried, M. R. (2001). *How therapists change: Personal and professional reflections.* Washington, DC: American Psychological Association Press.

Mitchell, S. A. (2004). My psychoanalytic journey. *Psychoanalytic Inquiry, 24*(4), 531–542.

Nuttall, J. (2008). The integrative attitude: A personal journey. *European Journal of Psychotherapy and Counseling, 10*, 19–38.

Safran, J. D. (2003). The relational turn, the therapeutic alliance, and psychotherapy research: Strange bedfellows or postmodern marriage? *Contemporary Psychoanalysis, 39*(3), 449–476.

Wachtel, P. (1977). *Psychoanalysis and behavior therapy: Toward an integration.* New York: Basic Books.

Yalom, I. D. (2002). *The gift of therapy: An open letter to a new generation of therapists and their patients.* New York: HarperCollins.

Chapter Two

Conducting Therapy for the First Time

Adi Avivi

No academic or intellectual exercise can truly prepare you to pick up the phone and schedule your first appointment with your first therapy client. After your client arrives in the waiting room, you must call them in. Everything is as if under a microscope: what you are wearing, your tone of voice, what you say or do not say on the walk to the therapy room . . . once you sit down. Who begins? And what will your supervisor think and say about your session?

This chapter describes the course of my first psychotherapy case and the process of mutual growth my client and I shared. I will describe the work with my client, my relationship with my supervisor, and my self-exploration in my own psychotherapy. The different roles I played in each circumstance enriched my work and development as a clinician, and each role influenced the others as I took my first steps as a clinician.

FIRST CONTACT WITH THE PATIENT

Being a novice often feels like a disadvantage, but in a profession like psychology, clinicians continue learning throughout their careers. Where we are in our professional progress, and who we are, could and should be a positive aspect of treatment. At the beginning of training, being new is who we are as students, and from this vantage point we have a unique opportunity to help patients grow. The support of wise and compassionate supervisors and our own therapy are powerful resources for making the clinical aspect of our training safe and rich.

Making that first call to Emil's parents, introducing myself as the new student therapist, and setting up an appointment for him to renew his therapy were my first difficult steps. At our very first session, I found myself spending most of the forty-five minutes watching Emil move around the playroom and arrange toys. Emil was eight when we met, and I was his third graduate-student therapist. During the second year of our doctoral program, students gave low-fee individual and group psychotherapy to the local community. At the end of the year, clients had the option to stay and see a new student therapist from the new crop of upcoming second-year students, or ask to be referred to an outside provider who could see them long-term. Emil himself chose to stay in our clinic every year. Although he was clearly mourning the loss of a psychotherapist every year, he also benefited from learning to connect with someone new and from the consistency of location and space.

Unlike me, Emil knew the playroom. In his years of therapy he had created a whole world among the dollhouses, puppets, and toys. Every session was an episode in the vibrant life of the playroom characters he invented. Rhode (2011) described the stages of a psychodynamic play treatment with a child diagnosed with Asperger syndrome. She detailed stages in the treatment, noting on the child's growing comfort in the playroom and increased richness of the fantasy play of the child. When I met Emil, he was in a far more advanced stage of treatment than I was. He was already using symbolic play and feeling relatively safe and attached to the space, though not to me. I was still trapped in my own autistic stage, unable to break through my anxiety and form a connection.

When we first met, I smiled cheerfully, introducing myself in my usual loud and verbose manner. Emil remained serious. He said "hello," and that one word revealed the odd intonation of his speech. Then he marched stiffly to the playroom, looked around, sighed, and started rearranging things while ignoring me. I had followed him in but found myself standing there feeling oddly shy, unable to think of anything to say.

WORKING WITH A CHILD WITH ASPERGER SYNDROME

I knew that Emil was diagnosed with Asperger syndrome, a "high functioning autism," but I did not have a deep understanding of this condition or how to work with a child who had it. I had some experience working with children, but not in a therapeutic milieu, and his age and diagnosis heightened my anxiety. Although I was supported and had excellent psychodynamic supervision, I had no idea what to do now that I was in the room with him. Different writers have recently discussed the tremendous benefits of psychodynamic psychotherapy with children and adults diagnosed with Asperger syndrome (Rhode, 2011; Cohler and Weiner, 2011; Goodman and Athey-

Lloyd, 2011). Cohler and Weiner (2011) argue, for example, that the psychodynamic perspective can shed light on the nature of such patients' anxieties, their desire to protect themselves from interpersonal intrusion and loss, and their avoidance of emotional stimulation. However, when actually meeting Emil, I felt overwhelmed myself. How was I supposed to "build a working alliance"? Create trust? Emil seemed to be busy, and I did not know how to start us off.

Emil's motions were fragmented and odd. He hummed to himself and never looked at me after our initial, awkward introduction. He placed little figurines in dollhouses' rooms, took puppets from the shelves and placed them in the puppet-show booth, and looked for specific toys in boxes and baskets that I had not noticed before he reached for them. While Emil continued to play, panicked thoughts flew through my head, and I wanted to run away from the playroom and hide. These emotions were new for me.

After a while I decided something needed to happen, so I began talking. I asked Emil what he was doing. He said he was organizing the toys in the playroom "the way they were last year." I asked him what bothered him about things being different. "Well, the raw meat will just have to be cooked at some point," he replied. My jaw dropped. Who was "the raw meat"?

I guessed it was him. My supervisor thought it was me. And my own therapist interpreted it as the relationship. So began the journey of cooking the raw meat. It was exciting and wonderful and remarkably difficult. More than anything else I learned about myself, but along the way I acquired knowledge about giving therapy, forming a working alliance, and saying goodbye. What is more, Emil and my other clients changed. Their ability to be in therapy, open up, tolerate the process, push themselves, and make clear gains were the greatest gifts I received from my training experience, and I will always be grateful to those clients for their trust and hard work.

STEPPING INTO EMIL'S WORLD

One of the difficulties I faced as a new therapist was my reliance on theoretical knowledge and intellectual processing. It was comforting to dwell on sophisticated and insightful debates about patients, their symptoms, their defenses, and the etiology of their diagnoses. Theory and intellectual analysis are essential to our work, but emotions—even insecurity that results from inexperience—are important informants in psychotherapy as well. Knowing how to discuss your work intelligently is quite different from getting to know patients, stepping into their world, and allowing them to be who they are. Allowing yourself to be who you are during therapy is another task that cannot be accomplished with intellectual tools alone. I am still wrestling with my desire to be a wise and omniscient psychotherapist, five years after experiencing my first session. This desire to avoid my own difficult emotions and insecurities manifests in attempts to fix my patients; if I can fix them, I can prove to myself that I am a skilled professional. I still feel a need to protect myself and my clients from the realization that change is a slow and painful process and that I do not have a magic wand that can easily make it all better.

Clinging to the fantasy that you can easily and brilliantly fix someone else does not leave much room for mistakes and the anxiety they evoke. It is painful but necessary to realize that therapists and the people they meet are far from perfect and that the shared therapeutic relationship is terribly flawed as well. To facilitate a true meeting between real people, each person must recognizes the other's humanity, power, and fragility and let the other be separate, different, and autonomous while holding the knowledge that the same applies to oneself (Benjamin, 1987). Such a meeting is anxiety provoking because a separate other can leave, and, if connected to you, might take over the relationship. Often it is easier to try controlling the other, denying your own desire for true closeness and even dependency—not in the sense of needing the other for physical survival, but for assurance that you are important enough that the other is willing to be connected to you. This makes you feel human and *known*. If no one knows you, you are alone, but when someone knows you, you are vulnerable. This paradox, when tolerated, is key to living a full life, with all its joys and pains (Benjamin, 1987). You cannot be omnipotent and in total control while creating a healing connection. However, new therapists often have an urge to control the therapy. I initially found myself unable to be playful and allow differences and incompatibilities to exist without constantly trying to impose my ideas about how therapy should be conducted with clients.

THE IMPORTANCE OF BEING AUTHENTIC IN THERAPY

One thing I had to learn was how to acknowledge the specific influence my personality and individuality had on different patients. I could not, and in retrospect should not, have tried to be anyone else but my novice self. Slavin (2010) claims that the analyst's individuality—her distinctive self—is essential to the therapeutic encounter and is itself a change agent for patients. Being in the presence of another person—another individual with a personality—is part of what makes therapy useful. Slavin emphasizes that although historically, psychoanalytic theory regarded the analyst's personality as distinct from her clinical work, it is actually impossible to entirely shed the personal. Nor is it beneficial to the treatment to try to do so.

By the middle of the year I was feeling more comfortable in my role as therapist. One day Emil was sitting with me in the playroom, and we were both drawing quietly. Drawing together helped us bridge the gap in our communication styles.

"What are you drawing?" Emil asked.

"I drew a turtle, next to this lake. And a fish. I think maybe they're talking to each other. What are you drawing?" I asked.

"I'm drawing what evolution has left behind. These are some animals before evolution, and I'm working on the animals after evolution," he answered. Emil had drawn the *Ice Age* animation movie characters on one side and on the other side, animals of the current era.

"I see. So animals evolve to be something else."

"Mm-hmm."

"Is something left of the old animal?"

"Uh huh." Emil remained silent, drawing for a long time.

"What do you think about evolution?"

"Hmm." Emil was silent. "I feel that the animals don't . . . don't like the change."

"What is it they don't like about the change?"

"They like things back to normal."

"They want things to stay the way they were."

"Mm-hmm."

"But things change anyways."

"Mm-hmm."

"That's difficult."

"It really is."

"It really is," I agreed. "What's the hardest thing about change? The most difficult?"

"The most difficult. . . you're going to miss things the way they were. That's the most difficult. You just need to stop thinking about it."

"When something changes and you can't have what you had before, the best you can do is stop thinking about it?" I asked.

"Yeah."

"Do you think you can think about it and be a little sad but also be a little happy that at least you had it?"

"Mm-hmm."

"Sometimes," I said.

"Yeah," Emil answered.

"It's a little bit like here. Every year you come here to the playroom, and it's different from the year before."

"Uh-huh."

"Every year you have a new therapist . . ."

Emil and I were quiet for a while, and then he lifted his eyes from his drawing and asked:

"Who's going to be here next year?"

His question broke my heart as I sensed his sadness and loss and his fear of change. Unable to protect him from the reality to come, I told the truth and replied, "I don't know yet." My limitations and the limitations of the situation were terribly painful. Though clients were explicitly told that the treatment would terminate by the end of the school year and student-therapists were instructed to address this throughout the year, the termination of treatment was a complex process.

Emil, strong and smart, was also fragile. Letting in someone new is a delicate process for most of us. For Emil, who was anxious and insecure in interpersonal situations and suffered a lot of rejection in his past, letting another person in was terrifying. The playroom, with its predictable routine, known schedule, and familiar frame made it somewhat easier. But the reality of the doctoral program's clinic presented a yearly loss and experience of separation for Emil—a recurrent process of letting go of someone dear, someone important. This process of loss that is part of every connection was ever present in my work with Emil. As I learned who we both were I was able to acknowledge the tremendous challenge of the closeness and separateness we were facing. But I also discovered that we could both tolerate it and survive, containing our deep feelings for each other, as well as the pain of saying goodbye.

My first sessions with Emil did not go as well as the interaction depicted above. The ability to sit together and share the painful truth of the playroom, along with the beauty and healing it offered, developed over the year. Both Emil and I changed. This process was made possible by the supervision I received from Dr. Danielle Knafo, whose guidance opened my eyes, as I allowed her to get to know me as Emil slowly allowed me to know him.

LEARNING THE THERAPEUTIC VALUE OF STILLNESS

My first lesson was learning to be quiet. Emil's shy and distant demeanor was in stark contrast to my easy-going, loud, and direct style. Coupled with his organic disorder, his presentation made communication that much harder, since he was anxious and scared of closeness. I, on the other hand, had a hard time giving him space. I wanted to be close and have a discussion that would make everything better. He was interesting and sweet, but he never shared or talked about his feelings. Meanwhile, I had been taught to get clients talking.

In supervision, I talked as well. I transcribed all of my sessions, seeing the visual proof that my verbiage was filling our time while Emil was quiet. When my supervisor noted it, I made smart and insightful comments about my sessions with the child. My supervisor was quiet. She allowed me to vent but then stopped me and took a stab at translating Emil's messages. Although Emil did not present himself verbally, he was also not one to leave his feelings unexpressed. Much like the raw meat comment, Emil's messages were cryptic and symbolic. He talked in play, drawings, and actions.

My domination of the verbal space and difficulty in deciphering other types of communication pushed Emil to the side. In my desire to "be a therapist" I was actually rejecting him because he would not just sit and chat with me. In fact, no child would. Nor would most adults. People have their own defenses when they are asked to build a new connection. As a therapist, it was my job to keep my own defenses in check and respect my patient's. But this was a theoretical notion. The task of monitoring myself with a patient radically different than I, and who needed an interaction radically different than what I imagined "therapy" ought to be, only became real with actual patients.

For example, Emil regulated his anxiety by counting, making lists, and at times, going to the bathroom. He would count toys, count pencils, count times of doing something. He would also walk around the room and make compulsive hand movements. In the first few weeks of treatment, he inventoried the playroom innumerable times. Often he started counting when I asked him too many questions. He went to the bathroom when I reflected on emotions. This appeared to be a common reaction for children with his diagnosis. In her description of psychodynamic play therapy treatment with a girl diagnosed with Asperger syndrome, Rhode (2011) stated: "She seemed to be taking refuge from fears of damage or from my murderousness by withdrawing into this autistic-like sleep" (p. 296). Escaping from frightening material or from the therapist's overbearing approach was not unique to Emil. However, I had to learn how to hear his unique message to me. Counting equaled "I need to tune you out," and going to the bathroom meant, "You're touching on a subject I need to run away from." My intellect grasped it quite quickly, but my need to act got the better of me again and again.

Since my supervisor asked me to transcribe the sessions, I had to listen to myself intruding on Emil every week. I would listen and cringe. "My God, I'm such a chatterbox!" I thought. But every time I entered the playroom I felt that I was supposed to do something, which translated into making comments and asking questions. I was hoping for some verbal breakthrough that would jump-start the therapy, but Emil hardly spoke. I had quickly developed deep feelings of care for Emil, and these benevolent emotions contributed to my wish to form an ideal connection with him. Still, it took time to open up to the kind of connection Emil could offer and benefit from.

Unlike Emil, my supervisor was not shy nor quiet. Actually she was an Israeli woman, like me: direct, forward, warm, and sharp. She delivered her help with passion and intensity, which worked well for me. She was reassuring, especially because I desperately wanted to learn how to help Emil and my other patients. Emil was smart and creative, and when he did talk, he was funny and quirky. A lot of adults loved and enjoyed him, but his peers were often mean to him, and he had a hard time at school. His parents reported stories of bullying and rejection, and I wanted to empower him and create an opportunity for him to better fit into the school world. In so wishing, I was actually asking him to be someone different and not himself.

The challenges I faced in giving therapy were echoed in my own therapy. At times I shared Emil's frustration about the nature of the world I found myself in. As a foreigner I found American culture at odds with my inclinations and style. My own therapist seemed fond of me, allowing me to talk and talk. His interventions pointed to realities I was avoiding and ways in which I was clinging to fantasies, trying my best to escape a painful truth. Wanting things to be different, ignoring unwanted realities, trying to escape emotional pain, and wanting to be loved as we are without needing to change are all human desires. Collectively these needs and desires could create patterns of behavior and interactions that are damaging and frustrating. My therapist told me there were fragile aspects of myself that I did not respect enough. He pointed out that I wanted certain parts of myself gone because they caused me pain and added that getting to know those parts rather than trying to rid myself of them might be more therapeutic. In addition, I began realizing how I used talking as a defense. As much as my therapist enjoyed my wit and insight, he also saw that talking helped me dampen my feelings.

THE HEALING POWER OF ACCEPTANCE

Work with my own therapist was not directly related to my work with Emil. Still, I saw parallels between my struggle to face my demons and mourn painful realities and the difficulties I was having as Emil's therapist. In both therapies, I was engaging in a challenging yet healing process to accept others as they are and not how I wished them to be. In both rooms, I had to accept my own self in relationship while learning more about my role in interactions. These therapeutic connections informed me about the joy and growth of being close to another, and also about the potential for pain and loss inherent in such closeness. I felt the theories I knew so well coming to life and making sense on a profound personal level.

By wanting to have a fantasy relationship with Emil, I was protecting myself from change, from knowing on a deeper level that he was different, and from caring more profoundly about the suffering caused by his oddness. I was also missing out on how unique, smart, and original he was. My supervisor, more realistic than I, trusted that forming a connection would be healing, all by itself. Being the two warm and noisy women that we were, we talked over each other and fought for space in supervision. That is a common form of interaction among Israelis. Although our cacophony could at times be challenging, my supervisor did not need me or our relationship to be different. Both she and my therapist modeled for me how it felt to be understood and valued. My supervisor and I created a safe space in which we were both known and appreciated. She was interested in me and invested not in changing me but rather in helping me find my path. By believing that I would be a good enough fit with the profession I was entering, she enabled me to make a real change in my work. This came about when I stopped talking so much and instead allowed myself to feel.

One day, after I had been probing Emil for most of the session, he presented a puppet show called "This Is Madness," which was about a monkey who needed to handle a "no monkey day" in the playroom. I asked him all sorts of questions to which he mostly replied, "I don't know." Then he sat down and started counting, ignoring me. He spent the rest of the session drawing in silence. He drew a huge dinosaur and a little soldier shooting at it. The soldier's gun was shooting orange lines at the dinosaur. On the other side he drew the dinosaur lying dead on the ground with Xs for eyes. I brought the drawings to my supervisor. She said "Oh my! Look what happened to the soldier! He became so small!" At first I did not know what she was referring to, so she showed me that next to the big, dead dinosaur was a tiny figure. I began crying. Emil felt that he needed to destroy me, which in turn left him too small for me to notice. Not only did he fear his anger and hostility toward me, but also he felt invisible in the room. He was scared that if he expressed his anger he would annihilate me and lose all presence himself. Worst of all was the terrible realization that I did not see the little figure on my own. My supervisor was compassionate, stating, "It is so awful for you, thinking that you are not helping Emil." I had not thought of it that way. I believed I was just a bad therapist. Busy with my anxiety, I did not see that Emil was trying to be known to me. I also did not realize how desperate I was to know I was helping. By not reading his cues, I made sure to miss any indication that he was engaged and benefiting from working with me.

Luckily, as therapists we have many opportunities for rupture and repair. You cannot be perfect, and as terrible as that notion seems to be, you can be "good enough" (Winnicott, 1953). My supervisor was able to teach me the signs that suggested Emil did want to be known. He wanted to be recognized, respected, and loved. My supervisor suggested that I allow his style to dominate the playroom. "Stop trying to talk to him about him," she said. "He cannot do that, and you're talking above his head. Play with him," she said. "Don't try to interpret his game. Work in the game. He needs that degree of separation. He needs that space." So I started to assume characters in Emil's plays and interact with him as different dolls and puppets.

Soon, however, my characters talked too much. Change is such a slow process. "Why don't you try to just sit back and let him invite you? See how he wants to use your presence," said my supervisor.

"But what if he doesn't?" I replied. "What if he just spends the hour ignoring me?"

"Well, then you can mention it to him," she said.

Novick and Novick (2000) have commented on the great relief many clients feel when their therapists verbalize the difficulties in building a working alliance and allowing for a growing closeness to form. Emil surprised me when I backed off and let him play. Usually I would pick up a doll and assume a character, trying to be involved. This time I remained quiet. "Just let things unfold," I told myself.

After a few minutes of play, Emil looked at me and said, "You are supposed to be someone!" I had been invited by this shy child to be a part of his play. And my pushy attitude, though not allowing him much room, had created a norm of my being involved. Emil chose to use this option. I was so happy. Of course, he closed himself off and drew back many more times, but he also invited me to play with him many more times. That was another great lesson. Even though I was being quite overbearing and Emil was uncomfortable, my good intentions and care did not go unnoticed. Although I did not know exactly what it was that made him want to communicate with me when I finally stepped back, I did something right. This was a wonderful realization.

My presence in the playroom changed. I felt internally quieter. I was able to look at Emil and listen to him. For his part, he learned to be more assertive with me. More than once he started doing something, and before I was able to get involved he said, "Don't ask!" Sometimes he would later say, "Now you can ask." We became better balanced. As our relationship unfolded, I began having strong feelings for Emil. I was excited to meet with him and enjoyed our interactions. I cared deeply for Emil and no longer wanted him to be different. Understanding how much we both benefited from my acceptance, I suffered a great deal when thinking about how he was suffering at school or how significant adults in his life wanted him to be different. These feelings made me concerned that perhaps I had transgressed some boundary. Was I supposed to think about my patient so much? Was I supposed to have such intense emotions? My memory of an old therapist and the experience with my current therapist helped me normalize these feelings, because I believed both therapists cared deeply about me. In examining the effect of my own therapists' love for me, I could only conclude that it was a good thing.

A boundary is not transgressed because of a feeling but rather when a feeling is rejected or denied and then comes into play unconsciously and without deliberation in the therapy. The appropriate and warm love that I received taught me that I was loveable in the therapy room. I believe that Emil felt the love I had for him and that it contributed to his sense of self and his healthy narcissism, even if it scared him at times. I also believe that my feelings for him gave him some familiarity with intense emotions. More precisely, Emil grew accustomed to my emotional presentation, which was radically different from his, and he found it to be (mostly) favorable. Though hard for Emil to tolerate without anxiety, those emotions helped him identify strong emotions within himself. In our very last session he was able to express himself in a manner that was characteristic of me and not of a young child diagnosed with Asperger syndrome. His ability to express himself in a novel way was an impressive step in growth and self-knowledge.

As Emil and I became more attuned, my relationship with my supervisor blossomed. I felt more secure and was able to discuss with her my feelings about Emil, knowing that I would not be judged and that we could explore together their meaning, their potential effect on Emil, and how to use them for the benefit of the psychotherapy. I was eager for her approval, but I was also able to appreciate her pointers and criticism. Students are often easily offended by their supervisors and feel devastated by criticism. It is of utmost importance for both students and supervisors to remember that and do their best to create an honest and open zone of communication. Students might benefit from developing a thicker skin that enables them to maintain curiosity even when they hear something negative. Supervisors might take heed that students need their support and belief in them. Their faith that students can become effective psychologists is crucial to the clinical training.

My own thick skin helped me make the most of supervision. Similarly, Emil's invitation to play and his ability to be more assertive taught me something important. He did not break under my "criticism" and demands that he act differently. In fact, once I adjusted myself to his style, he immediately responded, allowing for more closeness and talking much more. Though he sometimes showed me that he resented our mismatched communication, he also benefited from being in therapy with me. His resilience afforded him access to the parts of me he liked and needed. Similarly, my resilience in the light of my supervisor's direct style gave me access to her wisdom, guidance, and care.

In the playroom, Emil and I learned each other's communication style. We were each less afraid of the other, less afraid of getting close. We both felt dominant at times and tiny and worthless at others. We both knew that life after therapy would not be perfect but that therapy made life better. The richness of our playroom adventure was making a difference outside of it. I became more confident. My interventions became more deliberate as I saw Emil for who he was. He was not my project and he was not going to change into a different person. He was, however, delightful, smart, and able to grow. His parents shared stories of more meaningful interactions with his peers. His teachers reported that he was calmer and more cooperative in school.

I was also calmer and relating better to others. My supervisor did not have to work as hard to quiet me. As the year came to a close, she began directing me toward separating from Emil, which was difficult. Working with him had been a gift, and he was often on my mind. His play was rich and beautiful, easily lending itself to psychodynamic interpretations. In addition, I could sense that he liked working with me, too. The playroom, much like my own therapy and the supervision office, became a meaningful space for sharing. Toward the end of the year, I was able to sit through puppet shows, creations of whole comic books, and elaborate stories that had started three years earlier, as Emil imbued dolls and Lego figures with personalities and put them in relationships.

Once, Emil enacted the whole animated movie *Over the Hedge* through two sessions. The video recording of that session showed me with my back to the camera, facing the puppet-show stand. Emil's enactment of the movie was creative and emotional as he explored themes of loneliness, suspicion of others, friendships, and hunger. I showed my supervisor the tape, and we both became tearful. Then she said, "Is that your back? You sat there for twenty minutes without saying a word!" Indeed, I was able to just let the session unfold without leading it. There was no need for me to be directive or overtly active. Emil's play was fascinating, and giving him my undivided attention was easy. And it was healing. Being moved by him did not kill me or leave him feeling tiny and alone; rather it gave us both more space in the playroom, and that space, though challenging, was remarkable.

Emil continued to juggle his desire to form a connection and his deep fear of engulfment and loss. He knew how painful it was to lose what we were sharing, since he had said goodbye to two therapists already. Again, I was the raw meat. I had never said goodbye to a client before. Sensing my rawness, my supervisor instructed me to say goodbye in a prescriptive manner. Her firm and direct intervention was called for because my strong emotions confused me, and she could tell I needed containment. I did not want to end the year with her or with Emil, but it was inevitable. Of course, I had said goodbye many times before, but never had I explicitly stated to those I was leaving how much they meant to me and why. So simple but so foreign was the idea that goodbye could be made more meaningful if used to note what the relationship meant.

SAYING GOODBYE

In the second to last session, I told Emil exactly what my supervisor told me to say. It was easy, because she put into words something I felt but never thought about in such clear terms. I said: "Emil, you know, you're different from other children. And I know that it makes life difficult sometimes. But it also makes you special."

"I know!" stated Emil with pride.

"And it was special for me to know you. I will never forget you, and I will think about you when I see the movies we talked about, or when I think about evolution, or the animals you taught me about. Even though I will be sad that we can't play together anymore, I will always be happy that I met you."

Then Emil raised his eyes to me and said something wonderful and unexpected: "I feel the same way about you."

When I showed my supervisor the video of that moment, she repeated his words, imitating his little voice several times. That feeling of care and joy of what we shared and the sadness of goodbye were present in the supervision room. If I had been told at the beginning of the year that I would be able to feel such a spectrum of emotions toward this boy, express them with confidence, trust that he would understand, and be lucky enough to have him reciprocate, I would not have believed it. If someone were to tell me that I would proudly show my supervisor a segment of my work and that both of us would tear up, being moved together by a simple human encounter, I would have found it hard to imagine. Yet there we were, sharing closeness, tolerating separation, and balancing the paradox of recognition (Benjamin, 1987) in which no one was engulfed, no one annihilated. Knowing each other and accepting reality was worth it. It made life better, even if the world around us stayed as it was—even if we had to let go.

In our last session, Emil, who never said my name, walked into the playroom. Looking around, he stood in the middle of the room and said awkwardly, "Adi, today I am depressed because it is our last session." It was my turn to say, "I feel the same way." Emil shared his feelings by using my language and expressing himself explicitly. It was an adult, self-aware, direct statement, and I still consider it to be a present he gave me—a precious gift, because exploring and sharing his feelings in that way were hard for him.

After that, Emil took paper and pens and started expressing himself in his way. The balance we achieved during the year was apparent in the transformation of Emil's depiction of himself and me. For the rest of the session, Emil diligently worked on a comic page he titled, "What Happened in Psychology This Year." Cohler and Wiener (2011) describe the power of psychodynamic work with Asperger's patients in helping them create a coherent story from the bits and pieces of their experience. They argue that the relationship itself is enabling the patient and the therapist to understand the other in the room. In our last session, Emil was able to take the new knowledge of himself and of me and to create a story of us. Each little square in his comics strip had a scene from the playroom, of him and me playing, my watching him enact a movie in the puppet-show stand, us making a Lego version of *Star Wars*. No longer did Emil depict a dinosaur and a soldier ending up dead or invisible; we became us. We had become a story with a beginning, middle, and a happy ending.

NOTES

Names and identifying data were changed to disguise the identity of the persons involved.

REFERENCES

Benjamin, J. (1987). The decline of the Oedipus complex. In J. M. Broughton (Ed.), *Critical theories of psychological development* (pp. 211–244). New York: Plenum Press.

Cohler, B. J., and Weiner, T. (2011). The inner fortress: Symptom and meaning in Asperger's syndrome. *Psychoanalytic Inquiry, 31*(3), 208–221.

Goodman, G., and Athey-Lloyd, L. (2011). Interaction structures between a child and two therapists in the psychodynamic treatment of a child with Asperger's disorder. *Journal of Child Psychotherapy, 37*, 311–326.

Novick, J., and Novick, K. (2000). Love in the therapeutic alliance. *Journal of the American Psychoanalytic Association, 48*(1), 189–218.

Rhode, M. (2011). Asperger's syndrome: A mixed picture. *Psychoanalytic Inquiry, 31*(3), 288–302.

Slavin, J. H. (2010). Becoming an individual: Technically subversive thoughts on the role of the analyst's influence. *Psychoanalytic Dialogues, 20*(3), 308–324.

Winnicott D. W. (1953). Transitional objects and transitional phenomena; a study of the first not-me possession. *The International Journal of Psychoanalysis , 34*(2), 89–97.

Chapter Three

Guilt in the Beginning Therapist

Etiology and Impact on Treatment

Benjamin Gottesman

The first few years of graduate training in clinical psychology require students to tackle the daunting task of learning how to become a therapist. Like all novice therapists, I found the difficulties inherent in learning and applying complex theories and techniques compounded by the myriad personal emotions I felt while engaging with clients in the therapeutic relationship. Among the most prominent and powerful emotions that I felt was guilt. This guilt was induced by a variety of scenarios, ranging from terminating the therapy relationship with a client at the end of the training year to making an error when treating a client, both common occurrences among beginners. In turn, my clients reacted to my guilt with emotions and thoughts of their own. When I searched the literature, I found there has been little written about the beginning clinician's experience of guilt and how it impacts the therapist and the therapeutic relationship. This chapter takes a closer look at the emotion of guilt and considers the possible reasons it arises in training. It also describes how guilt affected my psyche and behavior and provides graduate student therapists with advice about how to cope with this common emotion.

THE ORIGINS OF GUILT

Sigmund Freud was among the first to write about the origins of guilt from a psychoanalytic perspective. Freud (1929/1962) attributed much significance to this emotion and its impact on society. In fact, his aim in *Civilization and Its Discontents* was "to represent the sense of guilt as the most important problem in the development of civilization and to show that the price we pay for our advance in civilization is a loss of happiness through the heightening of a sense of guilt" (p. 81). According to Freud, there are two origins of guilt. One arises from the fear of others' punishment or disapproval: a person has certain instinctual drives which he regards as "bad" because acting upon them would lead to the loss of love of another person and/or potential punishment. Over time, external authority becomes increasingly internalized and autonomous in the form of the superego, the second origin of guilt. Freud (1929/1962) postulated that man's innate tendency toward aggression is curtailed by his ability to internalize his aggressive instincts and direct those toward himself by developing a superego, which polices his aggressive impulses with the same harshness that he would like to act out against others in the external world. The tension between the inhibitory warnings of the superego and the aggressive urges is experienced as guilt. For Freud guilt is the fear of an inner policeman, formed by one's experience with a threatening parent and representing, in however distorted a form, the threats of that parent. In essence, guilt represents a fear of retaliation, either by external forces or by the internalized superego, after an imagined or real transgression against another.

Melanie Klein had another view on the origins of guilt. While she acknowledged the validity of Freud's idea of fear for the self, she called it anxiety. In contrast, in her nomenclature guilt refers to the fear of injuring a loved object. In her essay "On Criminality" (1934/1975), she conceived of two stages of superego development, later to be called the paranoid and depressive positions. Klein maintained that from infancy babies harbor aggressive and rageful fantasies of destroying their parents when their needs are not met. In the first stage, the infant's aggressive urges against its parents, which prove intolerable to the infant's psyche, are projected onto the parents, so that the parents are seen as the ones who want to hurt the infant. This leads to anxiety and paranoia lest they retaliate. In the second stage these aggressive fantasies lead to distress and guilt accompanying the infant's belief that it has damaged its loved object. Thus guilt is directly related to identification with and love of another (Klein, 1934/1975). The more one loves another person, the worse one feels thinking one has injured that other. Guilt, for Klein, is born of a fear of hurting another. Consistent with this stance, in her essay "Love, Guilt and Reparation" (1937/1975), Klein wrote of the "drive" toward reparation stemming from one's love and one's guilt over having damaged the objects of one's love. Klein was very clear that guilt and the drive to make reparation are not simply egocentric and self-preservative in nature but primary motivations based on love of another. In summary, Freud's guilt is egocentric and internally focused, consistent with his intrapsychically oriented drive theory, while Klein's guilt is other-focused, consistent with her object-relations theory.

A third common type of guilt that can be seen as an extension of Klein's guilt is survivor's guilt. Niederland (1961) first described this type of severe guilt experienced by survivors of the Holocaust. Typically, after struggling to begin a new life and often succeeding, these individuals succumbed to a variety of symptoms, including depression, anhedonia anxiety, identity disturbance, and psychosomatic conditions (Niederland, 1981). Niederland (1961) stated that the Holocaust survivors he encountered experienced an "ever-present feeling of guilt . . . for having survived the very calamity to which their loved ones succumbed" (p. 238) and concluded that his patients' pathology was not due to prior unconscious hostile wishes toward their loved ones, but rather to the patients' unconscious belief that merely remaining alive was a betrayal of the dead.

Psychoanalyst Arnold Modell (1965) broadened the concept of survivor guilt to include more subtle forms of survival accompanied by unconscious guilt. For example, one of his patients was a talented woman who had married well and achieved financial and professional success, rising far above the station of her parents. The patient undid her success by experiencing it as unreal, as if it were playacting. She provoked fights with her husband, which eroded her marital happiness, and allowed herself little pleasure in any of her activities. The patient's "deepest conviction was that she had no right to a life better than that of her mother, which was perceived by her as a life of hardship and degradation" (Modell, 1965, p. 326). Modell (1971) concluded that there is "in mental life something that might be termed an unconscious bookkeeping system, i.e., a system that takes account of the distribution of the available 'good' within a given nuclear family so that the current fate of other family members will determine how much 'good' one possesses. If fate has dealt harshly with other members of the family the survivor may experience guilt" (p. 340). Modell also wrote about "separation guilt" which is guilt based on a belief that growing up and separating from the mother will damage or even destroy a person. More generally, separation guilt is based on a belief that evolving one's own autonomy—having a separate existence from one's family or significant others or a life of one's own—is damaging to others. Modell's concepts of separation and survivor guilt are both based on the premise that some people hold the belief that their own welfare comes at the expense of another's. Both forms of guilt are occasioned by a belief that pursuing normal developmental or life goals harms a significant other.

Michael Friedman (1985) further elaborated that survivor's guilt arises when one believes that one could have helped—but failed to help—a loved one. It is a guilt borne of inaction as opposed to action, by people who believe they unjustly have better lives than those of their parents or siblings. The greater the discrepancy between one's own fate and the fate of the loved person one failed to help, the greater the empathic distress and the more poignant one's guilt.

GUILT AND THERAPISTS IN TRAINING

The aforementioned theories are relevant in elucidating the feelings of guilt that may arise in student therapists in training. Freud's guilt, based on the fear of retaliation from an outside force or from the superego, can be seen operating in a number of areas idiosyncratic to the training experience. Student therapists frequently report feeling like imposters or frauds when they start doing therapy. Often, the first year or two doing therapy is characterized by the sense that "I have no idea what I am doing." I believe that this can lead to feelings of guilt when students feel they have "done therapy wrong" and worry that the patient will recognize them as the imposters they feel they are. In addition, due to their inexperience, beginning therapists tend to be more rule-bound in their approach to treatment and may have a more punishing superego than more experienced clinicians. These tendencies, combined with fears of evaluation and fear of failure, create a perfect storm for feelings of guilt to develop. A potential outgrowth of this guilt is omitting details of the session, consciously or unconsciously, when discussing the case in supervision, for fear of being chastised by the supervisor. An additional guilt trigger, particularly for beginning therapists, is the development of negative transference on the part of the client. This commonplace occurrence, which is a normative part of the therapeutic relationship, often feels to beginning therapists like a personal attack. Rather than recognizing it as a transference reaction to be considered grist for the mill, students often attribute the patient's acting out to their own lack of experience and ineptitude, which leads to a feeling that it is their fault the client is acting out.

One can think of numerous ways in which the Kleinian perspective of guilt, centered on the fear of damaging or destroying another, can manifest itself in a student therapist's experience. First, feelings of incompetence and inauthenticity can also lead to fear of committing an error and harming the patient. In addition, the dislike that patients often elicit in their therapists can lead to a desire to hurt the patient, which will likely precipitate a feeling of guilt. There are a number of reasons a student therapist may come to dislike a patient. Novice clinicians often are required to juggle their caseloads with the demands of being a full-time student. When students are in the midst of finals and other academic responsibilities, it is sometimes difficult for them to give their full attention and energy to sessions with patients. They may resent patients for taking their time and energy, for little or no compensation, when they have a term paper due the next day and have had little sleep. In his landmark paper, "Hate in the Countertransference," Winnicott (1949/1994) says this about the analyst: "However much he loves his patients he cannot avoid hating them, and fearing them, and the better he knows this the less will hate and fear be the motive determining what he does to his patients" (p. 340). While experienced therapists can and do harbor hateful feelings toward their patients, it is likely that, due to the newness of the therapy endeavor, novice clinicians may be caught by surprise by their hateful feelings and may be more likely to enact a guilt-based response to their own hate.

Another source of guilt for student therapists is the short-term nature of the therapy they provide. This is where survivor's guilt and separation guilt come into play. One of the features of the training clinic in many programs is that students remain as therapists solely for the duration of the academic year. Thus, wherever the patient is in the course of his treatment, the student therapist has to terminate with the patient at the end of the year or transfer the case to a new therapist. Although in an ideal situation the therapist and patient discuss the termination date from the start of treatment and work over the course of the year toward a therapeutic parting of ways, this sudden and often premature end to the therapy relationship can lead to a sense that the therapist has harmed the patient by leaving him so abruptly. Moreover, the end of a training placement for most students marks an advance in their professional careers as they move one step closer to graduation and the start of a career. In contrast, the end of a therapy relationship for many clients marks a low point. Much of the time patients continue to suffer, to varying degrees, the maladies they entered therapy with, even as they lose an intimate confidante and are required to start the tenuous relationship-building process all over again with a new therapist. This discrepancy between the fate of the therapist and the fate of the client, whom the therapist has likely grown fond of, can easily lead to guilt.

IMPACT OF GUILT ON A THERAPIST

While guilt is a common human emotion, unchecked guilt in a therapist can lead to significant negative consequences that can affect the work of the therapist with a patient. One major pitfall of guilt is the potential for the therapist to develop countertransference reactions that lead to enactments. Jacobs (1986) wrote about the ways in which an analyst's countertransference reactions may be unconsciously expressed through his behavior in both overt and covert ways in the therapy. These instances of acting out on the part of the therapist are also known as enactments. It is well known that from the very outset of treatment, transferences are activated in both the analyst and patient. Whether overt or disguised, dramatic or barely perceptible, the analyst's transferences can exert a significant influence not only on his perceptions and understanding but also on the particular form and manner in which the patient's transferences emerge (Jacobs, 1986). Conveyed in tone and gesture as well as in words, these reactions may be expressed in the barest of nods, the most minimal of smiles, the scarcely audible grunt, or the slightest variation in words of greeting or farewell. The way in which thera-

pists listen, their silences and neutrality, their interpretations, and other facets
of their clinical work may contain concealed countertransference elements.
Therefore, a strong feeling of guilt on the part of the therapist can unconsciously influence his behavior and attitude toward the patient in overt and
covert ways.

Altman (2005) noted that guilt—acknowledging one has damaged or hurt
someone one cares about, either inadvertently or advertently—is an extremely painful emotion to bear. Therefore, there is a strong pull to resort to
defensive measures to avoid feeling guilt. One such defense is blaming the
victim: we tell ourselves and others that the ones we hurt deserved to be hurt
or that they brought it on themselves. In a variation on this theme, we objec-
tify those to whom we have caused damage, denying that they are people like
us. A third common defense against guilt is a manic defense, characterized
by "clinging to a sense of omnipotence, denial of psychic reality, an associated flight into action as opposed to thought, and massive projective identification" (Altman, 2005, p. 330). Manic defenses counteract depressive guilt by
keeping a person from reflecting on the circumstances surrounding the guilt.
Unreflective action replaces reflection as a way to get rid of unwanted feelings (Altman, 2005). Defensive maneuvers against guilt, left unchecked, can
prove disastrous for therapy if a therapist brings them into his work with a
client.

Furthermore, there may be idiosyncratic aspects of therapists' personalities that make them more prone to guilt and anxiety than other professionals.
Sussman (2007) explored in depth the unconscious motives therapists have
for practicing psychotherapy. He quotes Holt and Luborsky (1958) as stating,
"psychiatry attracts people who are in the process of mastering personal
problems. It may be from this source that one develops an interest in treating
people" (Sussman, 2007, p. 66). For many people becoming a therapist is a
reparative act intended to fix their family or make up for a traumatic event in
their past. In essence, their choice of profession is in some part related to
residual strong feelings of guilt. For example, Eigen (1998), whose brother
was hit and killed by a truck, noted, "My mother never fully recovered and to
say I felt guilty does not even come close. I suspect I became an analyst
partly to bring my brother back to life" (p. 81). Searles (1966) suggested that
many therapists may choose the profession of psychotherapy on the basis of
unconscious guilt over having failed to cure their parents. Sussman (2007)
wrote that, once understood and mastered, therapists' emotional conflicts can
actually aid them in their efforts to empathize and connect with clients.
Indeed, the archetype of the *wounded healer,* which presupposes that personal suffering is a prerequisite to becoming a shaman or physician who helps
others out of suffering, has a long and venerable history in cultures around
the world. Poal and Weisz (1989) suggested that therapists who faced numerous problems in childhood were more effective in empathizing with and

assisting their clients than therapists who had a more problem-free child-hood.

Finally, the flip side of every crime is punishment. If a therapist imagines that he hurt a patient, for any of the abovementioned reasons, and feels guilty, he may engage in self-sabotage in an attempt to atone for his "sin" and relieve his guilt. He may do something to make the patient angry at him, such as come late to a session, say something insensitive to the patient, or sabotage himself or the treatment in some other way. These actions, while perhaps satisfying the therapist's need for absolution, will likely adversely affect the client and the progress of therapy.

CASE STUDY

In my own work with a client I saw for analytically informed treatment at my graduate program's outpatient clinic for twelve weeks during a recent summer, I experienced some of the manifestations of guilt mentioned in the literature. My hope is that this case will serve to clarify and demonstrate the practical significance of many of the points made earlier. Mitch was a man who came to therapy presenting with depression. From the very start, the circumstances under which the treatment was conducted were less than ideal. While most of my classmates had finished their clinic practicum at the end of July, I was required to see Mitch until the end of September, as I had not sufficiently completed my clinic requirements over the course of the academic year. This fact elicited guilt, as I imagined that my delinquency had damaged my relationship with the clinic director and assistant director. In addition, while twelve sessions might have been enough for certain patients and theoretical models of therapy, it was quite a tall order for interpersonal psychoanalytic therapy, the modality I was being supervised in. Thus, from the very first intake session, I felt anxious both about having to remain in the clinic over the summer and about the thought of leaving the clinic, and Mitch, three months hence. This guilt was further complicated by a number of factors that developed in the first couple of weeks. In the first two intake sessions, Mitch described a severe history of abuse. This heightened my sense of guilt about leaving Mitch, since I felt that, by leaving him, I would join a long line of abusers and provide him with further confirmation of how abhorrent he was to others. Complicating matters was the fact that Mitch, almost immediately upon my meeting him, developed an idealizing transference toward me in which I could do no wrong. He was a model patient in the sense that he always arrived early for sessions and had his fee ready at the end, no small feat for a client in a training clinic, which I learned from my other clients. His frequent praise of my abilities and positive demeanor toward me strengthened my conviction that my eventual departure would be a major blow to him.

From a Kleinian point of view, those who cannot bear depressive guilt resort to defensive measures to avoid it. One such measure is splitting, or keeping separate those we love from those we hate, so that damage is never done to the loved ones. In this case, my inability to bear the guilt I felt about my relationship with the clinic director and assistant director, symbolic parental figures, led me to resent Mitch instead. I blamed him for having to drive out to Long Island once a week in traffic just to see him. I faulted him for the Sunday mornings I gave up weekly to receive supervision for his case. In addition, Mitch's primary defense mechanisms—intellectualization, rationalization, and reaction formation—had the collective effect of dampening and blunting his affect, leading him to minimize his symptoms and difficulties. Consequently, he spent a significant portion of sessions stating that all his troubles were behind him and how his difficult history had allowed him to help others. Although I was largely aware that these were defenses that masked a tormented soul—"Band Aids," as he himself described them—I still found myself wondering at times what he was doing in the clinic talking to me if all of his problems had been ostensibly resolved. This led to further aggressive feelings toward him for "holding me hostage" and taking my time and energy in the therapy room and in supervision when he claimed not to need help. My resentment of Mitch led to additional feelings of guilt about my thoughts toward him, as I feared my aggression toward him would emerge and damage him. Furthermore, I also harbored resentments toward those supervisors who "sentenced" me to twelve weeks of "penance" for my misdeed, which I largely did not acknowledge.

Although I am now able to identify in hindsight the extent to which I felt these guilty countertransferential emotions and the reasons behind them, at the time I lacked full conscious awareness of the strength of these feelings. Looking back on the treatment with Mitch, I recognize several enactments that occurred between us in the therapy. One of the more significant enactments occurred in the first session. As part of the clinic procedure, clients read and sign statements of informed consent. These documents describe the basic details of the treatment clients receive, the limits of confidentiality, and the therapy fee. Since these documents are somewhat lengthy and dense, students are supposed to discuss with their clients their details to ensure that they are understood. Therefore, among my first tasks was informing Mitch that I would be terminating with him at the end of September, at which point we would decide together whether he should continue treatment with one of the incoming therapists. In this discussion, I accidentally neglected to mention the detail about being transferred to another therapist. Instead, I said that in September we would evaluate whether he should continue to receive treatment in the clinic. Of course, Mitch assumed that I meant that at the end of

September, we would evaluate whether he should continue to receive treatment in the clinic *from me*. This inadvertent omission was a clear expression of my guilty conscience, which led me to defensively avoid the issue of termination instead of addressing it in a straightforward manner.

Another overt enactment that repeated itself weekly was invariably extending my fifty-minute therapy hour with Mitch. This deviation from the frame was uncharacteristic of my sessions with other clients in the clinic. I was aware of this at the time; however, I rationalized to myself that Mitch was a talkative person and had a hard time ending sessions. I realize now that this stance was in part a projection onto him of the difficulty *I* had ending sessions, and the treatment as a whole for that matter. Extending the sessions by five to ten minutes was a way for me to alleviate my guilt by giving him extra time, an attempt at reparation. I could not tolerate and stoically bear my guilt and, instead, acted out and extended the therapy frame. By extending the therapy frame, I unconsciously communicated to Mitch that I was willing to treat him in a special way, to make exceptions for him. These errors of omission and commission would have devastating consequences later on, when, at the urging of my supervisor, I finally told Mitch a month before termination that I would not be continuing to work with him past September.

The session when the issue of termination was finally discussed was among the most difficult ones that I have experienced thus far as a therapist. Mitch had been talking about the way in which his difficult childhood allowed him to help others who were going through difficulties. He said emphatically, "I don't think you could ever, ever . . . You can't reach out to people until you've suffered yourself." I sensed that he was addressing me with this statement and expressing concern about my ability to help him.

I stated, "Do you ever doubt my ability to empathize?" After a brief pause, Mitch began praising me and my abilities, stating how comfortable he felt talking with me. At this point I brought up the fact that September was approaching and we should discuss his continuing in the clinic or not. Once again, as in the first session, I did not say whom he would be continuing with, and Mitch assumed I meant we would assess his continuing in the clinic with me. After all, he had just expressed how much he liked and trusted me. In that moment, perhaps in an act of self-delusion, I had imagined in my mind that Mitch knew that we were not going to continue together. So when he spoke about continuing treatment with me, I became alarmed and extremely anxious that he appeared to have no idea that I was leaving.

Now I had no choice but to make my message explicit: "I am leaving the clinic at the end of September," I said.

"Where are you going?" Mitch replied sharply.

After I replied to his question, he said, "I don't know if I want to talk to anyone else but you."

I then said, "I know it's hard to switch therapists. I feel the same way, honestly, that I established a relationship with you and want to continue it, but clinic policy dictates otherwise."

What followed was a candid discussion with Mitch about how hard it had been for him to be in therapy. "It's like ripping your soul. It's like peeling parts of yourself away, exposing your vulnerabilities." After these observations, he continued to state how much he trusted me and felt at ease talking to me.

As I listened to the session recording afterward, I reflected upon the fact that I brought up the issue of termination immediately after I had elicited from Mitch an expression of trust of me. It seemed almost sadistic of me to lead him on into making positive statements about my abilities, only to state that I was leaving him. I can only conclude that it was an enactment of my hate toward Mitch, part of the splitting defense, as well as an attempt to provoke him so he would punish me and thereby alleviate my guilt about wronging him and the clinic administration. Subconsciously, I wanted Mitch to lash out at me, to yell at me for deceiving him and leaving him. After being flooded by guilt about harming him, however, I was unable to follow through with this provocation and tried to preempt further retaliation from Mitch by stating how upset I would be to leave him. Just as Melanie Klein's infant realizes that the object he hatefully destroys is also the object he deeply loves and, gripped by guilt, desperately repairs the object, so too I realized both my love and hate for Mitch and sought to repair Mitch, devastated by my news, by admitting my own regret and sadness to him. My attempt at reparation succeeded on a superficial level, as Mitch did not punish me and soon returned to his praise of me. In addition, despite his initial hesitation, he heeded my recommendation to transfer to another therapist in the clinic. However, I later learned that soon after beginning therapy with his new therapist he terminated his treatment. Upon hearing this, I found myself wondering whether my premature departure had affected his decision.

Stephen Mitchell (2000) distinguished between genuine guilt and guiltiness: "In genuine guilt . . . we consider the consequences of our actions on others and are moved to guilt. There is nothing to be done with these feelings; nothing can be done. We bear them and move on, informed and enriched as we encounter our next experiences. In . . . guiltiness, in contrast, we are trying to do something, and that effort fixes us in a static position" (p. 731–732). Throughout my treatment with Mitch, I was plagued by guiltiness. Unable to bear my guilt, I acted it out, whether through attempts at reparation, words and acts of contempt, or paralyzed inaction. However, with the historical and psychic distance and perspective that time has provided, and through reflecting on my experiences, I feel I have moved toward a sense of genuine guilt that is akin to remorse—a painful recognition of the consequences of my actions on others and the ability to enrich others and myself through this experience.

COPING WITH GUILT

There are various strategies clinicians can use to deal with their guilt. Although I have conceptualized guilt through a psychoanalytic lens thus far, it would be useful to think about strategies from other modes of thought that clinicians can use to cope with their guilt. The following suggestions have their roots in a number of theoretical perspectives, including psychodynamic, cognitive behavioral, and humanistic.

Supervision

The importance of supervision for all therapists, especially therapists in training, cannot be overstated. Being forthcoming and honest in supervision can be a very difficult task, especially in cases in which a therapist is feeling guilt or shame, since our natural tendency when feeling these emotions is to hide them. However, honest communication to a supervisor of guilty feelings about a client is the first step for obtaining help. A supervisor has a number of functions in helping a therapist cope with guilt. First, he can provide a supportive space in which the therapist can reflect on his experience and emotions. This space allows the therapist to process his feelings of guilt and reflect on where they originate. In addition, a supervisor can validate a therapist's emotions or provide direct advice about how to alleviate these negative emotions. Furthermore, supervision is an ideal time to spot any therapist countertransference that is being elicited by a client, which may include feelings of guilt. From his outsider's perspective, the supervisor is often in a much better position to catch countertransference than is the therapist, who is an active participant in the interaction. Once the countertransference is reflected upon, it may yield valuable clinical material about the patient that can aid in the therapy or illuminate blind spots in the therapist's psyche that should be more closely examined in therapy. The attitude one takes toward countertransference may depend on which school of thought within psychoanalysis the therapist most closely follows. The classical approach views countertransference as a hindrance to treatment, rooted in the analyst's neuroses, and indicates that further self-analysis is needed. More contemporary approaches see countertransference as an inevitable phenomenon in therapy that can lead to increased understanding of the patient.

Psychotherapy

As therapists we should value the use of therapy for our own development and mental well-being. Therefore, if one is plagued often by guilt, it might be helpful to seek out counseling to alleviate these feelings. Bringing up guilty feelings in supervision is certainly recommended; however, there may be personal issues the therapist is facing that may be difficult or inappropriate to bring up with a supervisor. These can include past traumas, global personality issues, and anxiety or depression, among others. In addition, the general focus of supervision is on the patient and how to best help him or her, as opposed to focusing on the therapist's personal difficulties. Many training programs encourage and require trainees to enter their own treatment because knowing oneself and one's conflicts and unconscious dynamics plays a significant role in being an effective therapist. This is crucial, as the emotions than can be stirred up in a therapist, left unchecked, "carry the full charge of repressed impulses suddenly bursting out from the depth. Thus they lead to real action, to over-strong emotion or to the opposite, to rigid defenses or blank spots" (Reich, 1966, p. 352). In contrast to other professions in which knowledge of a technology or use of a tool is the key, the personality of the therapist itself is the primary tool the therapist uses in therapy. As Freud stated, "diseases are not cured by the drug but by the physician . . . " (1912, para. 5).

Challenging Your Cognitions

The basis of cognitive-behavioral therapy is that thoughts can influence feelings, and that one's emotional response to a situation comes from one's interpretation of that situation. According to this perspective, guilty feelings are triggered by certain thoughts. Thus, if therapists can identify and challenge these cognitions, they may diffuse the emotions that the cognitions have triggered. Here are some cognitions that may underlie a therapist's guilty feelings and how I would challenge them:

Cognition 1: I damaged my patient by saying the wrong thing.

There are times that you will say the wrong thing and may hurt or offend the patient, just as there are times you put your foot in your mouth in non-therapy interactions. Remember that your patient is likely a remarkably resilient person who has gone through a lot and yet has the strength to come to therapy. So it is unlikely that anything you say will irrevocably damage him. In addition, the patient might not even register that you said anything problematic. Nevertheless, if you did say something offensive that the patient reacted to, part of the work of therapy is repairing the relationship with the client. A reparative gesture or conversation after a therapy rupture often leads to growth in the therapy relationship and can serve as a model to the patient of how to repair relationships that he has damaged in his own life.

Cognition 2: When I leave I am abandoning my patient.

It is important to remember that as significant as you are to your patients, they will continue to go on living after you are gone, just as they were able to live before they met you. Most patients have multiple social supports, of which you are likely a major support but by no means the only one. After bringing up my own guilt to a supervisor about terminating with a child client, she provided me with an apt metaphor for my role in my client's life, which helped to alleviate my guilt. She said that as the child's therapist I am one member of the team of people tasked with rolling a boulder up a hill. Each member of the team aids in the overall effort, but no one single member is essential in the task. Thinking of this metaphor allowed me to end my relationship with my client without fearing that he would "roll backward down the hill" without me, since I knew he had a lot of people working to push him up the hill of rehabilitation.

Cognition 3: I am too inexperienced to treat this patient; I have no idea what I'm doing!

If you were up-front with the patient in the informed-consent process, the patient is aware that you are a trainee. In addition, a recent study reported that clinically inexperienced student therapists providing cognitive-behavioral therapy who receive supervision from experienced supervisors can achieve treatment effects that are on a par with those of experienced licensed psychotherapists (Ost, Karlstedt, and Widen, 2012). The authors say that the key for beginning therapists is to seek out and accept feedback from supervisors. So chances are that you are helpful to your patient as a beginner therapist, even if you do not feel competent.

Cognition 4: It is my fault my patient left (if the patient prematurely left therapy).

This is a classic example of black-and-white thinking. There are many reasons why patients leave therapy, including financial reasons, scheduling challenges, and other personal reasons, including ambivalence about therapy. Sometimes patients are simply not ready to make the changes that therapy requires.

*Cognition 5: I am not devoting as much attention
and energy to this patient as I could be.*

Being a therapist is a demanding job, and you will have good days and bad days, like in any other job. Sometimes you won't be feeling well; other times you'll have a late event the night before or a sick child who keeps you up. What counts is making an effort to be present for your patient.

Cognition 6: My supervisor is going to be upset with me.

Disagreements with supervisors are never pleasant, but it is best to be candid and honest with your supervisor about your feelings or in explaining whatever you think you did wrong. Hiding information from your supervisor is generally not a good idea, as it will probably adversely affect your relationship and create unnecessary tension.

*Cognition 7: My patient is upset with me because
I did something wrong.*

Patients get upset with therapists for all sorts of reasons. As stated earlier, it is common in therapy for a negative transference to develop between the patient and the therapist, in which the therapist can never do enough for the patient or satisfy the patient. Furthermore, at times you will have to set limits in therapy that the patient will not be happy with. The patient's upset with you is not necessarily a reflection on anything you are doing wrong. Depending on what the patient needs, it may be an integral part of the therapy process for the patient to be upset with you.

*Cognition 8: I could have done more to help my
patient in our time together.*

This is a thought that often comes at the end of a therapy relationship. You will find yourself thinking about what might have happened if you had you done X, Y, or Z, or if you had more time together. A difficult realization that all therapists face at one time or another is that in the time-limited therapy relationship, they won't accomplish everything they seek to accomplish with their patients. If you think that at the end of therapy the patient is completely cured of all pathology, you are deluding yourself. Instead of focusing on what you didn't accomplish with your patient, think about what you did accomplish. Ask yourself, is my patient better off today than when I first met him? How has he changed for the better? Most of the time, you will be able to identify real changes the patient has made since starting therapy with you.

CONCLUSION

Not only is guilt deeply embedded as a reaction in the human psyche, but conflicts inherent in human affairs tend to make guilt inevitable. Our values often are conflicting, so to act under the influence of one set of values can lead us to betray another set of values and thus provoke guilt. For example, many of us wish that our loved ones have the best possible educational and material opportunities available to them. We also feel responsible for the homeless and the downtrodden in society at large. But in particular instances we make choices to provide comforts to our families when we might otherwise be able to make contributions to social-service agencies. Guilt, at least in the background, is unavoidable in such a case. If we had made the opposite choice, some guilt with respect to family members might have been inevitable. In short, guilt is inherent in living and choosing. Moreover, guilt is an essential emotion in the maintenance of an orderly society. Freud stated that guilt is the linchpin holding civilization together. Without guilt there would be only sociopathy (Freud, 1962).

It is paramount to remember that therapists are people too, subject to the same emotions as their clients, including guilt. Moreover, the very experiencing of these emotions can actually enhance therapists' abilities to understand and help their clients. However, as the people to whom others turn to for relief and emotional support, it is incumbent upon therapists to examine and master their guilt and find ways to overcome it if it is interfering with treatment. My hope is that this exposition will encourage readers to think more about their guilt and its impact on their work with patients.

NOTE

Names and identifying data were changed to disguise the identity of the persons involved.

REFERENCES

Altman, N. (2005). Manic society: Toward the depressive position. *Psychoanalytic Dialogues, 15*(3), 321–347.

Eigen, M. (1998). Shivers. In J. Reppen (Ed.), *Why I became a psychotherapist* (pp. 77–88). Northvale, NJ: Jason Aronson.

Freud, S. (1962). *Civilization and its discontents* (J. Strachey, Trans. and Ed.). New York: W.W. Norton & Company, Inc. (Original work published 1929)

Freud, S. (1912). *Selected papers on hysteria and other psychoneuroses* (A.A. Brill, Trans.). New York: The Journal of Nervous and Mental Disease Publishing Company. Retrieved from http:// www.bartleby.com/280/

Friedman, M. (1985). Toward a reconceptualization of guilt. *Contemporary Psychoanalysis, 21*(4), 501–48.

Holt, R. R., and Luborsky, L. (1958). *Personality patterns of psychiatrists: A study of methods for selecting residents.* New York: Basic Books.

Jacobs, T. J. (1986). On countertransference enactments. *Journal of the American Psychoanalytic Association, 34*(2), 289–307.

Klein, M. (1975). Love, guilt and reparation. In *Love, guilt and reparation and other works 1921–1945* (Vol. 1). New York: The Free Press. (Original work published 1937)

Klein, M. (1975). On criminality. In *Love, guilt and reparation and other works 1921–1945* (Vol. 1). New York: The Free Press. (Original work published 1934)

Mitchell, S. (2000). You've got to suffer if you want to sing the blues: Psychoanalytic reflections on guilt and self-pity. *Psychoanalytic Dialogues, 10*(5), 713–33.

Modell, A. H. (1965). On having the right to a life: An aspect of the superego's development. *International Journal of Psychoanalysis, 46*(3), 323–31.

Modell, A. H. (1971). The origin of certain forms of pre-oedipal guilt and the implications for a psychoanalytic theory of affects. *International Journal of Psychoanalysis, 52*(4), 337–46.

Niederland, W. G. (1961). The problem of the survivor. *Journal of the Hillside Hospital, 10,* 233–47.

Niederland, W. G. (1981). The survivor syndrome: Further observations and dimensions. *Journal of the American Psychoanalytic Association, 29,* 413–26.

Ost, L. G., Karlstedt, A., and Widen, S. (2012). The effects of cognitive behavior therapy delivered by students in a psychologist training program: An effectiveness study. *Behavior Therapy, 43,* 160–73.

Poal, P., and Weisz, J. R. (1989). Therapists' own childhood problems as predictors of their effectiveness in child psychotherapy. *Journal of Clinical Child Psychology, 18,* 202–5.

Reich, A. (1966). Empathy and countertransference. In *Annie Reich: Psychoanalytic Contributions* (pp. 344–60). New York: International Universities Press.

Searles, H. F. (1966). Feelings of guilt in the psychoanalyst. *Psychiatry, 29,* 319–23.

Sussman, M. B. (2007). *A curious calling: Unconscious motivations for practicing psychotherapy.* Northvale, NJ: Jason Aronson.

Winnicott, D. W. (1994). Hate in the counter-transference. *The Journal of Psychotherapy Practice and Research, 3*(4), 348–56. (Reprinted with permission from The International Journal of Psycho-Analysis, pp. 69–74, by Winnicott Trust and American Psychiatric Press, Inc., 1949.

Chapter Four

The Novice in the Therapist's Chair

Samantha Shoshana Lawrence

We set the time and date for our first appointment. For her it was one of many first appointments, since she had been a patient at the psychotherapy clinic for years. She had seen more than half a dozen therapists already, with each therapeutic dyad enduring just under one year, as her therapists moved on in their training and left her to teach the next crop of novice clinicians. In stark contrast, this appointment was my first, in which I would sit, for the first time, in the therapist's chair across from another person who sought my help. How would I manage my new role as healer, I wondered, when I felt like an imposter? What would I say to my new patient who was thirty years my senior and had experienced unimaginable trauma?

This chapter explores my experience as a novice clinician encountering my first individual patient during doctoral training. These initial therapeutic encounters served as a catalyst for my doctoral research, since I chose to study beginning therapists. Thus, I will also present data from my research participants and document the challenges of being a first-time therapist in a clinical psychology doctoral program.

THE EXPERIENCED PATIENT AND THE INEXPERIENCED THERAPIST

My first patient, a Hispanic female in her early sixties, presented with anxiety and depression. Mary claimed that she was depressed all of the time and that she did not "experience elation." She had come to the realization that she had been depressed all of her life, but that she had only realized it a few years ago, and reported trouble sleeping and unhappiness with her weight gain in recent years. Additionally, Mary felt overwhelmed by her anger and her inability to control it, oftentimes "flying off the handle" at people who angered her. Most of all, Mary was disappointed with her marriage.

Mary had grown up in a strict traditional family with a verbally and physically abusive alcoholic father who terrified her. She described her mother as a subservient, doting wife. During our first session, Mary mentioned that her father had sexually abused her for years, beginning when she was a small girl, but she never shared the details of her incest history. She remarked that those sexual interactions with her father were the only time that he was "nice" to her. She never mentioned a word about the abuse to anyone, but, after several years of victimization, she finally threatened to tell her mother, and the abuse ceased. This left Mary with an enormous amount of guilt, since she felt she could have stopped the abuse sooner if she could have mustered the courage to speak up.

Throughout her teenage years Mary dreamed of attending college but was never able to do so, and as a result she felt intellectually inferior to others and self-conscious about her lack of education. Mary met and married her first husband when she was just a teenager because she wanted to move out of her parents' house. She characterized their relationship as volatile. Her first husband was an alcoholic like her father, with a penchant for sadomasochistic sex. Mary bemoaned the fact that he was unable to communicate on either an emotional or intellectual level. The only kind of intimacy they shared was physical intimacy, which often left Mary feeling used because of her husband's perverse demands. The couple raised four children together, two of whom became alcohol and drug abusers.

After three decades of marriage, Mary's husband left her, and she felt completely devastated by his abandonment. After he left, Mary found out that he had had a string of mistresses throughout their marriage. Mary met her second husband only a few months later, and they married shortly after despite disapproval from her family. This marriage solved the problem of the silence that had filled Mary's home after her first husband left. Mary was the sole financial provider, which enraged her. She felt emotionally neglected and unfulfilled. Both Mary's first husband and her second husband called her "sick" and told her that she "needed help."

Mary had primarily sought help at low-cost psychology training clinics, which resulted in a high turnover in therapists; she had seen seven or eight already by the time she arrived in my office. Throughout her treatment history, Mary tried several antidepressants, many of which caused her to experience negative side effects. She finally found one that was helpful and had been taking it for a couple of years when we met. In addition to beginning individual therapy, Mary had sought psychological relief by attending various self-help groups and reading a voluminous number of self-help books. Her constant attempts at self-improvement caused her to intellectualize her feelings as she relentlessly reframed her experiences in an effort to deal with them. She would often act as her own therapist despite the limited amount of insight that she had.

I knew much of Mary's history before we met, since my supervisor advised me to familiarize myself with the information in her chart that had been collected by her previous therapists. As I perused a thick pile of papers stuffed into a fraying manila folder, anxiety began to overtake me. I was overwhelmed by her history and the diagnosis of borderline personality disorder that she had been given by previous therapists. Here was someone with an incest history, depression, anxiety, and a personality disorder. How would I possibly be able to help this woman who had suffered so much? She had seen so many therapists—all of whom I was certain knew more than I did about conducting therapy. As I sat clutching Mary's chart in my office in the school clinic, a place in which I did not feel even remotely comfortable, I became keenly aware of my young age. My very first patient had been married to her first husband longer than I had been alive. Was it fair for me to act as this woman's therapist when I felt so ill-equipped in that role? I was jealous of my classmates whose first cases were college students having a hard time adjusting to school or women in their twenties with relationship issues. Was everyone as nervous as I was?

My stomach turned as I picked up the phone to schedule our first session. She was excited when I introduced myself as her new therapist and said that she had been waiting to hear from me. Her enthusiasm increased my anxiety. She spoke rapidly and sounded somewhat anxious herself. Five days later I walked down the long corridor of the clinic and encountered Mary in the waiting room. She looked up, smiled, and jumped out of her chair. Mary was surprisingly petite. Her voice on the phone had conjured up an image in my mind of a larger woman. She had dyed blond hair and big brown eyes that looked like they had lived through and seen more than most people. I had rehearsed many times what I would say to begin our first session: "Hi. I am Shoshana. It's nice to meet you. I have familiarized myself with your information on file, but it would be helpful if you could tell me in your own words what brings you here today." But I was not prepared for Mary to begin our session in the hall. She immediately started chatting anxiously with me, and I never had a chance to recite my prepared remarks, since Mary continued talking as we sat down.

ANXIETY AND BOUNDARY ISSUES

Mary filled the session from beginning to end. Her speech was pressured and her thought process circuitous, as she told me about her incest history, her alcoholic father, her strict upbringing, her ex-husband, and her current husband in what seemed like one long, convoluted sentence with no pause. My head was spinning, and I felt like it hardly mattered whether I was in the room. Mary needed to talk regardless of who, if anyone, was listening. I felt guilty ending the session. After I said, "We have to stop for today," Mary began to fumble for her checkbook. She slowly filled out her check and continued talking as she walked through the door. We agreed to meet again at the same time the following week.

At my first supervision session, which took place before Mary's second appointment, I shared my anxiety with my supervisor, who reassured me that it was normal to be anxious. I was also nervous about what my supervisor would think of me and wondered if all first-time therapists felt the way that I did. My supervisor conveyed that I would learn a great deal working with Mary, but that Mary would not be an easy first case. She asked that I transcribe my sessions so that we would have the opportunity to analyze them together.

At our next session I asked Mary for her permission to record our sessions, and she obliged. She continued to begin our sessions in the hallway, so the recording always started a couple of minutes into the work. During the first few months of my work with Mary I simply listened, although I had a difficult time following her thought process. Mary's sentences ran together without pauses. Her anxiety was palpable, and my anxiety when I was with her was oftentimes overwhelming. I was unable to determine if my anxiety was a result of inexperience or whether I was trying to contain the anxiety Mary induced in me. Maybe it was both. However, I was well aware that Mary's uninterruptible discharge of information and minutiae left me feeling completely helpless, hopeless, and incompetent. The concept of counter-transference was still something I did not fully grasp.

Oftentimes, I felt like a helpless victim during Mary's treatment because she did not allow me to get a word in edgewise. She diverted any attempt I made to intervene in the sessions by simply finishing my sentences and raising her voice to talk over me. My patient was subtly invading my boundaries by beginning our sessions in the hallway and not leaving when the session was over. I began to feel angry and victimized as a result of my inability to intervene in our sessions and by her not adhering to the boundaries of our session time. I was pervaded by anxiety and dread before each session, and each week I spent six hours transcribing our sessions, which forced me to hear her breathless chatter all week long.

My supervisor urged me to interrupt Mary, to comment on her anxiety, to ask her how she was feeling, and to get a sense of what she was experiencing. Mary seemed compelled to provide me with every detail about her life, seemingly unable to decide what was important to share. For example, if she told me about an incident that occurred at the supermarket with a cashier, she would also tell me which groceries she purchased, although these details had no relation to the overall point of her story.

ROADBLOCKS TO EFFECTIVE TREATMENT

Since Mary was overly anxious and at times did not make sense, my supervisor suggested that Mary see a psychiatrist for a comprehensive psychiatric evaluation. Mary had actually not seen a psychiatrist in years as her general practitioner had been prescribing her antidepressants. I was acutely aware that Mary would likely experience this suggestion as my way of telling her that she was "sick" and "needed help," as her immediate family had done. I desperately wanted to be helpful but did not feel that I had the authority to make such a suggestion to her. Nonetheless, I had no choice and managed to make this suggestion in a gentle and kind way. To my relief she was not disturbed by my suggestion and went for the evaluation, and the psychiatrist prescribed an antipsychotic in addition to the antidepressant to help with her disorganization. The antipsychotic medication made a notable difference in Mary's thought process, and she was able to remain more focused in the sessions instead of haphazardly jumping from one topic to another. However, soon after she began to experience bothersome side effects, so the psychiatrist prescribed a different drug. Meanwhile, she began taking pain medication for back pain, so she could not take the new medication. She tried two additional antipsychotics that the psychiatrist thought might also help control her anger, each one for less than a week because of uncomfortable side effects. Mary never allowed herself to acclimate to the medications, which was a pattern for her throughout her psychiatric history.

Mary had a hard time letting people help her. She did not adhere to the psychiatrist's suggestions and did not let me speak, or perhaps I was not brave enough to make myself heard. Several months into our sessions I felt as if Mary and I had established a working alliance. I began to feel less victimized and more comfortable in my role as therapist, and Mary began to trust me to some degree. Nevertheless, for the majority of the treatment, Mary was unable to stay focused on a topic, and her quick jumps from topic to topic allowed her to avoid experiencing any meaningful and painful emotions. Her concerns were primarily her relationship with her current husband, occupational and financial issues, and problems with her immediate family. Since I was feeling less threatened by her, I attempted to address her resistance and point out moments of anxiety—noting that it seemed difficult for her to remain focused on one topic. Mary experienced my comments as criticisms and became defensive, often responding by anxiously saying, "I do?" as if she had done something wrong. Her response made me uncomfortable because I felt as if I were hurting her, even when I made what I thought were fairly benign comments. I also commented to Mary that she often got caught up in the details of what she was relating to me, which prohibited us from delving deeper into the issue at hand. Mary nonetheless did not change her behavior. It appeared that she felt that I would not be able to understand what she was going through unless she communicated every single detail to me. She wanted me to know exactly what happened, whether it was a fight with her husband or an embarrassing experience at work. I continued to experience anxiety and also felt guilty about hurting Mary.

TRANSFERENCE AND COUNTERTRANSFERENCE ISSUES

Later in the treatment, my countertransference began to change. I had an omnipotent wish to rescue her from her abused childhood and felt enormous sympathy for the hardships that she endured. Looking back, I believe I also experienced some survivor's guilt for having had the idealized childhood that she never had and for which she had actually begun to mourn. Although her capacity to truly experience and tolerate her feelings was limited, she none-theless started to mourn her lost childhood. For me this was quite moving, and I found it difficult to tolerate her anguish as well as my inability to take away her pain. The more I empathized with her, the more comfortable I became confronting her resistance. I realized that my inaction was not always helpful and that it would benefit her if she could begin to tolerate my input. I commented gently, "I notice that you often interrupt me when I am speaking, and that at times you finish my sentences. What is it like for you when I speak during our sessions?"

She was narcissistically wounded by this and again answered in disbelief, "I do?"

It had been difficult for me to sit through months of being spoken over and not being permitted to help. My supervisor had urged me to tell Mary that her behavior made it difficult for me to help her. However, I did not convey my feelings of frustration and sadness about this to her.

The end of the treatment was difficult and sad for both of us. Mary commented that I had truly listened to her and that she could see the care that I had for her in my eyes. I was sad that the treatment had to end and felt guilty about abandoning her. This abandonment served several functions for Mary. First, it recreated the abandonment that she experienced when her first husband walked out on her. Second, it was an unconscious punishment for all of her perceived wrongdoings. And, third, she used it as a resistance to making meaningful progress in her treatment. She knew that by seeking treatment at a training clinic she would never have to get so close to her therapist because he or she would be leaving. She could thus avoid delving into the horrors of her abuse and avoid experiencing the associated feelings. The calm and closeness that had at times characterized our sessions during the last few months of our work together would be replaced by pressured chatter once again when Mary would begin with her new therapist the fol-lowing academic year. In addition, it is noteworthy that Mary formed an institutional transference to the clinic and that her relationship to the clinic and the graduate student therapist put her in the position of victim once more. She informed me during our final session that she felt good about helping me in my training and hoped that what I had learned from her would be helpful to others. I did learn a great deal from her, but I felt that the training aspect of our relationship was exploitative, thus recreating her experience of being a victim. However, when I realized how much our time together had meant to her, I felt that she had begun to internalize a positive object relationship. Unfortunately, I had to abandon her and repeat an old pattern.

Our last session was difficult for both of us. She left my office crying, and after she left, I sat down on my couch and also cried. About two minutes later, Mary knocked on my door. When I answered she was all cleaned up and asked me if someone would be contacting her in September. I told her "yes." She then said goodbye and left. Her actions seemed to indicate a need to leave me instead of having me leave her and also seemed to be a way to show me that I had not affected her that much and that she was looking forward to seeing someone new. On another level, perhaps she was taking care of me and wanted me to know that she was okay and not damaged by this abandonment.

Working with Mary was difficult for me, not only because she has many serious mental health issues but also because she was my first patient. I was extremely anxious during the first few months of her treatment, which made it challenging for me to listen to Mary. I was overcome with counterproductive thoughts such as "I do not think that I can help this woman," and "I have no idea what to do or say." Months passed before I was capable of working up the courage to interrupt her ceaseless monologue. Although she appeared unable to tolerate even minor confrontations or interpretations, my non-interventional approach was not particularly helpful; my silence did not come from a place of case conceptualization or therapeutic thought but rather was a result of anxiety. Upon reflection, I would not have pushed her too much further, but I would have explored much earlier her need to ramble, her intolerance of silences, and her experience of me and my interventions. If she seemed hurt or wounded I would have tried to gently and without criticism explore those feelings with her and relate them to her experience with significant others in her life. Perhaps I was also afraid of her turning the extreme anger that she demonstrated towards others during our sessions on me, as I was not prepared to receive it. Although we established a working alliance and by the end of the treatment were able to have a dialogue, we could have gone further had I been more assertive and confident.

COMMONALITIES IN NOVICE THERAPISTS' EXPERIENCES

My work with Mary continued to impact me throughout my training. I felt more competent with each succeeding patient and learned to use countertransference to benefit treatment and help me understand the patient's experience. Anxiety, anger, sadness, boredom, and a variety of other emotions became sources of information rather than paralyzing experiences. Nonetheless, I continued to wonder whether my experience with Mary was particularly unique or if other beginning therapists shared similar feelings. After many discussions with my professor and upon his urging, I decided to use a qualitative research design for my dissertation to further explore this question.

My study was designed to examine the range of emotional experiences that beginning therapists (student therapists) had during the start of their clinical training, where it was expected that they learn how to treat patients while simultaneously traversing a clinical psychology doctoral program (Lawrence, 2008). Following Auerbach and Silverstein's (2003) qualitative research methodology as the basis for data gathering, coding, and analysis, I interviewed seventeen second- and third-year students in an American Psychological Association (APA)–approved clinical psychology doctoral program in four focus groups. The focus-group interviews were recorded and transcribed, and the transcripts served as the data for analysis. As the primary researcher, I analyzed the data along with two coders. We organized the data into repeating ideas, themes, and theoretical constructs. As might be expected, the theoretical constructs that emerged depicted the beginning therapist as a narcissistically vulnerable novice experiencing the tumultuous process of becoming a clinician and cultivating a therapeutic identity. The five constructs consisted of Narcissistic Vulnerability, Countertransference Difficulties, Supervisory Triad, Disillusioned Therapist, and Developing a Therapeutic Identity.

Narcissistic Vulnerability

When the novice-therapist research participants began treating patients, they experienced a myriad of feelings, many of which were unexpected and surprising. They went through a process of development in which the road was bumpy at times. The foray into therapy challenged the novice therapists' self-esteem, and they found themselves narcissistically vulnerable. Their competence and self-assurance was compromised, which in turn added to and caused an overwhelming amount of anxiety. Most of the participants explicitly expressed a sense of incompetence, insecurity, self-doubt, and anxiety. Many were overcome by these emotions and felt that they were the defining characteristics of their experience as a beginning therapist. Here are some of the comments they made:

"I remember feeling really overwhelmed, like, what am I going to say to this person? Am I going to have the right things to say? Are they going to come back? Did I learn enough to be able to be in this room? I was anxious."

"I just remember feeling like a fraud."

"I think that [thinking about the patient] would have been way too much to think about. I could barely think about how I was going to get through those next forty-five minutes, and if I even considered the thought of somebody else's existence in the room I just don't think I would have done it."

"Anxious is like an understatement. [I felt like] there is terror going on in the room right now because I don't know what to say to this person."

In addition to such feelings, novice therapists were also particularly prone to self-deprecation and self-blame. They were unable to see that aspects of the training process might not be related to them. As one participant stated, "I'm so inclined to interpret it all as my fault." Some unnecessarily began imposing meaning on ordinary situations; they personalized events that had no particular relevance to them. One participant recalled that there was a paucity of clients in the school clinic when her training year started. Many of her classmates had been assigned new cases while she had not been. She remembered thinking, "Already I don't have clients; they [my professors] don't believe in me."

Countertransference Difficulties

Already narcissistically vulnerable, the new therapists then had to deal with the vast range of emotions that all therapists have to contend with in their work. These emotions were exacerbated because of their novice status. In particular, the participants were apprehensive about their feelings toward their patients, many of which were unexpected to them. They experienced a wide range of feelings in their countertransference with patients, including anger, boredom, annoyance, and sexual attraction. One participant shared, "I get really angry and annoyed—not just angry—because I think anger would be easier to deal with, but annoyed. And I really feel like it's petty, and so that kind of thing doesn't strike me as what a good therapist would be like, and that's hard for me to sit with."

The combination of the participants' inexperience and the intensity of their countertransference reactions evoked a fear that they would somehow unintentionally hurt their patients. One participant succinctly noted, "My main focus was 'I hope I don't mess up this person more than they are.'"

One predominant emotion for these novice therapists was guilt, a feeling that the majority of participants admitted to experiencing. Many felt guilty that people were coming to them for help and they had never helped anyone before. They had a small and circumscribed repertoire of interventions to employ with little belief in themselves as effective therapists. As one participant stated, "It's guilt for not knowing more, not being more." In addition, the participants were privileged in comparison to their patients. The student therapists may have been struggling financially at the time, but they were in training to receive their doctorates. Many of their working-class patients in the low-cost training clinic had not received higher education. Additionally, some of the study participants reported having deeply fulfilling lives outside of their training work. This left many of them feeling guilty for not only having what their patients did not have but also for having what their patients desperately wanted. The therapists also reported feeling guilty about having to terminate treatment with their patients at the close of the training year.

All of these emotional experiences and challenges set the stage for these novice therapists to question their chosen profession, as many searched for faith in therapy's effectiveness. As noted earlier, the therapists lacked confidence in their ability to help others and were afraid of causing harm to their patients while trying to help them. Therefore, it seems only natural that they would contemplate whether there was any value in their work. One participant shared, "My anxiety has shifted more toward 'Am I really doing anything for this person? Is this even effective? Are we just two people sitting in a room talking, or is there actually some kind of valuable outcome in this?' So I think it's kind of moved from the immediacy of 'How am I going to get through this?' to 'Is there a point to what I'm doing? Is there a value in what I'm doing?'" Clearly, some not only questioned their own efficacy but also began questioning the efficacy of psychotherapy.

Issues with Supervision

An essential part of training for all beginning therapists is supervision, during which the therapist is forced to share with an experienced therapist what he or she is doing and saying in sessions with patients. Sometimes the supervisor is also the student's professor. While supervision is supposed to be a helpful experience, the beginning therapist's novice status contributes to the power differential between supervisees and supervisors. Study participants expressed concern about being judged and evaluated. They were anxious about revealing what they were actually doing in sessions with patients and also felt compelled to do something in sessions. Many had this recurring thought: "What is my supervisor going to think?" In addition, the already complicated supervisory relationship was made more complex when the supervisor was a faculty member and professor of the supervisee. The many hats of the faculty supervisor made it more difficult for these beginning therapists to share their concerns and self-doubts with their supervisors.

Regardless of the supervisor's status, novice therapists simultaneously desired and were adverse to criticism from their supervisors. They felt ambivalent about what they wanted from their supervisors. Many of the supervisees felt persecuted as a result of perceived criticism. On the other hand, some of those same supervisees felt that they had learned from the criticism that they received. One participant commented, "If I don't have a supervisor that's challenging like that, then I feel bored and underutilized as a therapist."

Disillusionment

All of the previously mentioned anxiety-provoking aspects of therapy were not something that these new therapists had expected. Some had unrealistic ideas about what it would be like to be a therapist, while others simply did not anticipate all of the vulnerability, countertransference difficulties, and supervisory issues that would arise. Most of the participants were disillusioned once they began clinical training. For the majority there was a significant discrepancy between reality and what they imagined therapy and the therapeutic relationship would be like. One participant said, "I had an idealized version of what a therapist should be." This idealized version did not leave room for negative countertransference reactions toward patients and instead imagined a "neutral" therapist devoid of unique human experience.

These beginners also conjectured about what their patients would be like. One participant stated half-jokingly, "How come they're not all high-functioning—we've been meeting twice a week for the last three months! Why are you not out there doing the things you need to be doing?" A beginner's idealized image of a patient is a high-functioning person who does not experience conflict about change and who experiences only positive transference.

Some therapists did not realize that they would be working so hard. As one informant noted, "I didn't expect it to be so draining." The participants expected the process of becoming a therapist to be easier and were humbled by their lack of knowledge and experience.

One of the most difficult aspects that these beginning therapists had to contend with was the contrast between their desire for their patients to change and their patients' ability to make progress. The beginners were frustrated and angry with their patients for their slow and sometimes imperceptible progress or their lack of progress. Two comments along these lines included, "Just the amount of progress they make doesn't compare to the progress I want them to make," and "Some really don't want to change. That's even more frustrating for us because we're so change-oriented at times that we don't sometimes focus enough on the acceptance part of things or maybe not pushing as much. I think especially when you're starting out, [you believe it is your job] . . . to help change people." The therapists were unprepared for the very gradual visible progress that patients make in therapy, and one study participant said, "You want to see change, and change is so gradual." Many beginning therapists worked hard on adjusting their expectations for change and had to learn to appreciate the minor changes that patients were capable of making.

Developing an Identity

As in other professions, these novices were not born therapists. Becoming a therapist takes work and includes both positive and negative aspects of training. The participants were all engaged in the process of developing a therapeutic identity, and they spoke about several components of their development. The participants reported incorporating aspects of their supervisors that were consistent with their own personalities into their identity as therapists. Some eagerly grasped at anything that their supervisors said because they wanted to have something to offer their patients. Moreover, some realized that their own personal therapist was affecting their therapeutic identity. As time went on, the beginning therapists happily noticed that they were growing professionally. They were forming their identities and becoming more comfortable in their new roles. As one novice said, "I started to be more flexible and competent." Nonetheless, most still found it difficult to balance their new identities with their non-professional identities, an idea that one participant captured by stating, "Being authentic to who you are and being a therapist is such a challenge."

The therapists in my study were trained in a program with a dual focus of cognitive-behavioral therapy (CBT) and psychodynamic psychotherapy, and they noticed that each orientation affected them differently as they practiced. Because of the structure inherent in CBT, many of the novice therapists felt more competent and self-assured when practicing in that orientation. While a few did feel more authentic and comfortable working from a psychodynamic perspective, others felt more anxious because of the abstract and unstructured nature of a psychodynamic orientation.

Beginning therapists navigating the tumultuous terrain of professional training and development found different ways to handle their stress. For some, the support of family and friends who were not involved in their professional development was indispensable. In addition, many realized the importance of taking care of themselves and making sure their own needs were met. Some accomplished this by separating from their work for a while. One individual expressed that her own therapy was helpful in coping.

Throughout their training process, the novice therapists learned key lessons about being a therapist and practicing psychotherapy. Unlike other relationships, where the verbal give and take is often equal, the exchange in the therapeutic relationship is not. One participant quipped, "It was really just a lesson in learning to shut up." Not only did these novices have to learn to remain silent despite wanting to speak, but they also had to come to terms with the idea that the session and the therapy belonged to the patient. "It's not about me," one therapist remarked. Despite all the knowledge about doing therapy that they acquired from professors, supervisors, and their own therapists, these novices had to come to terms with the fact that there were many things they did not know and had to learn to sit with the discomfort of that. One therapist astutely observed, "I think also being comfortable with the 'not knowing.' That's part of what I have started to understand is actually happening in therapy everywhere."

GROWING PAINS

Each therapist-patient dyad is unique and exceptional. The therapeutic relationship that develops within the confines of the four walls of the therapist's office is a world unto itself. Mary and I created a world in which we both at times felt chaotic and overwhelmed. As time went on, I became more comfortable in my new role as therapist and was able to contain some of our chaos. Our world became relatively more tolerable and peaceful. The beginning therapists interviewed also created distinct and special worlds with each of their patients. Similar to my experience with Mary, these novice therapists were overcome with a great deal of emotion. Anxiety, insecurity, self-doubt, and a host of other difficult emotions reigned supreme. The process of developing a therapeutic identity can be arduous and painful, but those growing pains are a necessary part of that development which ultimately leads to one becoming comfortable sitting in the therapist's chair.

NOTE

Names and identifying data were changed to disguise the identity of the persons involved.

REFERENCES

Auerbach, C. F., and Silverstein, L. B. (2003). *Qualitative data: An introduction to coding and analyzing.* New York: New York University Press.

Lawrence, S. L. (2008). *Understanding the experience of beginning therapists: A qualitative study* (Unpublished doctoral dissertation). Long Island University, C.W. Post Campus, Brookville, NY.

II

Navigating the Personal and Professional during Doctoral Training

Chapter Five

Clinical Psychology Training and Romance

For Better or for Worse?

Silvia Fiammenghi

In January of 2006, after spending two years in an expensive, long-distance romantic relationship, my boyfriend, Brad, moved from Seattle, Washington, to Pavia, Italy, so that we could begin our longed-for life together. Soon after we married, Brad found a job, and we furnished our apartment and adopted two cats. Life seemed to be sailing smoothly for us newlyweds until one spring night, when I confessed the desire to pursue a doctorate in clinical psychology in the United States. I had been a licensed psychologist in Italy for some time and had been working in the field of health psychology. Trained accordingly to the Italian model of academic psychology instruction, I was at this point well versed in the areas of assessment and psychology research, but had not received any type of training in therapy. After considering various postgraduate options in Italy, I realized that I simply wanted better, more intensive training than what my country had to offer. I was determined to fulfill my potential as a clinician, but I did not know when or how this plan could materialize. We had just started to settle together in Italy, so I thought that my dream would have to wait a few years.

Swayed by his love for me and a bit of the recklessness typical of some courageous people in their early twenties, Brad thought it was a great idea and said that he believed in me and would support my academic pursuits. He saw no reason to wait, since we were young, had no children, and would always have the option to move back to Italy after I completed my doctorate and secured a second license to practice psychology in the United States. It would not be Brad's first time starting over in a new city, and for him moving back to the Unites States felt like a new adventure rather than a challenge.

MOVING TO NEW YORK CITY

After much talking, thinking, feeling, deciding, planning, and sharing with family and friends, I began looking into programs. I learned about the difference between the PhD and PsyD; investigated tuition, financial aid, and immigration laws; procured countless documents; had my academic credentials converted into the American system; obtained letters of recommendation from Italian professors who did not know that such attestations existed or why they were necessary; prepared for the TOEFL and GREs; and underwent several phone interviews, complicated by poor international phone connections and a difference in time zones. Applying for graduate school became a second full-time job, which put some strain on my marital relationship. I was busy, stressed, and constantly anxious about some aspect of a complex and unfamiliar application process. Meanwhile, Brad began feeling sad about leaving the life he had just started and grew anxious about becoming the sole breadwinner during the long training period ahead of us. Nonetheless, we expected that, after the move, I would begin school, Brad would find a job, things would settle down, and all would go back to "normal."

In the winter of 2007 acceptance letters began to arrive, and one day in April, while sitting by a canal in Venice, I left a message of acceptance with the coordinator of the PsyD program at Long Island University, C. W. Post, for a spot in the incoming class of 2007. We were moving to New York City, and I had committed to five years of study in a clinical psychology doctoral program. The four months that followed were hectic and exciting, with a million tasks to complete before we could start the next chapter of our life together. Brad left in July with two pieces of luggage and a letter of recommendation from his boss. Fortunately, he found a new job in his field quickly. The pay was not princely, but it would have to suffice. Three weeks later I packed up our two cats along with two more pieces of luggage and joined Brad in a Brooklyn sublet. Although feeling sad and a bit guilty about leaving my family and friends behind with no clear sense of what the future held, I was full of excitement and expectations for my new life in New York. After two weeks of searching for an apartment on our very small budget, I secured a two-hundred-square-foot studio in Bedford-Stuyvesant, Brooklyn. Although I thought I was ready for my doctoral journey, like most students I could not truly conceive of how long five years of training would really be, and I was oblivious to the many ways in which the journey ahead would affect me, Brad, and our relationship.

ALIGNING LIFE EXPERIENCE WITH A
DOCTORAL RESEARCH TOPIC

Two studies by Legako and Sorenson (2000) and Cymbal (2004) indicate that doctoral training in clinical psychology is likely to have a significant and complex impact on the romantic relationships of students. In certain cases the training improves the perceived quality of couple interactions, contributing to strengthening the relationship; in other cases it strains the bond between the partners, and the relationship eventually deteriorates. This topic—the impact of training on relationships—was relevant to my personal journey and through an interesting chain of events eventually became the subject of my doctoral dissertation (Fiammenghi, 2011).

By the fall of 2008, I was entering my second year of training as a busy and stressed-out doctoral student in clinical psychology and novice therapist. I was dealing with patients, supervisors, teachers, assignments, train schedules, and, of course, Brad. My circumstances at the time were certainly not in line with what I had previously pictured for myself as a twenty-eight-year-old woman. Financially, I was dependent on my husband and still had to rely on my parents to some degree. Professionally, I had plunged back into student status after having previously been licensed as a psychologist in my own country. Developmentally, while my friends were beginning to talk about starting a family and buying a home, I felt years away from such milestones. I was determined not to take one day longer than necessary to earn this doctorate, regain professional status, and begin making money again. When the opportunity arose, I sought to speed up my degree by using a project in my Research Methods class as my dissertation proposal.

The quest for a topic that could be further researched for a dissertation added a new layer of pressure to an already complicated doctoral-student existence. As the days went by, my anxiety grew as I struggled to find a suitable subject. One night I thought it might be helpful to share my concerns—most likely not for the first time—with Brad. He had just gotten home from work. Over the course of the prior year, he had adjusted to a new job and to living in a small basement apartment in a rough neighborhood in Brooklyn while dealing daily with the fear of losing his job in the midst of the worst economic crisis since the Great Depression. Meanwhile, I was mostly "too busy," or simply too exhausted to do my half of the daily household chores, had gotten into the habit of coding psychotherapy sessions at the laundromat on weekends, and no longer watched TV without typing something on my laptop.

After going into great detail about my concern over not yet having found a dissertation topic, I realized that, while nodding and periodically producing "umhum" sounds, Brad had kept his eyes on an episode of *South Park*. I asked him to repeat what I had just finished saying, which confirmed that he had indeed not been listening to a single word. My initial reaction was the usual mix of anger, frustration, and sadness; then, after a moment of silence, and to Brad's surprise, I did not engage in a tirade using abstruse psychological jargon. Instead, I thanked him for giving me a great idea. I spent the rest of the evening researching the topic of involvement in a romantic relationship while also training in a clinical psychology doctoral program. By bedtime I had found my dissertation topic.

QUALITATIVE RESEARCH ON ROMANTIC RELATIONSHIPS

My qualitative research on the impact of clinical psychology doctoral training on students' romantic relationships (Fiammenghi, 2011) featured four focus groups of seventeen doctoral trainees who had been in a relationship six months prior to enrollment in the doctoral program and had stayed in the relationship for at least the first two years of training. Participants, at different stages of their lives and their relationships, shared the many complex ways in which their loving relationships and their doctoral training had become interwoven, mutually affecting each other.

Impact on Finances and Quality Time

Enrollment in graduate school signifies the beginning of a challenging phase of life (Butler, 2014). The graduate student must be willing to delay gratification of financial stability and professional accomplishment, while devoting significant amounts of personal and financial resources to the academic goal, which in turns negatively affects their wellness level (Pierce, 2005). The longer the course of study, the greater is the demand for devotion and commitment (Brannock, Litten, and Smith, 2000). While most begin their graduate journey somewhat aware of the academic effort that will be required, few are prepared for the personal sacrifices that will result from their decision to pursue further education. In discussing the effect on her romantic relationship, one clinical psychology trainee said, "There was not a deep discussion about it, [such as] 'if this is something that you want to do we'll make it work.' We never thought about how it would impact our relationship [until] later on."

Another shared, "There was not a discussion, and I think organically it kind of worked out okay, but what I think could have been helpful is a discussion of what it would mean financially and what it would mean emotionally, which I don't think I realized either one of those."

Concerned with meeting academic demands, graduate students often lack the personal resources to devote to family and friends, thus reducing their leisure time and limiting social interactions (Butler, 2014; Gerstein and Russell, 1990; McLaughlin, 1985). This is especially relevant when the trainee is committed to a romantic relationship at the time of enrollment and/or throughout graduate training (Carter and McGoldrick, 2005). Although career fulfillment positively affects personal fulfillment and enhances family financial stability (Young and Long, 1998), long years of training stand between grueling training and the doctorate itself. As Carter and McGoldrick (2005) pointed out, enrollment in a graduate school program often forces couples to restructure their relationships. The couple must revisit their relationship in terms of priorities, time, energy, commitment, and financial resources (Gerstein and Russell, 1990; McLaughlin, 1985; Sori, Wetchler, Ray, and Niedner, 1996). Among the many issues that graduate-student partners have to face are financial strain, possible geographical relocation, adjustment to a different schedule and social life, sexual dissatisfaction, role conflict, and lack of shared leisure time (Gilbert, 1982; McLaughlin, 1985). Graduate school often becomes more of a family task than an individual responsibility (Brannock et al., 2000). One trainee who was approaching the end of her doctorate candidly said,

> I was a little naïve going into it. I thought: "Well, we thought about it, everything will be fabulous, because we said that it will be stressful, then it won't be stressful!" So, even though it was thought and planned and discussed, I don't think either one of us realized how stressful, how much time, how much money, it was going to take. . . . what type of commitment this was going to be.

The impact of graduate training on the relationship varies from couple to couple. Factors such as the presence of children, financial circumstances, and the need for relocation played an important role in overall couple satisfaction in many relationships (Gilbert, 1982; McLaughlin, 1985). Furthermore, relationships may be affected differently when both members of a couple are attending graduate school as opposed to when only one of the members is pursuing further education (Bergen and Bergen, 1978). Couples are defined as symmetrical when both partners are students and asymmetrical when only one of them is a student. Even though early results indicated that symmetrical graduate-student couples are disadvantaged because both partners are exposed to school demands (Price-Bonham, 1972), more recent findings suggest that symmetry benefits graduate-student relationships, in which shared priorities, interests, and lifestyle are associated with high satisfaction of the student partners (Bergen and Bergen, 1978; Scheinkman, 1988; Brannock et al., 2000). One student in a symmetrical relationship said, "So for us it was . . . a very logical decision. We were both in undergrad . . . so it kind of made sense for both of us to move to New York, so we just decided to apply to schools."

Maclean and Peters (1995) pointed out that in asymmetrical graduate-student relationships, the premise on which the relationship was founded may be strongly challenged by enrollment in a graduate program. For example, the nonstudent partner may be required to relocate and relinquish an established professional and social status. For example, in my relationship, Brad did not fully realize how established he felt in Italy and at his job as a mobile producer in Milan, until he left both of them to follow me in my doctoral adventure and join the employee ranks of competitive corporate America. Such sacrifices may later become reason for resentment when, due to program demands, the student partner becomes unavailable as a source of concrete and emotional support (Butler, 2014). One trainee said, "I might feel guilty if I can't go to something, or I'll be like, 'Hey don't you realize that I have all this work? Stop making all these plans every night!'"

Another shared, "He is free on weekends, and I can't really do things on weekends. I am really busy, so I guess that impacts us. It's hard not to be able to have that free time. . . . Most people who work Monday through Friday have their weekends free, and I don't really feel that I have that."

A period of five years is a long time to constantly feel "on call." During my training I experienced guilt every moment that I was not doing work. On weekends Brad and I would sometimes have brunch in Brooklyn, and I would wistfully look around at people enjoying their eggs and bacon with their dogs sitting by their chairs. I fantasized about them having a whole day with nothing to do and money to spend, after working an entire week at a paid job. Maybe—I imagined—they would go to the park or the museum, or maybe they would take a nap. Instead, by the end of my meal I was already uneasy about the time that I had "wasted," guilty about the cost of the food, and sad about leaving Brad to find a cafe where I could get work done, or sit alone at the laundromat and type papers while Brad cleaned the apartment alone. Before the check for brunch arrived at our table, we'd be bickering about this or that aspect of one of the above plans, and I would feel guilty for neglecting Brad and ignoring his need to enjoy the weekend with me. Often, torn between the relationship and academic responsibilities and aspirations, the student partner alternates between choosing the relationship over the program and the program over the relationship. One student said, "I am *making* free time by choosing, you know, to hang out with my partner and not do the readings," but this comes at a cost for driven, ambitious doctoral students.

One trainee commented: "If you are not doing something you feel like you should be doing something, and I feel that is a lot of stress, and I feel that it could definitely be a strain on the relationship."

At other times, when feeling guilty for not fulfilling relationship-related responsibilities, the student partner may forgo academic and career-related opportunities to preserve the relationship and, consequently, develop resentment toward the nonstudent partner. One student shared, "I limited myself based on my relationship, and it just was so important, like location was so important to me that I was not going to apply to these sites on Long Island, even though that was going to be the best opportunity for me and you know . . . I don't know if that was the smartest decision . . . I question that . . . but I know that it was due to my relationship."

Relationship Imbalances

Another trainee, whose partner had dropped out of her residency program while he was in training, made these comments:

> With externship, instead of picking maybe the one that best suits my style, like I passed on one that was maybe a little bit more dynamic, a little more the way I work. I picked an externship that is more in a big hospital, that has a bigger name and that maybe will have a bigger influence on internship. And I would have totally not done this if she had not dropped out of residency. You know I would have been like, "I am going to pick what is good for me because we are going to be OK." Now it's like, "We may not be OK, if I don't have, you know, good credentials."

In addition, the imbalance that arises in the couple from enrollment in a graduate program does not necessarily resolve with the completion of the degree. In fact, this imbalance may grow after the student partner completes the program. A gap in educational level and professional status, which may result from only one of the partners acquiring a graduate degree, may reduce the perceived commonality within the couple and raise feelings of inferiority in the nonstudent partner and/or superiority in the graduated partner (Pederson and Daniels, 2001). Depending on cultural background and personal values, it can be uneasy for one or both of the partners when wedding invitations arrive addressed to "Dr. and Mr."

Effects of Differential Personal Development

Not every field of graduate study is the same, and not every type of training presents students and their partners with the same challenges. Polson and Nida (1998) argued that programs such as psychology, social work, and family therapy, by means of combining classroom work, research, and clinical training, create more potential stress than other graduate programs and have a complex effect on students' personal lives. Clinical psychology doctoral programs present an especially significant challenge to students and their partners. Becoming a clinical psychologist often results in a considerable amount of personal development on the part of the student partner, whose growing expertise in "human nature" and development in "psychological mindedness" may affect the dynamics of the couple's interactions in a variety of ways (Polson and Nida, 1998). Personal and professional development, promoted in clinical psychology training, includes the enhancement of students' awareness of beliefs about themselves and others and of how these can affect their behavior and interpersonal perception (Butler, 2014; Mearns, 1997).

Clinical psychology training programs are designed to promote individual growth and self-awareness, which accounts for the subjective perception of personal development reported by experienced psychotherapists (Guy, 1983). Farber listed increased assertiveness, self-assurance, self-reliance, introspection, self-disclosing abilities, self-reflection, and expanded sensitivity as positive aspects of personal growth ensuing from the practice of psychotherapy (1983, as cited in Guy, 1983, p.111). While these changes are usually gratifying and positive on an individual level, they may not be entirely positive for relationships. Such positive individual consequences of the educational experience in clinical psychology may lead to increased couple satisfaction, or have little effect on the student's romantic relationship, or actually have a negative impact on the graduate student's love relationship (Pederson and Daniels, 2001). One trainee said,

> This is one of the only fields where you are forced to think about thinking. You know what I mean? Your life and the people that you are around, and you are sort of forced to look at your life, and I think this is kind of unique . . . like when you argue about something, you are also better at doing it, because your job is to understand situations, and see things in a different perspective, and that makes you a better arguer.

Another student commented: "It changed for the better in the sense that we became more psychologically minded and able to communicate more constructively and insightfully."

One student whose relationship had fallen apart during her training commented, "Just by being in classes and learning about relationship and couple dynamics, I was able to break down what was happening to us as a couple, I could put words to things that were happening, that before I had not known how to articulate. So to me things seemed very clear, when the breakup happened."

The personal growth that can result from doctoral-level psychology training may be compared to the individual change that often results from personal therapy. Individual changes made by one spouse or partner as a result of therapy may cause unhappiness among others close to this person who are not accustomed to and even disturbed by major interpersonal changes (e.g. Hurvitz, 1967, as cited in Margolin, 1982, p. 789). Aspects of personal therapy are often interwoven with therapy training. For example, classwork may push the trainee to reflect on the dynamics of his or her family of origin, and supervision may touch upon personal issues of the graduate-student therapist (Aponte, 1994). This effect may be enhanced when a psychology graduate-student partner enters personal therapy while in training but the nonstudent partner does not. At a time when the student is devoting her heart and soul to become a doctor in psychology, she inevitably becomes keen on understanding the human mind. By the end of my second year in training, I had spent eighteen months in individual therapy and two years in supervision, had completed a family genogram and two ethical autobiographies, and had participated in countless academic conversations that had stirred up personal matters. All of it profoundly impacted the way in which I spoke to Brad about myself, about his role in my life, and about our relationship. He happened to be an open-minded and curious person whose main response to my change was to enter therapy himself. Yet, there still were many occasions in which he appeared exasperated by my newly developed constant need for *understanding* and said things such as "Can we just enjoy this movie instead of pausing it every five minutes to turn it into a discussion about our life?"

Reconciling the Roles of Therapist and Partner

As the student partner struggles to reconcile her personal identity with the new professional one, she may encounter difficulties in separating the role of therapist from that of romantic partner. In such a case, the student partner may tend to focus on the intrinsic meaning, unconscious motives, and hidden causes in everyday situations (Guy, 1987). While I tried to refrain from sharing with Brad the complex case studies that I was running in my head about him, myself, and our respective families, sometimes I could not help myself. By the end of my first year of training, the word "dynamic" had been officially banned from my household, as its use on my part would immediately lead to a fight, which would usually start with *"Stop trying to be a psychologist with me!"* The student partner may be tempted to apply recently learned psychological constructs to analyze a romantic relationship that may already be strained by many other stresses related to graduate school. If the nonstudent partner experiences this process as if he or she is deficient in some manner or feels "pathologized" or judged, the relationship is going to suffer. Describing her tendency to use her psychology skills inappropriately on her partner, a trainee said, "I say something about his sister and he says, 'Stop doing that; it's my sister!'"

Similarly, another shared, "I know that I have totally inappropriately used skills on him . . . that just is not what I am supposed to be doing with my partner, but I do." When the nonstudent feels this type of relationship threat, he or she may adopt a rigid coping style, which can result in further damage through retaliation and distancing (Pederson and Daniels, 2001). Significant theoretical knowledge of interpersonal relationships may lead some to expect that psychologists are more successful than the general population in their romantic relationships (Guy, 1987). Yet, psychologists are no different than any other people, and several studies show that practicing psychologists experience couple distress and failure of their relationships at an equal or greater rate than the general population. Wahl (1986, as cited in Guy, 1987, p. 107) found that about 40 percent of psychologists surveyed had been divorced at least once. Wahl reported that 20.4 percent of the surveyed psychologists listed couple distress as a source of personal distress (p. 107). In the same study 36.7 percent of those surveyed perceived that their personal distress decreased the quality of the therapeutic services they provided. Similarly, a recent international survey of psychotherapists showed that clinicians perceive their personal sense of well-being as a determining factor affecting their therapeutic alliances (Neissen-Lie, Høglend, Havik, Monsen, and Rønnestad, 2013). Guy, Poelstra, and Stark (1989) found that psychologists' couple distress is not only a personal matter but also a potential source of professional impairment.

The Emotional Strain of Therapy and Its Effects on the Relationship

Several factors have been investigated as contributing to couple distress among psychotherapists. Emotional strain caused by spending considerable hours of the workday listening to others' problems may cause the therapist to be emotionally withdrawn and unavailable for his or her partner (Butler, 2014). Also, patient confidentiality demands that the therapist's relationships with clients remain off limits to his or her partner. Under such circumstances the non-therapist partner may feel excluded from the work life of the therapist partner. Finally, clinical psychologists who spend much of their professional life conducting psychotherapy can experience a sense of grandiosity from their work and take an "analytic stance" into their romantic relationships (Guy, 1987; McWilliams, 2004).

Among the challenges encountered by beginning therapists in training is the strong emotional impact of being exposed to and expected to contain the traumatic stories and emotional distress of patients. One main task of being a clinician is containing emotional pain, and this is a skill that can be learned only slowly and painfully. Often working with marginalized, underserved populations, novice clinicians may witness for the first time a degree of emotional violence, despair, and suffering they had not previously encountered. They may witness circumstances that previously were unimaginable to them. This type of experience is inevitably brought back into the student partner's relationship in a variety of ways. For example, often in response to having to bear for many hours the new role of professional caretaker, trainees seek emotional support in their partners to a greater degree than they had before. The way in which the partner responds to this demand is in turn very important for the relationship itself. One student explained,

> You have to be "on" so much that I really like having space to just totally regress and also have space to be a baby . . . and be babied, and I guess I totally realized it when we were talking about regression in class. A friend and I both looked at each other and both were like . . . "Is it bad that we do that all the time to our significant others?" And I said, "No—no, it's okay, better be okay!" . . . So I think having that kind of space to fall apart when you have to be so "on" [is a good thing].

A second trainee shared: "I work in the emergency room, psychiatric ER. It's really intense. The first few weeks of rotation, I was crying all the time and just like a total mess. And because my partner is really good at those intense emotional things and he does not get [overwhelmed]. . . . If he was the kind of person that would get freaked out and not know how to handle it, it would be really bad for our relationship."

As the student partner deepens her understanding of interpersonal dynamics and developmental processes, she most often witnesses firsthand clinical cases of people for whom these processes were upset by a variety of dysfunctional circumstances leading to a detrimental clinical outcome. This likely worsens the student's sense of guilt for neglecting her partner and family to pursue the very career that stresses the importance of family and interpersonal relationships. This experience is especially heightened for students who are parents (Pierce, 2005). This experience was well portrayed by a student who became a parent while in training:

> I was having guilt as a mother, and guilt about not being home, and here I am at school, learning about—you know—mothering and attachment process and all of this and [thinking] "What am I doing?" I had a really tough [time]. I wrote my whole dissertation about a really tough case with a kid that brought up so much countertransference for me, about attachment and mothering, and I was [thinking], "Why am I torturing myself?"

APPLYING THE MODEL OF THIRDNESS TO RELATIONSHIP CHANGE

I chose to interpret the data I had collected within the framework of intersubjective psychoanalysis and particularly according to Benjamin's model of *thirdness* (2004). When understood within this theoretical frame, clinical psychology training can be viewed as a type of life stressor in a relationship that pushes the partners into an interpersonal impasse but also as one that gives partners a unique set of tools to then move out of this impasse.

One of the premises of intersubjective psychoanalysis is that meaning in each individual is not created independently, but it is entangled in the inevitable interactions with others (Gerson, 2004). Dyads, including couples, are subjected to intersubjective processes. However, any given dyad originates from the union of two separate individuals, each bringing a separate subjective experience to the relationship. The two separate subjects of the dyad do not always easily and spontaneously develop the harmonic synchrony of mutual recognition. To the contrary, Benjamin explained how relationships, as part of a developmental process, often grow to be Benjamin (2004) described the development of *thirdness* as the process through which a relationship can move away from rigid complementary and co-dependent roles and evolve into an exchange between two differentiated minds.

When the partners become rigidly co-dependent, often as a result of major life events such as the death of a parent, the birth of a child, relocation, or a similar event, they fall into an impasse, an unconscious symmetry, in which conflict is not processed but rather acted out at the procedural level between polarized partners. When stuck in such a predicament, the two participants in the relationship shift from identifying with the position of the doer to identifying with the position of the done-to. At this stage, the participants remain stuck in complementarity, a psychic experience of a *one-way street*, in which one person is the subject and the other is the object (Benjamin, 2004). Aron (2006) explained that for a more flexible arrangement to arise, one of the participants on this seesaw must step off, transforming a straight line into a triangular space, thus opening a new space in which each member of the dyad moves with relational freedom, no longer bound to the other's position. Progressive adaptation to the other's needs allows for the development of a stage in which the participants in the relationship begin to consider the other's position and, by taking it into account, put forward effort to accommodate it (Benjamin, 2004; Aron, 2006). Subsequently, each person progressively grows to acknowledge his or her contribution to the relationship's co-created reality, further moving away from the psychic experience of a one-way street. A new vantage point of observation is created outside the dyad, and both individuals begin to recognize their participation in the "confusing traffic of a two-way street" (Benjamin, 2004). As the two-way perception strengthens, each member of the dyad acknowledges that the interaction is based on reciprocal influence.

Practicing Multiple Roles

Elements of clinical psychology doctoral training play a significant role in fostering the potential evolution of some students' relationships from twoness to thirdness. I propose that the key to this transformation is the novice therapist's growing expertise in forming and closely observing multiple unique relationships with patients, supervisors, teachers, peers, mentors, and so forth. All student partners in a clinical psychology doctoral program find themselves enacting multiple selves because in each one of their relationships they are expected to play a different role: therapist, supervisee, student, and, of course, romantic partner. When these students are assigned their first clients and take on the role of therapist, they are thrust into a new type of relationship, in which they are assigned the role of expert caretaker.

In my first encounter with a patient, I felt like an impostor in a "professional's costume," faking a role that, despite my previous experience in Italy, I did not yet perceive as fitting me. Relationships with clients are different from any other interpersonal interactions students have experienced before, as they are governed by unique and specific clinical responsibilities. For the beginning therapist, it is often challenging to find a balance between personal and professional selves in relationships with clients. Partly because this is a new role and responsibility, novice clinicians are prone to participate in rigid transactions with their patients to minimize their anxiety about being in this novel and intimidating role. In this situation it is not uncommon for beginning therapists to establish and remain stuck in a dynamic of complementarity with their patients, falling into a doer/done-to impasse (Benjamin, 2004; Aron, 2006). This fruitless therapeutic predicament is especially evident when therapist and patient remain focused on the content that is brought in by the patient, without venturing to explore the process that takes place within the therapeutic dyad. Davies (2003) described this situation as "cases of apparently inescapable therapeutic impasse . . . [in which] patient and analyst become prisoners of the coercive projective power of each other's vision; each becomes hopelessly defined by the other and incapable of escaping the force of the interactive pull to act in creative and fully agentic ways" (pp. 15–16). This is especially true for novice therapists, still too narcissistically vulnerable in their shaky professional selves to consciously address the therapeutic process. For student therapists, recognizing and facing vulnerability and mutual enactments can be especially intimidating (Blount and Glenwick, 1982; Hogan, 1964; Stoltenberg, 1981).

From Objective Observer to Observing Participant

However, as the training proceeds, trainees have the opportunity to examine the complex dynamics ruling their relationships with their clients. In an ideal situation, the difficulties encountered by the student therapist are explored in the safe space of supervision. As the training progresses, the novice therapists are confronted time and time again with the challenging reality that they are not only mere observers in the therapeutic relationship but also involved parties participating in a two-person, co-created reality within the therapeutic process. Novice therapists have to face the fact that the position of therapist as objective observer must be modified to therapist as participant observer, and then to observing participant (Mitchell and Black, 1995; Hirsch, 2011).

Moreover, when a supervisor encourages the student therapist to "bring the therapy back into the room" (i.e., focus on the therapeutic process rather than on the content), the supervisee may come to realize that the patient's responses, at least partly, include the feeling that the therapist is "doing something" to him or her. As novice clinicians "own" responsibility for contributing to their relationships with each and every client, they begin to acknowledge that the dyadic unconscious transactions taking place in the therapy room are more than the mere product of transference but are actually mutual transactions in which both parties are "doing something" to the other and also feeling like "something is being done to" them.

In observing and experiencing the evolution of therapeutic relationships with clients, students may be confronted with the shortcomings of a doer/done-to dynamic and with the fact that they too are active participants in co-created therapeutic realities with certain patients. If their clinical supervision experience is seen as occurring in a safe environment, there is the potential for student therapists to observe their own participation in the therapy and supervision process (Berman, 2000). For the trainee to grow in the direction of understanding interpersonal processes, the supervisor may lead the way, sometimes even identifying similar dynamics within the supervisory relationship. If the trainee's professional growth slowly unfolds during the course of training, the beginning therapist may very well accept her contribution to the therapeutic relationship and see this situation as a mutual, co-created therapist-client relationship. It is through this slow recognition of participation in the therapeutic relationship that the beginning therapist often finds a way out of impasse in client relationships.

Not surprisingly, therapeutic and supervisory relationships do not happen in a vacuum but instead become an integral part of the trainees' lives and profoundly impact their way of understanding and participating in all interpersonal interactions. If student therapists are able to discover the value of this approach in moving relationships out of stagnation, they may be able to apply this knowledge, gained in the role of therapist and supervisee, to other relationships, especially when these similarly involve moments of impasse brought on by the challenges of the doctoral program. Armed with such first-hand professional experiences, the student partner may be the first to step outside of the seesaw dynamics in a romantic relationship. In other words, student partners may be able to recognize a dynamic in their romantic relationships similar to one they have already seen in therapist-patient and supervisee-supervisor relationships. If the relationship is polarized by the many strains brought about by the doctoral experience, their familiarity with the dynamic can potentially begin to open a space of *thirdness* for themselves and their romantic partners.

Participant Data on Relationship Growth

Of the seventeen participants in the study, thirteen reported improvements in their romantic relationships as a result of enrollment in a clinical psychology doctoral program. This is consistent with what Truell found in 2001. In that study, of the six students interviewed, five reported that their relationship struggled as a result of their training, but five also reported that the relationship eventually improved by the end of their training experience. One of the sources of such improvement could be the students' use of a relational approach to challenges they experienced in their romantic relationship, once they recognized that a two-person process was at play. For example, one student in my study noted, "I won't say, 'You are anxious,' but rather, . . . I would say, 'I feel really anxious about this, and I wonder if you do too.'"

Another student said:

> I noticed doing more of the validation thing . . . just being more validating of what is going on for him. But also the same thing goes for everyone that I feel I have been interacting with . . . I feel that has been a change for me, from when I started graduate school, so I feel that has improved the relationship. So I feel I [am using] more of those "I feel angry when you . . ." sentences instead of "That is pissing me off!" I feel that has shifted over the years too.

Another student shared these thoughts:

> It actually has been really great for my relationship, because my partner is really guarded about her emotions, and I used to not know how to deal with them in the way that I do now. I used to [say], "Tell me what you are thinking! Why don't you tell me?" Now, after being at the clinic, I say [to myself]. . . "You can't do that to people, whether they are clients or family members or a spouse. You just can't do that to people's emotions and feelings." So I have been more laid back with her, like a little bit calmer, and it has been really good. I think it has had a really good impact on our relationship.

However, while the student partner may be the first one to step outside of a one-dimensional seesaw dynamic, the nonstudent partner must also participate in a two-person process analysis. For accommodation and differentiation to take place, nonstudent partners also need to master sufficient personal resources to overcome the struggle of dealing with the student partner who is now different from the person they knew before clinical training began. He or she must be willing and able to welcome a new two-person approach to the relationship and follow the student partner's lead in this interpersonal adventure. As four of the participants recognized, it was pivotal for their partners to change along with them as they progressed through the program. Also, four participants recognized that their partners grew into more psychologically minded individuals. Similarly, two participants acknowledged that they became closer to their partners as a result of the significant other's ability to relate to their clinical work. Some of the students appreciated how their significant others were able to recognize and eventually even welcome the student partner's newly developed clinical skills as a new side of his or her personality and as a tool that could benefit the relationship. For example, three participants in the study reported that, while initially their partners were annoyed by their newly developed analytic qualities, they became more accepting of them, and actually welcomed the student partners' new style of involvement in relationship-related matters. One trainee beautifully summarized it in this way:

> I find that my partner over the years has become so much more psychological-ly minded. He is like a mini-therapist. . . . Like he is in his own therapy . . . and [is also] an analyst . . . it's awesome! And even the language that he uses, and the way that he speaks back to me or even when I hear him on the phone with his friends, I go, "Ha . . . ha!" It's wonderful because I feel he has . . . adapted. He has always been my rock, but we can have deep conversations, and I feel that he can really . . . and he even reads my papers so . . . it has been cool.

Similarly in my relationship with Brad, after the initial ban on the word "dynamic" was lifted, he began to enjoy the idea of becoming progressively more psychologically minded and curious about the human mind. His personal experience in therapy unquestionably helped.

From Twoness to Thirdness

Thanks to their clinical training, especially when it is informed by "two-person" supervisors, student partners may experience the value of exploring two-person dynamics in their personal relationships and moving these relationships out of a doer/done-to impasse. When the significant other shows the ability and willingness to accept this new model of relating, moving the relationship from twoness to thirdness becomes possible. Of course, while psychology doctoral experience might have the potential to foster this progression, this is not the only possible outcome for couples. Students and their partners, depending on many factors (such as age, stability of the relationship, partner's psychological mindedness, type of supervision, and so forth) might experience a wide array of outcomes regarding their relationships. For example, some couples might be challenged in their complementarity, become polarized, and never recover. This was the case for one of the participants, who described how her relationship, also strained by distance, did not get around the roadblock of her doctoral training and fell apart. She reported that she and her partner became more and more polarized over time. In addition, some nonstudent partners may lack the psychological resources to welcome a complex, interpersonal understanding into their relationship. Other couples may be at a more mature stage of development and may feel less of an impact from the doctoral experience.

Also, even couples that "achieved" thirdness as a result of their experience as doctoral trainees in a clinical psychology program should not view this as a stable achievement; rather, it is part of an ever-evolving dynamic that continues working to strike a balance between mutual recognition and polarization (Davies, 2003). Thus, when a couple develops into moral thirdness, a strategic battle, not the war, is won. If the relationship is to survive, going forward the partners will continue negotiating the new differences thrown at them by the exigencies of life. Similarly, the journey for the participants in my study did not end when they found a way to open the space for doctoral training in their relationships. However, something that participants gained from winning the "doctoral-training battle" was faith in the relationship itself.

LESSONS LEARNED: A RETROSPECTIVE

Brad and I certainly experienced a generous dose of polarization while I was in training. He felt analyzed and pathologized countless times, and we had endless discussions filled with "I can't believe you don't get it! Aren't you supposed to be a psychologist?" I felt guilty for our financial situation, for my absent-mindedness, and for giving all of my care and attention to my clients while being largely unavailable to my husband. During the first three years of my training and personal therapy, I revisited my identity, my purpose, and my roles. Brad stood by me like a rock in this storm. Our relationship was shaken by resentment, by my seeing dysfunctional dynamics everywhere, and by the fact that my training became on obsession for both of us. Most of the time it felt as if there were three of us in the relationship: Brad, the program, and me. I was deeply affected by the stories of severe interpersonal violence that I was exposed to every day through my inner-city clinical placements, so I could not tolerate much evening TV programming beyond HGTV. When I would indignantly protest that shows such as *Breaking Bad* were nothing like entertainment, as they portrayed something that to me was daily reality, Brad would tell me he feared that we could never be "normal" again. Many times we came close to giving up, but, in the end, we made it through. In school I learned a lot about interpersonal dynamics and working with highly sensitive, severely mentally ill clients. For most of my training years I experienced firsthand how relationships are always inevitably two-way processes. Despite the many difficulties, and thanks to our undying desire to communicate and share, Brad remained open to learning with me, and we spent two years in couples' therapy. When I got my first choice for internship, we cried from joy together as *our* doctoral adventure was coming to a close.

I am now aware of just how much, during the years of my training, Brad kept me grounded on a daily basis, reminding me that there still was a whole world of grocery shopping, TV shows, politics, and world news outside of my clinical psychology training life. Brad helped me keep matters in perspective and contributed to making me a better therapist. Looking back on those years I see that my training catalyzed our journey from twoness to thirdness. I was the one who, using the vantage point of my training, led the way and showed Brad how our relationship could also get out of the impasse and evolve into something more. We made this transition together, and eight years after that day in Venice when I officially committed to my doctoral training, we are back in Italy, where I am working as a psychologist for an American institution in my home country, just as we had planned. As for Brad, in New York he broadened his professional skills and strengthened his position within his company. He is now working remotely from Italy, maintaining a role of international liaison for the regional branches of his company, a job that he enjoys very much. As we begin to prepare for the next big steps in our relationship, we know that we will have to brace for the next polarization storm. We hope that what we learned about ourselves during my doctoral training will assist us in making the process just a bit smoother.

NOTE

Names and identifying data were changed to disguise the identity of the persons involved.

REFERENCES

Aponte, H. J. (1994). How personal can training get? *Journal of Marital and Family Therapy, 20*(1), 3–17.

Aron, L. (2006). Analytic impasse and the third: Clinical implications of intersubjectivity theory. *International Journal of Psycho-Analysis, 87*(2), 49–69.

Benjamin, J. (2004). Beyond doer and done to: An intersubjective view of thirdness. *Psychoanalytic Quarterly, 7* 3(1), 5-46.

Bergen, G. R., and Bergen, M. B. (1978). Quality of marriage of university students in relation to sources of financial support and demographic characteristics. *The Family Coordinator, 27*, 245–50.

Berman, E. (2000). Psychoanalytic supervision: The intersubjective development. *International Journal of Psychoanalysis, 81* (2), 273–91.

Blount, C. M., and Glenwick, D. (1982). A developmental model of supervision. In *Psychotherapy supervision: Expanding conceptual models and clinical practices.* Symposium conducted at the APA Convention, Washington, DC.

Brannock, R. G., Litten, M. J., and Smith, J. (2000). The impact of doctoral study on marital satisfaction. *Journal of College Counseling, 3,* 123–30.

Butler, M. (2014). The impact of providing therapy on a therapist: A student's reflection. *Journal of Clinical Psychology, 70*(8), 724–30.

Carter, B., and McGoldrick, M. (Eds.). (2005). *The expanded family life cycle: Individual family and social perspectives* (3rd ed.). Boston, MA: Allyn and Bacon.

Cymbal, S. R. (2004). Married to the shrink. The impact of doctoral training in psychology on marital satisfaction. *Dissertation Abstract International: Section B. Sciences and Engineering, 65*(6-B), 3150.

Davies J. M. (2003). Falling in love with love: Oedipal and postoedipal manifestations of idealization, mourning, and erotic masochism. *Psychoanalitic Dialogues, 13*, 1–27.

Fiammenghi, S. (2011). Doctoral training in clinical psychology and romantic relationships: For better or for worse? (Unpublished doctoral dissertation). Long Island University, C.W. Post Campus, Brookville, NY.

Gerson, S. (2004). The relational unconscious: A core element of intersubjectivity, thirdness, and clinical process. *Psychoanalytic Quarterly, 73*(1), 63–99.

Gerstein, L. H., and Russell, N. (1990). The experience of medical school: A major life crisis. *College Student Journal, 24*, 128–35.

Gilbert, M. (1982). The impact of graduate school on the family: A system view. *Journal of College Student Personnel, 23*, 128–35.

Guy, D. G. (1983). The impact of conducting psychotherapy on psychotherapists' interpersonal functioning contents. *Professional Psychology: Research and Practice, 17*(2), 111-14.

Guy, D. J., Poelstra, P. L., Stark, M. J. (1989). Personal distress and therapeutic effectiveness: National survey of psychologists practicing psychotherapy. *Professional Psychology: Research and Practice, 20*(1), 48–50.

Guy, J. D. (1987). *The personal life of the psychotherapist.* New York: Wiley.

Hirsch, I. (2011, April). Analytic co-participation—the essential model for the new century. Paper presented at the Division of Psychoanalysis (39), 31st Annual Spring Meeting, New York, NY.

Hogan, R. A. (1964). Issues and approaches in supervision. *Psychotherapy: Theory, Research, and Practice, 1*, 139–41.

Legako, M. A., and Sorenson R. L. (2000). Christian psychology graduate school's impact on marriage: Nonstudent spouses speak. *Journal of Psychology and Theology, 28*, 212–220.

Maclean, A. P., and Peters, R. D. (1995). Graduate student couples: Dyadic satisfaction in relation to type of partnership and demographic characteristics. *Canadian Journal of Behavioural Science, 27*(1), 120–24.

Margolin, G. (1982). Ethical and legal considerations in marital and family therapy. *American Psychologist, 37*(7), 788–801.

McLaughlin, M.C. (1985). Graduate school and families: Issues of academic departments and university mental health professionals. *Journal of College Student Personnel, 26*, 488–941.

McWilliams, N. (2004). *Psychoanalytic psychotherapy*: A practitioner's guide. New York: Guilford Press.

Mearns, D. (1997). *Person centered counseling training.* London: Sage.

Mitchell, S. A., and Black, M. J. (1995). *Freud and beyond. A history of modern psychoanalytic thought.* New York: Basic Books.

Nissen-Lie, H. A., Havik,O. E., Høglend, P. A., Monsen, J. T., and Rønnestad, M. H. (2013). The contribution of the quality of therapists' personal lives to the development of the working alliance. *Journal of Counseling Psychology, 60*(4) 483–495.

Pederson, D. J., and Daniels, M. H. (2001). Stresses and strategies of graduate student couples. In S. Walfish and A. K. Hess (Eds.), *Succeeding in graduate school: The career guide for psychology students* (pp.171–85). Mahwah, NJ: L. Erlbaum Associates.

Pierce, L. A. (2005). The experience of wellness for counselor education doctoral students who are mothers. *Dissertation Abstracts International: Section A. Humanities and Social Sciences, 67*(07), 157.

Polson, M., and Nida, R. (1998). Program and trainee lifestyle stress: A survey of AAMFT student members. *Journal of Marital and Family Therapy, 24*, 95–112.

Price-Bonham, S. (1972). Student husbands versus student couples. *Journal of Marriage and Family, 35*, 33–37.

Scheinkman, M. (1988). Graduate student marriages: An organizational/interactional view. *Family Process, 27*, 351–368.

Sori, C. F., Wetchler, J. L., Ray, R. E., and Niedner, D. M. (1996). The impact of marriage and family therapy graduate training programs on married students and their families. *The American Journal of Family Therapy, 24*(3),259–68.

Stoltenberg, C. D. (1981). Approaching supervision from a developmental perspective: The counselor complexity model. *Journal of Counseling Psychology, 28,* 59–65.

Truell, R. (2001). The stresses of learning counseling: six recent graduates commented on their professional experience of learning counseling and what can be done to reduce associate harm. *Counselling Psychology Quarterly, 14*(1), 67–89.

Young, M. E., and Long, L. L. (1998). *Counseling and therapy for couples.* Pacific Grove, CA: Brooks/Cole.

Chapter Six

Clinical Psychology Doctoral Students with a History of Eating Disorders

Brianna M. Blake

Embodiment, for most people, is unequivocal. It is the experience of being clearly defined, having mastery over the discernment of internal and external experiences, and inhabiting the space where the self makes contact with the world. For those struggling with an eating disorder, however, these boundaries may be far less clear and even distorted by symptomatic behavior. In the world of clinical psychology, the body is the quintessential tool used in relating to and establishing a language between therapist and patient. While the manner in which the therapist uses her body to communicate empathy, agreement, or avoidance is an important topic of discussion in clinical training, the relationship the therapist has with her own body is seldom explored.

Most individuals who have struggled with an eating disorder have done so in secret, almost mechanically denying the presence of a problem and the gravity of the illness, even to themselves. Moreover, being known to others who share this painful and oftentimes shameful history is like shedding light into the innermost corners of one's being—places that have long been shrouded in an impenetrable darkness. But such an act can be liberating and self-defining.

In my experience as a clinical psychology doctoral student, I was surprised to learn how many of my peers shared my history of an eating disorder. Fearing being judged by teachers and supervisors, many of my peers were reluctant to make such history known within the program. In training to bear witness to the psychological pain of others, trainees are often reticent about their own history of suffering because they feel pressed to present themselves as unwaveringly competent and emotionally balanced. Furthermore, working with patients who present with an eating disorder may reignite some of the clinician's issues surrounding body image, which can complicate the countertransference and the overall therapeutic work.

This chapter—drawing on my own experience as well as the personal accounts of other clinicians in training who consider themselves largely recovered from an eating disorder—will address the difficulties of navigating a clinical psychology doctoral program and developing a professional identity in the shadow of an eating disorder history. These narratives, filtered through the lens of a personal experience with an eating disorder, are intended to convey the unique difficulties and transformations that occur among trainees as they wrestle to make meaning of their own histories alongside the wounded patients they are being trained to treat.

For these psychologists in training, learning to harness personal experiences in the service of individual growth and for the purpose of connecting with patients can prove both complicated and enlightening in the context of a training program that consistently confronts and challenges their self-identities.

INITIAL ENCOUNTERS

The heavy summer air pressed against my skin, further stifling my already shallow breathing. Radiating excitement and anxiety, I entered a large conference room and looked on a sea of unfamiliar faces. Scuttling to find a seat, I was eager to embark on my clinical journey. It was day one of orientation into the clinical psychology doctoral program and huddled together in one room were the people who would shape my life for the next five years. After a few hours of general introductions, instruction about the program layout, and the articulation of many anxiety-driven questions, the clinical director announced, "Let's break for lunch." Sweet smells wafted in the air as the vibrant colors of the food blanketing the table before me arrested my senses.

Instantly I was struck with panic. Would they discover my secret? Would they see so soon my imperfections? While I was not yet hungry, my fear of being quizzically observed impelled me to fill my plate with food. Heaving and churning with emotion, I believed every bite, every morsel, delivered me one step closer to being "exposed." Feelings of insecurity, uncertainty, and helplessness were reinvigorated—emotions I had fervidly tried to avoid for the majority of my young life by imposing structure and following a plan of being "the best." While this perfectionist drive made me into a diligent student and guided me in the direction of success early on, it also propelled me in maladaptive directions. As a result, for two years of my childhood, I struggled with an eating disorder.

EARLY STRUGGLES WITH ANOREXIA

The exact moment it all started is hard to pinpoint, but the illness thrived and quickly took hold of my existence—invading most every thought and dictating most every action.

Within six months, I was severely restricting my food and had limited my intake to a meager list of items I had categorized as "good" or "acceptable." At the height of my illness, I had devised an intricate system for protecting my eating disorder which involved evading mealtimes, disposing of food, and deceiving people into believing I had eaten. In effect, I had become a master at concealing the utter torture I was inflicting on myself. I was ten years old.

As an only child living with my mom, the task—sad to say—was relatively simple.

Struggling with her own demons and disappointments, my mom's focus failed to reach beyond the scope of her own pain. I was cast in the role of parent, nurturer, and protector all the while absorbing the sadness around me until it became my own. The more I focused on food and exerted control over my body, the less mental space I had to think of the profound sorrow I felt.

The more I attenuated myself, the more empowered and masterful I felt; the more empowered I felt, the less power I wielded. My sickness was embedded in and a representation of a bruised and impoverished family system collapsing under the weight of its own hurt. Through the destruction of my body, I attempted to express what words could not: I need you to be strong enough to save me. But the salvation did not come, and I was left to wonder if I would survive attrition. As if bound in a collective family denial, my eating disorder went largely unaddressed or even noticed. It was not until the seventh grade that teachers began to recognize that the young girl occupying their classes and roaming their halls was but a ghostly shadow of the girl who had once existed in her place. But their concern went only so far as monitoring me at lunch and weighing me in the nurse's station every so often until I artfully convinced them that I was well some months later. It is amazing how quickly people will see what they want to see.

Upholding this charade was exhausting, and by age twelve, I was sufficiently drained. One evening as I got ready for bed, I leaned over my bathroom sink, eyes swollen from crying, and gazed at an ashen and unfamiliar face. "No more," I uttered to myself. It was then that I made the choice to try to get better, to fight against the eating disorder rather than for it. Truth be told, I'm not sure if this decision should be attributed to a miraculous recognition of self-worth or merely to the fact that the eating disorder no longer served its purpose. After all, if the goal was for my pain to be noticed or the family dynamics to shift, neither was happening. Regardless of the motive, I had committed to breaking free of my self-imposed imprisonment. The road to recovery, however, was long and rocky. Throughout high school, I continued to scrutinize my body, some days reverting back to old behaviors. It was not until I reached my early twenties that I began to form a more healthy relationship with my body, accepting and appreciating it for what it could do as opposed to denigrating it for its perceived flaws.

Coming into the doctoral program, I held a host of preconceived notions about the people I would meet: bright, driven, socially developed with a strong sense of self, products of a cohesive family, gentle but determined. Few, if any, did I believe would appreciate the depths of my experiences or know what it meant to have struggled with an eating disorder. To my astonishment, many of my classmates not only understood but also shared in this rather painful history. In a small study conducted of students who attended my clinical psychology doctoral program, 50 percent of first- and second-year students admitted at least some degree of personal experience with an eating disorder—either themselves directly or through witnessing a close other (Blake, Nadell, and Demaria, 2011). While there is no way to know how representative these numbers are of other doctoral programs, they nonetheless speak to the necessity of considering how experience with an eating disorder may affect novice clinicians themselves and, eventually, their clients. Interestingly, the overall picture of many of these students is a familiar one. They reported that beginning in pre- to early adolescence, an unhealthy relationship with their bodies emerged, and, ill-equipped to tolerate the emotional burdens they faced, they sought refuge in behaviors that eventually evolved into an eating disorder. One clinician in training, Sharon, recalled that she first started worrying about the size of her body at age thirteen:

> There was a classmate who told me I had a big butt. I had never looked at my butt before, so I was surprised. It was around that time that I started going to the gym, becoming more worried and self-conscious about [my body]. Gradually, it worsened and, by 14, I really started exercising a lot and cutting out different foods. At one point, I was only eating squash—some fad diet I had read somewhere. I was crying all of the time and spent endless hours in front of the mirror just hating myself.

Another clinician in training, Rob, recounted a similar story of the emergence of his poor body image and disordered eating:

> I never received a formal diagnosis of an eating disorder but I would say that I started restricting my eating in sophomore year of high school when I was about 14 or 15. I would pretty much not eat throughout the school day and eat only one meal a day. A lot of my friends were doing something very similar and they were all thinner than me. It wasn't something they ever pointed out but I feared being regarded as the "fat one" in the group. At the time in my life, that wasn't an option for me. By the time I entered college, the problem

became severe. I was restricting my eating almost entirely, essentially living off diet pills and water.

Complicated relationships with caregivers, ranging from enmeshment to neglect, also characterized the early experiences of many of these clinicians in training and were credited as creating an environment in which emotions were avoided or unacknowledged. Caregivers were painted as figures that, for various reasons, could not bear to witness the battleground that had become their children's bodies. For example, Sharon recalled, "I had to be perfect for somebody else, essentially. My emotions could never be out in the open. I always had a hard time because my mother, while she loves me to death, couldn't tolerate my emotional distress. She'd become overwhelmed by it and blame me for it." Rob described a similar state of unrest in his family at the time when he was struggling most with his eating disorder:

> It was during my sophomore year of college when my eating disorder was probably most severe. During that time, my brother was in and out of jail and my father was sick so a lot of my family's energy and money were dedicated to them. I didn't want to put more pressure on them than they were already dealing with. [It wasn't until years] later that they acknowledged having noticed [my eating disorder] and I was a little resentful. It made me wonder, "Why did you wait until *now* to say something?"

Such life experiences can leave an abundance of unanswered questions in their wake. Gravitating toward and even entering the field of psychology can be a way for many individuals to gain insights into their family dynamics and aspects of their character. My own path to self-understanding began in my freshman year of college when I decided to pursue psychology. I thought it was something at which I would excel, especially because I was an astute observer. I was captivated by the dramas of people's lives and consumed by the desire to help them make sense of their stories. At seventeen, I had yet to contemplate, or perhaps was not ready to contemplate, the true complexities underlying this career choice. True to the perfectionist that I was, I committed myself to being "the best" so that I could quickly advance to a doctoral program. I earned my bachelor's degree, with distinction, in three years and completed my thesis on the eating attitudes of college females. I hurried through much of my college experience, a phase of life notably contemporaneous with self-exploration, and successfully removed *myself* from the process. I kept my interest in eating disorders at arm's length, examining it from the perspective of how it manifested in and impacted others as opposed to myself. I knew at that time that I wanted to work with young people with eating disorders and believed I had the tools to help guide them away from the treacherous road I knew all too well. But it wasn't until pursuing my master's degree that I began to view my passion for helping others through a more genuine and intimate lens. I recognized that it was a way of mending parts of myself that had yet to be healed, of filling in lines that had been ill-defined. Once so disconnected from my body that at times it felt alien, I knew that working with eating disorders in my adulthood was a way of reconnecting with the experiences I had detached from. Through studying others, I would come to understand more about myself. My study eventually allowed me to see my mother through different eyes as well; in time, we would rebuild our relationship into one that would be insightful and inspiring to me.

Sharon cited similar reasons for entering the field of clinical psychology: "I think a lot of the way my mother was motivated me to help others. Another part of it was that I just wanted to understand myself . . . *needed* to understand. Perhaps unconsciously, entering the field of psychology served as substitute for therapy." Through the pursuit of psychology, the "wounded healer" can, to quote Jungian contemporary Karl Kerenyi, "be at home in the darkness of suffering and there find germs of light and recovery" (Levy, 2008, p. 37). A painful journey can be transformed and used in the service of not only helping others but in reaching personal enlightenment as well.

As budding clinicians, we learn to become aware of the ways in which we use our bodies to communicate to our patients; we begin discerning when we are nervous, intrigued, moved, and engaged. However, the ever-evolving relationship and history we have with our own bodies are seldom explored outside of the scope of individual therapy. Given that a large number of novice clinicians seem to have struggled with an eating disorder and continue to confront and revise what it means to inhabit their own bodies, it is important to explore the ways this unique history plays out in the clinical realm. When both clinician and patient are in search of a more cohesive self-definition, is effective treatment possible?

WORKING WITH CLIENTS

Providing psychotherapy, particularly to individuals who have endured struggles similar to our own, can be like holding up a mirror to the most monstrous and tender parts of ourselves, reigniting long-buried emotions. Especially for novice clinicians who may lack the experience of creating and maintaining therapeutic boundaries, the urgency to somehow reach or "fix" the person sitting across from them can feel stifling and unbridled; it is through the patients' improvement that inexperienced clinicians believe they can heal themselves. While a patient's achievement of insight and psychic growth can be mutually transformative, as both clinician and patient gain added perspective, improvement must be in the service of the patient and not the rectification of the clinician's past burdens. A real danger of working with patients who share our defining characteristics and experiences is the potential to become overinvested, violate boundaries, or incorrectly assume knowledge of the patient's experiences. When I began working at a residential treatment facility as a milieu therapist for young women with eating disorders, just prior to entering the doctoral program, I was instantly confronted with emotions I believed were long resolved. Almost like seeing myself from the outside, I was faced with a concrete representation of the quest for annihilation on which I had set out ten years earlier. Witnessing the gaunt appearance of many of these young women, their extreme devotion to their eating disorders, and the intense sadness and anger that percolated beneath their frail surfaces, I experienced a flood of memories. Was I ready to face this? I wondered. For the first month I became more focused on my body shape and at times was even comparing it to the patients around me. If I can become so easily triggered, I thought, perhaps I *can't* make meaningful contact with these women. As with my experience at the doctoral-program orientation, I feared my inner thoughts and conflicts would somehow be projected for all to see and criticize. If they knew my body image was imperfect and I was questioning my ability to help, would they brand me a fraud?

One patient in particular, Emma, a nineteen-year-old college student attending a prestigious local university, stirred many of these doubts and anxieties in me. Her ash-blonde hair veiled her large brown eyes, protecting her from seeing and being seen. Buried under layers of timidity and a contrived smile was a sad story she narrated in slightly above a whisper: an insatiable drive to achieve perfection, an uncontrollable sadness that went mostly unnoticed, an absentee parent struggling with alcoholism, and a hope to save a family on the verge of collapse. Emma's story, which was not unlike my own, inspired me to feel not only instantaneously connected to her but as though I understood the depths of her as well. Yet I would become extremely nervous around her—perhaps fearful that she could somehow see parts of myself I had hidden from others, perhaps scared that her sickness meant something about my own. I sat across from this young girl, hoping there was something I could say to save her; if I saved her, I could somehow save the helpless, silenced young girl I once had been. If I saved her, I could assign positive meaning to the traumas I not only witnessed in life but had also inflicted on my own body.

As a milieu therapist, my duties consisted of assisting the women through mealtimes, managing crises as they arose, reinforcing the use of positive coping skills, and functioning as an ever-present shoulder to lean on as they fought against ravenous urges to binge and purge. Perhaps more than with the other girls, I would invite Emma to participate in discussion and games during downtime, encourage her when she did something well, try to make her laugh, and welcome late-night chats in the hope that she might connect with genuine feelings she kept largely hidden. Nearly two months into her stay, she sat alone one night at the kitchen table, her head hung low and despair tugging on her face. I sat down next to her and, after a moment of shared silence, she began to cry. "I can't do this anymore!" she exclaimed, "It's like they don't even care. And here I am, going to treatment, and I'm even more fat and miserable than before." I remembered Emma saying weeks earlier in passing that her sister also struggled with an eating disorder but, unlike Emma, would severely restrict her food intake to the point of hospitalization. In Emma's view, she failed even at her eating disorder, and such failure came at the cost of her parent's attention and care, which had been dedicated to the "sicker" child.

"It must feel exhausting when your sister's pain is given the attention it deserves and you're left alone trying to pick up the pieces," I ventured.

She paused and, gently sweeping a tear aside, uttered, "Wow. How did you know that?"

I replied, "I listened." Throughout my conversation with Emma, I wrestled with the urge to scream out, "I understand! I've been through it and you're not alone. Things can get better!" I wanted so badly to connect, believing that through my own admission she could feel supported and her pain would be eased. But it was remnants of my own pain rather than Emma's that was fueling this desire. Observing and reflecting upon this nudging feeling, I recognized that it stemmed from my own unfulfilled wish to be noticed as a child. Perhaps the most important lesson Emma taught me was that even without revealing that I too had struggled with an eating disorder, I could still help her feel heard and understood. Further, I realized that I could use my experiences to build empathy without allowing my emotions or cravings to intrude on the needs of others. Working with people like Emma in my clinical training who have presented with eating issues, self-injurious behaviors, and poor self-image has allowed me to view parts of myself from a safe and healthy distance. I could feel empathy for the small child whose devastation went unnoticed—an empathy which I draw upon in my work as a clinician.

Other colleagues in training have described similar experiences of fear and self-doubt when working with patients struggling to make sense of and exist in their bodies. One of the greatest fears of such novice therapists is that they will overinvest in their patients, particularly when they are unsure about whether they have fully resolved their own body-image issues. While they generally believe they are better equipped to assess for the presence of an eating disorder than novice clinicians who have not had this personal experience, they question their ability to remain objective when providing treatment to these patients. One of Rob's earliest clinical experiences with a patient who struggled with an eating disorder illustrates the internal conflict new clinicians can feel when faced with issues similar to what they have personally endured.

About three years into being a therapist, I met a patient, Steven, while working on an inpatient psychiatric unit. While he was bulimic, and not restrictive like I had been, there was still an identification that I had with him that I could not escape. No one on the treatment team seemed to be taking his eating disorder seriously. Instead, they were focusing on and treating his drug use. I protested, saying, "We have a much bigger issue here. He's going to the bathroom to throw up his food." The team was almost confused that I seemed to care so much, likely because he wasn't even my individual patient (I had only known him in a group therapy setting). Even Steven was confused that I seemed to care so much and, in fact, asked me about it. I had to answer in this very therapeutic, blank way, "I'm concerned about all of my patients." But, truthfully, I was a little extra concerned about him. And that was part of the problem that I felt I had with Steven. I felt I was *too* empathic, *too* attuned. It was probably a burden on him because it was evident that I really needed him to be okay.

Just as the boundaries between the self and the body become loosened in the presence of an eating disorder, so too many clinicians who have endured such difficulties with embodiment question their ability to maintain firm therapeutic boundaries. Identification with a patient may lead to an overinvestment of emotions and resources, as was the case with my initial experience with Emma and Rob's experience with Steven. Changes in one's own behavior can provide information about the permeability of boundaries between clinician and patient. Rob recounted:

> According to my friends at work, I was a little triggered by Steven. I remember one day, I was just going through life, working, and probably forgot to eat that day. One of my peers who knew my history said, "You're acting like Steven. You have to go eat something." It was then that I realized that I can become triggered when I work with these types of patients. Apparently there are some limits to all the help I can give.

On the other hand, when aware of one's own pitfalls and fixations, a clinician's identification with a patient's struggles can help with building an alliance and compassion.

Sharon recalled one of her most difficult yet rewarding experiences working with a patient with an eating disorder:

> I really pick up on enmeshment because of the relationship I had with my mother. Working with people who are extremely needy, it has been difficult for me to maintain therapeutic boundaries at times; it's something I'm dealing with in supervision. I have a client now who is obese. For twelve years she has been in the forensic system—a system which provides mental health services

to people diagnosed with a mental illness who have a history of incarcera-
tion—and she's getting ready to move toward discharge. She's done a lot of
growing, and now she's ready to face her body. She's put on all of this weight
to protect herself; she was a victim of sexual abuse. I can understand the
motivation to destroy yourself in a warped effort to protect yourself. I can
really help my clients in a very concrete way to work on moderation, drawing
on my own journey where I had gone from one extreme to the other with food.

Drawing from one's own life experiences can be a way of gaining additional insight into the experience of those we treat; however, working with
patients with similar histories to our own can spark unforeseen emotions in
novice clinicians that may potentially cloud their clinical judgment or bring
about regressive thoughts or actions. The goal is to recognize both how to
harness past experiences as a way of making connections and attune oneself
to the blind spots that may result from these experiences.

RECONCILING PROFESSIONAL
AND PERSONAL IDENTITIES

One of the greatest internal conflicts I have faced in my clinical training has
been whether to reveal my eating-disorder history to peers, professors, and
supervisors. These would be my colleagues, evaluators, and, ultimately, the
people deciding my fate as a psychologist. To be potentially seen as somehow less than capable of pursuing the discipline that I loved was a devastating notion. While it seemed reasonable to assume that many people who
become psychologists have either wrestled with mental illness themselves or
endured its effects alongside a loved one, I remained uncertain about the
acceptability of revealing my experiences in a doctoral program. Moreover,
if I did reveal them, in whom would I confide and when? Should it be only in
the context of how these experiences might impact clinical work with a
particular patient or should discussion of all relevant life experiences occur in
the service of individual growth? This dilemma took on particular significance when considering the almost total immersion of trainees in their clinical training for several years and the potential consequences of disavowing
critical parts of the self along the long journey to becoming a clinician and
forming a clinical identity. These unanswered questions, along with both the
fear and reality of evaluation by peers and professors, kept me at odds with
aspects of myself and spawned an internal battle between self-acceptance and
self-repudiation.

In my first clinical supervisory encounter at the doctoral level, my history
was almost immediately thrust to the foreground for examination, "I see from
your CV that you're interested in eating disorders," my supervisor affirmed.
"Why is that?" Unsure of how forthright to be in the presence of someone

who would evaluate my competency as a clinician and even more uncertain of my own readiness to visit this topic with a stranger, I answered in a truthful but equivocal manner: "I have both a personal and an academic interest in the topic." Although I had confessed to very little, I left this encounter feeling incredibly raw and exposed. I felt I had lost control over when and how this information would be used and shared; the more my supervisor pressed to learn, the more I retreated, believing that if I sheltered the facts of my history, I would be safer from criticism or misperception. Over the course of our first few months together, I filled the supervision space with clinical material, questions about treatment, and my conceptualization of patients but rarely did *I* enter the room. Of course, the "therapist" parts of myself showed up, but the most authentic parts—what irritates me, what drives me, what disheartens me—had been relegated to some hiding place even I had trouble accessing.

It is often said that the thing we fear the most is what we ultimately bring about for ourselves. I learned this lesson firsthand. The more my clinical self tried to disown my past experiences for fear that they would paint me as a less-than-capable clinician, the more disconnected I became from my patients; in turn, I became less effective at using myself to understand my patients' internal lives and emotional needs. More simply put: I became a less effective therapist. As I continued on in my training and forged new supervisory relationships, I chose to be more open about sharing areas of vulnerability even beyond my history of anorexia and discussing when patients elicited unexpected emotions or impulses in me. Although still not something I typically divulge in the nascence of a professional relationship, as I grow more confident in my clinical skills, I am now more willing to explore the ways in which my early experiences show up in the therapy room, shaping my reactions and guiding my focus on particular topics. I learned that, despite how hard I have tried to keep them separate, my past experiences were invariably connected to and constituted my clinical identity. This realization, with time, brought me great solace and pride.

In a position of limited power, novice clinicians can find it daunting to decide what information to divulge. Sharon said, "I originally wanted to write my dissertation on the topic of eating disorders in the first year. But I eventually realized that, for my own sake, I had to go to my professor and say, 'I don't really need to be close to this right now. I need to stay away from thinking about eating disorders for a while." Sharon further explained that, while it was difficult to confess this to her professor, she was ultimately glad that she gave herself permission to not be "Wonder Woman." Relying on the support and feedback of other colleagues in training can help combat the pressures of graduate school life. Further, it is through exchanges with peers who are similarly straddling personal and professional identities that novice clinicians can begin to assess their level of comfort in revealing intimate parts of themselves. "While in training, we live and breathe psychology, and much of our relationships are with fellow trainees. Together, we cried about feeling overwhelmed when we first started seeing patients and felt largely inadequate," Sharon said. "My classmates were the ones to contain my stress, not only about treating patients but of having little money or time to eat healthy and exercise." Like Sharon, by gradually exposing myself to my classmates and experiencing how they exposed themselves to me, I gained a new appreciation for the unique ways in which personal experiences lead people down the path of helping others. From academic discussions, social gatherings, and friendships unfolded harrowing stories of loss, parental abandonment, trauma, and mental illness. Suddenly, I was not so alone, and my experiences were no longer as anomalous as I once thought.

Particularly in my conversations with novice clinicians who so bravely shared details of their experiences with an eating disorder, I recognized that if they could remain preserved in my mind as skilled and faithful clinicians, then I could begin to see myself in that way as well. While the rules and expectations about the permissibility of disclosing a history of mental illness in clinical training remain largely unclear, particularly to incoming students, the process of knowing and being known to other novice clinicians can help dissolve the naïve misconception that to be a psychologist means to be free from emotional scars. Moreover, the experiences underlying these scars often propel people into the helping professions; when a clinician enters a room, she invariably takes the past in with her.

COPING AHEAD: IS RESOLUTION POSSIBLE?

For anyone who has wrestled with an eating disorder, maintaining a healthy relationship with one's body can prove challenging even after recovery. During times of high stress or uncertainty, self-deprecating thoughts and old preoccupations can furtively slither back into one's mind like the lyrics of a song one can't seem to forget. A tool for regulating painful emotions, neurotic behaviors can paradoxically serve as a comforting refuge to which a person can return in times of need to help distract, to gain control, or to find companionship. In a program in which one feels like almost every aspect of personhood is being assessed—academic work, clinical work, and peer interactions—the pressure to not only excel but also maintain an air of equanimity while doing so can feel overpowering. While I have long abandoned the severe behaviors of my past, there are still times in which I experience the urge to skip meals or become highly critical of my weight—persecuting my body as though it is somehow a reflection of my success, my intelligence, and my worth. At first I was ashamed of these thoughts and feelings, believing that they meant I was unfit to be a psychologist. What I learned through training and experience, however, was that I needed to amend my idea of what it meant to be a psychologist, a chimerical figure who I fashioned in my mind as someone always in control and aware of her emotions, unwaveringly brilliant, and seamlessly related. I had created a fictional standard I could never live up to and then punished myself for failing to meet that standard; it was an all-too-familiar cycle that forced me to ask the question: why was I so unwilling to grant myself the space to be imperfect, when I so generously afforded it to my patients?

Given my own history, it is important for me to be aware of events, emotions, and even people that can prompt negative thoughts about my body or instigate urges to behave in ways that are ultimately harmful. For me, being aware of feelings of inadequacy when they surface helps me recognize when I need to call a friend, watch a movie, or go for a walk in an effort to regain balance. Sharon also experienced feelings of inadequacy in the resurgence of negative thoughts about her body. "I notice these thoughts more when I'm feeling inadequate as a therapist, inadequate as a student," she shared. "That's where my brain goes, my heart goes, and then I feel my body is inadequate. But I've learned a lot of little strategies. I practice yoga and emotion management techniques I learned [from dialectical behavior therapy]. I also think that doing this work has helped me to put a lot of things in perspective. I have worked with people who have endured some of the most horrific emotional, physical, and sexual abuse. It helps you slowly, but certainly, let go of your ego. Now, I can accept not being perfect."

When working to succeed in academia, thrive in clinical work, and overcome the personal pressures of completing a doctoral program, it can be easy for novice clinicians to minimize or dismiss their needs. Knowing when to step outside of the superhero role and rely on the support of others is an important part of not only avoiding the use of old, harmful behaviors but of becoming strong clinicians as well. Admittedly, being the self-reliant person that I am, asking for emotional support has been a continual challenge. For Rob, knowing when to reach out to others has helped him cope with the stresses of being a doctoral student and burgeoning clinician. "I have gotten much more comfortable with expressing how I'm actually feeling to peers, friends, and family as opposed to just holding it in. Particularly since beginning in the doctoral program, I've noticed a lot of progress in my ability to reach out for help," he explained. "When I'm having difficulties I actually speak a lot more about it than I ever have. I also have a lot of strategies to help regulate myself, like art and music."

Regardless of whether we have a history of an eating disorder, the way we mentally represent, regard, and relate to our bodies is continually changing as we grow, mature, enter new stages of life, and reflect on ourselves from novel perspectives. As someone who has struggled with the acceptance of my body for the greater portion of my life, I am aware of the propensity for that nagging voice in my head, eagerly waiting to whisper captious remarks, to emerge during times of change and worry; it is a voice I believe I will long hear and fight to silence.

When considering the evolution of his body image, Rob remarked:

> I don't think those [body image] issues are ever resolved. I believe this type of thing is one you must deal with forever because we are in our bodies. You can amend this distorted view but stress and anxiety can send you back to where you once were; and in a lot of ways your [eating disorder] is a safe and familiar place. So while I do feel that my relationship with my body has greatly improved, I don't know what might trigger some of those old negative thoughts and feelings—perhaps the death of a family member or a particular type of patient. However, unlike in the past, I now know what to do when I'm feeling triggered so as to avoid acting on those negative thoughts.

While the pain of living with an eating disorder is often palpable and far-reaching, the lessons learned from the journey can serve as assets for novice clinicians. As the famous aphorism by Terence says, "I am a human being. Nothing that is human is alien to me" (Lefèvre, 2013). My experiences have allowed me to develop a greater compassion and understanding for my patients as I search within myself to find the connection even when it may not seem apparent upon first glance. Alongside traces of familiarity develop a gentle curiosity and a will to uncover others' truths. Before beginning my training on an adult inpatient psychiatric unit in the inner city, I wondered how I—a young, White female who on the outside appeared unmarred by the events of life —could form any alliance with my patients, many of whom were members of minority groups. Sharon, having also worked on an inpatient unit, perhaps summarized this experience best:

> [My history] has helped me not to be so judgmental. When working with the type of people I work with, some of whom have committed violent crimes such as murdering their mother, there is a tendency to differentiate between "me" and "them," as though we were two different breeds. There's a big danger in saying he's *there* and I'm *here* and we can't meet because therapy will then likely fail. Reflecting on my own experience of madness has really helped to bridge that gap.

For better or worse, we are all contained within and cannot escape the boundaries of our bodies. Every experience, every sensation is filtered through it. As such, it is the common denominator uniting us all. Most all "disorders" are characterized by problems in the relationship between the body and the inner self—schizophrenia, substance dependence, posttraumatic stress disorder, body dysmorphic disorder, somatizing disorders, and eating disorders, to name a few. Familiar with what it feels like to be at odds with and disconnected from your own body, I can use my history of anorexia as a way to "bridge the gap" between myself and patients with seemingly dissimilar ailments. Like other novice clinicians who have wrestled with an eating disorder, I must be alert to when negative thoughts or urges resurface and active in considering the ways in which these impulses may impact my clinical work. Moving forward in my clinical and professional development, I can find solace in knowing I'm not alone.

CONCLUSION

More clinical psychology doctoral trainees have had an eating disorder than might be expected. The narratives of these novice clinicians share prominent themes of familial disruption, strivings for "perfection," acts of self-destruction, and a passion for helping others. The drive to succeed that often accompanies an eating disorder, particularly one that is mainly restrictive, may represent an underlying trait that also makes for an individual who can manage the rigor of clinical training. As a budding clinician, sitting across from and attempting to aid someone who has experienced similar issues as you can be both terrifying and inspiring; it allows you to see parts of yourself, perhaps for the first time, through less distorted and more patient eyes. Bearing witness to the pain of others can help training clinicians form a new understanding of their own experiences, and heal old wounds through the healing of others. Given the inherent and inescapable presence of our bodies as a means of perception, expression, and connection and its essentiality in the art of psychotherapy, novice clinicians who have struggled with the acceptance of their own bodies must be cognizant of the ways certain patients and life events can reignite self-defeating patterns. While it may feel frightening to consider revealing these experiences to professors and supervisors, gradually sharing personal information with peers can be a less threatening way of beginning to work through the anxieties and hurdles that accompany a clinical psychology doctoral program. Through listening to and participating in the defining experiences of others, shameful and tender aspects of the self are transformed into experiences of value and substance—at last unveiling a self that is healthy and defined.

NOTE

Names and identifying data were changed to disguise the identity of the persons involved.

REFERENCES

Blake, B. M., Nadell, N., and Demaria, T. (2011, August). *Impact of personal eating disorder history on the professional development of psychology graduate students*. Poster presented at the 2011 Annual Convention of the American Psychological Association, Washington, DC.

Lefèvre, E. (2013). Heauton timorumenos. In A. Augoustakis and A. Traill (Eds.), *A companion to Terence* (pp. 243–261). Oxford, England: Blackwell Publishing Ltd. doi: 10.1002/9781118301975.ch13

Levy, P. (2008). The wounded healer. In D. Pinchbeck and K. Jordan (Eds.), *Toward 2012: Perspectives on the next age* (pp. 37–48). New York: Penguin Group.

Chapter Seven

Life as a Juggler

Work, Family, and Study inside a Doctoral Psychology Program

Matthew G. Liebman

Graduate students in a doctoral clinical psychology program spend a great deal of time sitting in a mildly uncomfortable chair, listening to lectures about how to effectively help people in distress. We all probably spend even more time feeling guilty about the work we *should* be doing while we're sitting at home, watching a half-hour of television, and trying to catch up on happenings in the world outside of graduate school. As the years have progressed, it has become easier to live the lifestyle that doctoral training requires. My days are exhaustive and challenging, exciting yet terrifying, and thought-provoking yet droll. The life of a full-time graduate student is alluring and difficult. As I enter my fourth year of study, I am juggling a sometimes staggering level of responsibility as a result of my life both inside and outside the program. This chapter will describe the difficulties I encounter while juggling the various aspects of everyday life and my doctoral work. As a full-time student, full-time musician, newly married man, and someone who struggles to maintain a sense of individuality through it all, I hope to shed light on both the positive and negative aspects of life as a doctoral student.

Everyone involved in doctoral training in clinical psychology stresses the importance of self-care, both in personal and professional practice. We try to impart the same message to the patients we are privileged to treat. Is it possible, or even fair, however, to expect this from patients while actively engaging in a daily schedule that seems to rule out that possibility for ourselves? Even with financial and/or emotional support of others through this work, it is still difficult to juggle all the balls we must keep in the air. While my complicated juggling routine has been a struggle over the last several years, I have chosen it willingly, and it has actually enhanced my graduate training experience. Ironically, my choice to take on so much has allowed me to *maintain* my sense of individuality, not diminish it. The juggling act is an important factor in my emergence as a unique and proficient professional. It makes me who I am.

MY LIFE AS A MUSICIAN

In third grade I was given the choice to join the orchestra and play the violin, cello, or viola. If I wanted to play a band instrument like the clarinet, I had to wait until the fourth grade—apparently one year was crucial in developing the maturity required to play wind instruments, though it was never explained to me why. My teacher passed around a sign-up sheet for choosing the instrument we would like to play, and nearly everyone wrote down the word "violin" next to their names. The sheet made its way around the room and came to me second to last. I glanced at it for a second, tilted my head to the side, and then simply passed it to the girl sitting next to me.

She turned to me and said, "You forgot to write."

I said, "No, I didn't."

A few weeks earlier, I had been watching a television movie with my dad. On screen was a scene that depicted the coolest cat I had ever seen. He was wearing a sharp, black zoot-suit, black sunglasses, and a pinstripe fedora. As he stood on stage in the haze that engulfed the nightclub, he picked up a saxophone and played the smoothest, most elegant music I had ever heard. I turned to my dad and said, "That's what I'm gonna do. I'll play that." I didn't want to be sidetracked by picking up a violin, even if it meant missing a period of class each week. It was the saxophone or nothing.

At that moment, music became a lasting and essential part of my life. I ended up playing in every band my schools had to offer, played in a jazz quartet with a few buddies to make a couple of dollars on the side at some local cocktail lounges, and even sang in a punk-rock band through high school. In college, I had a double major in psychology and saxophone performance. In my spare time I sat at the piano and wrote a few songs. I composed to express heartache, and I composed to get the girl. Music was an essential part of my life.

After I returned from college to live with my parents before launching myself into full adulthood, I happened to run into my music teacher's son at a local deli. It happened that he owned and played drums for a tremendously successful, fifteen-piece band, and he also owned the entire company the band worked for. I had met him a few times and recognized his face.

I turned to him. "Dave, right?"

"Right. Matt, right?"

"Right. How's things?" I asked.

We spoke for probably four minutes before my sandwich was ready. On my way out, I jokingly said, "By the way, I'm back in town now in case you ever need a horn player."

His eyes opened a bit wider as he responded, "Actually, I'm putting together a new band. It's a twelve-piece. Our company is getting too busy, and we need to expand. Why don't you come and jam with the guys next week and see what you think?"

It has now been six years since that first rehearsal. I work for Dave and his fabulous entertainment company where I am privileged to meet some of the most talented and warm individuals in the business. I took the gig even before going for my master's degree—and we played seven weddings that year. Last year I played fifty-five. This year we will play over sixty weddings, primarily in the spring, summer, and fall, with two to three weddings per weekend.

I'm still not sick of eating lobster and calamari every weekend, but when I first decided to pick up the saxophone, I wish someone had warned me about the bad hours (although admittedly it probably wouldn't have made a difference). For a five-hour affair that typically begins at seven, I usually leave around three o'clock in the afternoon to set up. Then I dance, play, sweat, and sing all night, getting back home around two or three in the morning. I am tired. All the time.

THE DEMANDS OF STUDY

Ironically, the hours for playing are the only hours in the day that I've got left after graduate work, or at least it feels as if all the other hours are consumed by graduate work. When I am not in school or at the hospital for an externship three days each week (twelve-hour days working with no immediate paycheck), I am working on my doctorate at home—or should be. If I am not reading, I should be writing. If I am not writing, I should most certainly be studying, or at least reviewing something clinically relevant so that I can be more prepared for my externship than I was the day before.

If it weren't for music, I would be doing nothing but graduate school work. That is, I would either be doing something of an academic nature, or actively *not* doing something related to graduate school and feeling guilty while thinking about how much I really *should* be doing something more "productive."

Our orientation as graduate students reminds me of something that happened in the movie *John Tucker Must Die*. John's four ex-girlfriends are in the same room arguing over how much they hate him, when one stops to reflect on their process in that moment: "Don't you all see what's going on? It doesn't matter whether we're all talking about loving him, or talking about hating him—we're still talking about him. Either way, it's still always just about him."

Sometimes it feels like my life as a doctoral student is exactly like that—except that my obsession is the doctoral work. Graduate work has a way of invading every crack and crevice of waking life. Music gives me reprieve from its pervasive and exhausting demands. For that I am eternally grateful. I am grateful that the thing that I would be doing for my self-care *anyway* is also the semblance of a career. I am grateful that this thing I'd be doing anyway is something I get paid for. Most of all, I am grateful that I have a support system that allows me to keep music in my life.

MUSIC AS SELF-CARE

From the beginning, my lifestyle as a musician would serve either as an obstacle to my success in graduate school and ultimately get in the way of completing the work I was required to do, or it would exist as a complement to my new full-time gig. Thankfully, it has been the latter. More often than not, the hours do not overlap. Patients rarely want to hold session Friday and Saturday nights, which lets me enjoy as I please the splendor that is other people's weddings.

In truth, the hours simply do not matter to me. It does not matter that after a full day of working as an aspiring psychologist, I have to throw on a three-piece suit and work another full day until three in the morning; it energizes me. It rejuvenates me. Without it (and I have been without it before in my life), I am not whole. It was this understanding of what it takes to become a well-rounded, complete person that brought me to doctoral work in psychology in the first place. To discount that knowledge and not allow music to remain an integral part of my existence would not only be negligent to my own well-being, it would be hypocritical in light of the message I hope to convey to the patients I meet with.

Not everyone gets to have a hobby that turns into a career and also counts as their self-care. But everyone needs to develop complementary aspects in their lives, because the interplay among them will be far more productive for their overall emotional and psychological health. It is because I allow my work in music to continue bringing me joy that I remain enthusiastic and passionate with my patient work.

In my case I *allow* my work in music to bring me joy. This distinction is crucial with regard to integrating the parts of a whole. It is not enough to simply do the things that *should* function as complements to one another. In my case I take a few extra moments during each performance to observe, understand, and appreciate the moment I am privileged to be in. If those moments simply pass by, they remain fleeting instances of non-productive work in relation to graduate school. However, if I am able to capture the feeling of relaxation and escape from daily stressors, then playing is much more potent. So, I remain vigilant in my effort not only to keep music as my self-care but also to appreciate the joy that music brings me. I take the time to understand the happiness I am actually experiencing. In doing so, the reprieve is more fulfilling, and my developing psychological prowess remains more focused and pristine.

NOVICE CLINICIANS BEHAVING BADLY

Graduate students in a doctoral psychology program train to help others. Specifically, we aid in the development of more mature and healthy interpersonal relationships, social skills, in building insight and awareness, and in facilitating healthy communication between individuals who struggle to find common ground. But sometimes we expect too much from ourselves.

I am told that I am not a stereotypical male because I spend a lot of time in the affective realm. I talk about feelings. I think about feelings. I *feel* about feelings. I help others communicate and aid in practicing effective and productive ways to say difficult things to other people. As a psychologist in training, I am expected to be good at "the relationship thing." Am I not supposed to be better at it than the "average" man? I analyze the impact of words and actions on individuals in others' lives. I help conceptualize functionality of behavior so that individuals can gain more insight into *why* they do what they do. Shouldn't I absolutely be able to do that for myself in my own relationships?

It is not that simple. The following story illustrates how woefully unprepared I can be in addressing stressful situations that arise in my relationships. Before I was married I took a vacation to Mexico with my fiancée and her family. We were traveling together to spend a full week at a resort, which was to be a perfect "getaway" from it all. Since it was the first time I had ever been away with what were sure to be my future in-laws, I wanted nothing more than to continue making the good impression I had worked very hard to establish up until that point.

My fiancée and I arrived at our room and began unpacking our bags. There were only a few hours until dinner, and since we did not have time to go to the pool and relax, we decided to explore the grounds and then shower and change for the first meal of the week. As I opened my suitcase, I smelled something rather delightful. A fruity, pleasant scent gently wafted up from my bag.

It was emanating from my clothes.

For a brief second, I thought, "Oh, what a pleasant thing!" Then I realized that my SPF30 Australian Gold sunscreen with island coconut infusion had opened and leaked all over my clothes. It had been open for so long that it soaked its golden color and coconut infused scent through every piece of expensive clothing I had brought. My everyday clothes were just fine—plain white tee shirts, khaki shorts that I'd held onto since the eighth grade—those were good to go. The designer shirts that I had purchased *specifically* for this trip, on the other hand, did not fare so well. The bronze-toned sunscreen had soaked a stain as large as a grapefruit through the chest of every single one of them.

I do not have the words to describe what I did in that moment, so let me say that I simply "freaked out." In retrospect, it was silly, but I wanted nothing more than to feel a part of things on this vacation and, at that moment, my ability to feel accepted was taken from me. If a patient were describing this story to me, I would without question begin dissecting it piece by piece to highlight the level of "catastrophizing" that he was engaging in and how this common yet powerful thinking trap can get in the way of enjoying the moments that so often escape us. But it wasn't a patient—it was me—and I was angry. All I wanted to do in that moment was scream and talk about how terrible everything was. I knew that I was doing it, and I didn't care. It felt empowering, and I just wanted to let my anger run wild for a bit.

My intellectual self knew exactly what was happening. All it would have taken was some thought-stopping techniques to reactivate the executive portions of my frontal lobe long enough to figure out that the hotel had a dry-cleaning service and everything would be fine. I could have practiced a bit of mindfulness, taken a few deep breaths (in through the nose, then out through the mouth for longer than the duration of the inhale), moved from "emotion mind" to "wise mind," and regained some composure before attempting to problem-solve or engage in acceptance strategies. But I did not feel like thinking intellectually. I didn't feel like thinking at all. I just felt like feeling. I felt like being mad and letting myself get carried away. After a while I cooled down and sent my clothes to a dry cleaner, and they were back within hours.

While this story illustrates a particular point, it is not meant as a comparison with the potentially heavy and trauma-based material presented to me daily in my work with patients. Rather, it simply shows how even in everyday situations our thoughts affect our feelings and actions. If I, someone who *should* be "good at relationships," can fall victim to something so banal, then who am I to ask the same (if not more) of my patients facing a reality laced with powerful trauma? It is a reminder that what we ask of our patients is no easy task, especially considering our own propensities to fall victim to the very same pitfalls that we conceptualize as their determining sources of distress. This idea has significantly impacted my life and my work. It is likely that many people who do graduate work in clinical psychology feel pressure to be "better at relationships"—and for good reasons—and it is one of the more important ways in which the training has changed me.

IMPERFECTION AS AN ASSET

Moments like that give me perspective. In graduate school it is easy to forget that everything you learn has to do with people. None of the theory is any good unless it can be applied to helping a person in need. And when that person is sitting in a chair across from you, looking at you with a bizarre mix of desperation and hope as if the next thing out of your mouth could potentially have the power to make it all better, the pressure may be enough to shake loose every bit of information you've learned in the past several years all at once, creating a flood in your psyche. Alternatively, everything you've learned thus far may simply disappear.

Change is one of the hardest things for a human being to bear and or to accomplish. Sometimes I forget how difficult it is to change and what it is we ask of patients, particularly in times when emotion runs high. Graduate school teaches us to expect a lot of our patients, to truly engage in therapy as a commitment to much more than just one hour per week. Change is difficult, and it takes work. That work happens over time, and to enact change in the lives of those that ask for and/or require it, the work needs to be done by both the patient and the therapist.

It is a fallacy to think that since I am the one that sits in a chair and is privy to others' life stories—which they share in the hope that I can provide an effective catalyst for change, through my words and my actions—that my work is done at the end of a session. I also have to change, and my own personal life is not "spick-and-span." So, the question remains, how is it that I can be expected to help others when in fact I am just as vulnerable to missteps and errors in judgment in my own day-to-day life?

The answer to this question is complex and does not deserve an "either/or" approach, but rather an "and" or "in addition to" mentality. For example, some cardiologists smoke. A professional architect may cut corners with the contractor who builds his own home just to save a couple of dollars, despite the fact that doing that very thing is the opposite of what he would advise a client to do. A lawyer might make a right turn on red even when there is a sign present telling him he cannot. Yet somehow, when it comes to the profession of psychology, people feel pressure to hold to a standard that may be unrealistic in their personal lives. Perhaps the lawyer or the architect has a twinge of guilt, and the cardiologist may know he is setting a bad example, but I doubt people in these professions go through soul searching every time they commit a faux pas in relation to their chosen profession. However, each time I get into an argument with someone with whom I have an intimate relationship, I feel that I have failed myself and my professional ideals and should even stop trying to be a therapist.

Perhaps I am exaggerating; I will not drop out of graduate school just because I had a spat with my wife. The guilt, however, is real, and I am not exaggerating when I say I feel an overwhelming sense of failure each time I do exactly the opposite of what I would advise a patient to do in similar circumstances. As I navigate this pressure that has reared its ugly head at several points throughout my graduate work, I have found a certain idea effective in coming to terms with this problem. I can be an individual who helps others with their distress, trauma, and struggle, *and* at the same time be vulnerable to the very thing that patients seek treatment for.

Possessing this knowledge is (or should be) empowering. To know that the very thing that patients seek professional help for is a capacity that I own is what allows me to relate to them. It reveals my humanness. If there is one thing I *do* know about this work, it is that being true to myself—both the positive and negative aspects of my emotional and psychological well-being—is what has the power to make me a proficient psychologist. We all learn the same theory, discuss the same cases, and engage in the same type of conversations. Does a hypertensive Darth Vader as a Rorschach (ink-blot) response have a historical quality to it according to the Exner model of scoring and assessment? In theory, we should be similar as clinicians, but in actuality, nothing could be further from the truth.

Bringing my actual self into the room is what makes me effective. To not acknowledge the different facets of my life that exist both in and out of the graduate school realm is neglectful and makes me less whole as a professional. More important, I believe a patient will always know when a therapist is not being genuine. In that instance, there exists the possibility for him or her to feel patronized and less than, even if that is not the intention of the therapist. Understanding who I am and being true to each aspect of my personality constellation allows me to avoid inauthentic interactions with patients.

Graduate school has given me every tool to become a more refined, competent, and clinically capable psychologist. I would be deficient without every single class that I have taken, every patient I have seen, and every supervisor that has guided my work. It is also true that under the shiny lights and allure of the graduate-student world, an individual holds onto the aspects of himself that drew him to graduate school in the first place. It is *that* piece of me that enhances my training beyond anything inside a textbook.

My choice to "spread myself thin" by working in music and psychology is what makes me genuine. I can identify with feeling overwhelmed, and my reactions are real. I can feel what a patient feels when they tell me they don't quite understand how they let things get so out of control. While I do not know their particular and individual feeling, I am not without solid ground for my empathy to root in. Insight based on my experience keeps me engaged with patients, and I am grateful for it.

THE DIFFICULTIES OF POSTPONING THE FRUITS OF A SUCCESSFUL CAREER

Another aspect of my life that both adds to my growth as a clinician and also makes my training more arduous is the fact that I am a newly married twenty-eight-year-old. I have been married for nine months and live in a one-bedroom apartment with my beautiful wife. On Facebook, her friends post about moving into bigger and better apartments in Manhattan. They are discussing when to have their first child, or they have already had one and have begun to live life in a whole new way.

I want it all, and I want it now. Perhaps it is selfish, especially in light of the difficulties faced by many of my patients, but because of my background and upbringing, I did think that at my age I would be more financially independent and doing well enough to start thinking about putting money away for my first house and first child. But the life of a part-time musician and full-time doctoral student doesn't contribute to fulfilling my earlier expectations.

Sometimes I feel emasculated in the life I have chosen, as the following story illustrates. Recently my wife threw a beautiful party for two of our friends who recently got married and are moving to follow his work. There were ten of us at the party, and we were set up in my in-laws' backyard. The pool was refreshing, and all the men (myself included) were cooling off in the shallow end—because it was simply too hot to be out of the water for too long. As we caught up with one another, the topic of golf came up. After all, the Masters was on, and Tiger was behind only by a couple of strokes. They all played, and I do not. Even if I *did* play, they all had *time* to play, and I do not.

One of the guys asked another if he had ever played on some course out on Long Island. All four of their eyes lit up as the reminisced on how challenging that course was, but how relaxing and enjoyable it was to have the luxury of spending a day trying to conquer the difficulty it brought. After a few minutes, they had all noticed I was quiet because I did not have much to contribute. One of them turned to me and said, "So—have you played there?"

"Nah. I don't really play."

"Oh, okay. Have you ever?"

"No. I mean, I've worked at every course you guys are mentioning. Just never played any holes." That was my response. All I could come up with to relate to men who were my own age was that, at the lush, amazing golf courses that they frequented whenever they'd liked because they had the time and financial means, I had been the help and could tell them about whether the venue served decent calamari.

I felt ashamed. I *feel* ashamed, sometimes. Why is it that other men my age don't have to worry about gigging until 4:00 a.m. on the weekends, every single weekend, just to make some money so they do not feel *totally* useless? Just as important as acknowledging shame's existence is the idea that the very thing that triggers shame can also grant the boundless joy referenced earlier.

I grant myself the satisfaction that they cannot do what I can do. I am a musician. I have chosen a different lifestyle; it is the road less traveled within the bounds of my particular socioeconomic class. For this, I remain torn and experience daily dissonance. My two truths, at odds with each other, are that my lifestyle choices bring me boundless joy and optimism but also restrict what I can do in comparison to those around me. I offer the idea that the very acknowledgement of this fact allows for acceptance and adaptive coping necessary for the maintenance of a healthy lifestyle.

Earlier I said that music is something I would have done, no matter what the circumstance. Thankfully, it has been a career that never interfered with my studies, and it also pays the bills. At this point in my life, as a nearly thirty-year-old man, I would like to be doing more than just paying the bills. I'd like to be living life more comfortably, and I feel pressure to do so. While all of my friends are having babies, it seems, I am in a living space in which it is hard to imagine a baby. While each couple with whom my wife and I socialize moves out of the city and into bigger, more lavish living quarters, we lease our one bedroom apartment because "it works for us." Of course, this pressure is ultimately self-imposed. Intellectually, I am aware that my situation is temporary. I have no doubt that I will be able to set my sights on some particular niche within the field and have success. I simply intend here to highlight that the sacrifices I make are new to me, and although I have accepted the reality that they must be made, an element of resentment and jealousy exist in tandem.

I am not unhappy in my life so far, and I have many things I am grateful for. Rather, my purpose is to share honestly the personal struggles that have arisen for me as a result of the graduate lifestyle. Sometimes I just want to go out to dinner without having to worry about whether we're ordering the most expensive thing on the menu. In short, pursuing a career in psychology is time-consuming and life-consuming, and anyone who embarks on this training should reconcile themselves to that fact from the beginning.

CONCLUSION

I am still working on acceptance regarding the fact that my friends were able to start careers before me, and that other couples are able to have children, and we have to wait a bit. It is important to understand that just because one reconciles oneself to the realities of training, it does not make it any less stressful when the opportunities to experience distress present themselves. The two exist concordantly, and it is important to acknowledge that they will often do that. Without awareness of my contradictory feelings I would not be able to cope as effectively as I do with the potential life delays I am experiencing.

Everything that I do in my life—music, performance, teaching, socializing, externship, class lectures, all of it—I accept. They are choices I have made to maintain all of the aspects of my life that keep me driven, focused, hardworking, and motivated. A schedule that is reflective of time for everything but sleep (meaning, I get little sleep) is something I have grown accustomed to, and on some level even like. I use these strategies to help me accept what I had chosen: First, I figured out potential stressors (i.e., friends posting baby pictures on Facebook and Instagram while I am reading articles that won't even make it to my dissertation's literature review). Then I figure out how to cope with them ahead of time—that is, decide exactly how to approach those stressors *when* they arrive. For example, if I begin getting more tired more easily in the future, I will evaluate my circumstances early enough to see what can be changed before the problem gets out of hand. Right now juggling my various activities works for me. This life is not for everybody.

If you *think* you can stomach something but have to make excuse after excuse for what you feel, eventually the cognitive dissonance will catch up with you. The longer I can maintain the different facets of my busy lifestyle, the more confident I feel in my ability to handle the various responsibilities a psychologist must shoulder. It is the juggling that allows me to be who I am both in and out of the therapy room. The juggling makes me feel accomplished and exhausted—most of all, it makes me feel like myself. I wouldn't have it any other way.

Chapter Eight

Experiences of a "Black Sheep" in a Clinical Psychology Doctoral Program

Noel Hunter

As a student returning to graduate school in her mid-thirties after more than a decade of pursuing other interests, I have faced some uncommon challenges. Although I eased the potential shock of returning to school after such a long period of time by first acquiring a master's degree, I was less than prepared for the demands of a doctoral program. Before beginning my doctoral studies, I had acquired life experiences, opinions, and research interests that informed my worldview and direction in life. I had grown used to autonomy and acting as my own boss and had been rewarded for my innovation and tendency to challenge the status quo with promotions and advancements. My pursuit of justice and a constant striving to improve had helped me to excel, gave me purpose, and eventually culminated in my embarking on advanced studies and research in psychology. Yet, it was not long before I learned that all of the qualities that had helped me advance thus far would not necessarily help me in the role of "student." Although it was necessary for me, as a student, to acquiesce to authority and open my mind to new ways of thinking, it was neither good nor necessary to ignore the lessons I had learned through life experience and independent research. Nevertheless, I found myself frequently in the position of having to do just that, as my prior experiences were often not compatible with the views espoused by the current paradigm in the mental-health field. My experience as a graduate student was a curious process of finding myself a dissident in a field that values conformity, and struggling to find a balance between submission and integrity.

I am by nature opinionated and stubborn, and these traits are both positive and negative, depending on the context. Moreover, a fine line exists between unnecessarily promoting one's opinions for narcissistic reasons and being an informed contributor to a discussion and scientific debate when one's perspective is unwelcome. I have believed myself to be in the latter position in many of my struggles as a student; however, I have found that successes have blossomed as well, as a result of my critical and outspoken position.

WHY I ENROLLED IN GRADUATE TRAINING

Before entering graduate training, I successfully ran my own business as a personal trainer. This was a job that required working very closely with individuals to help them grow, develop insight, learn healthy coping tools, and alter long-standing bad habits and addictions. My work was mostly with individuals struggling with morbid obesity and the effects of old age and stress, and many learned new ways to manage emotions, find inner strength, and engage in self-care. Through this work, as well as through countless personal encounters, I frequently heard stories of how the mental-health system had let someone down. On the other hand, these same individuals found much of the help they were looking for through alternative support; being a part of that alternative, I had begun to form educated opinions on ways to help people. It is not an exaggeration to say I had hundreds of conversations with individuals who had similar stories of desperately seeking help from psychotherapy and not being able to find it, and these were individuals who might be considered "normal," not those deemed "mentally ill." I had had my own negative experiences with mental-health professionals, but nonetheless was aghast when, over the years, I continued to hear similar stories of disappointment, shame, and fury. Something was not right, and for reasons that would take the most talented Freudian analyst to understand, I felt the call to enter into what I believed was a very broken field.

When I first began studying clinical psychology, I was certainly skeptical and aware that sometimes there were negative outcomes as a result of psychotherapy. It was my understanding that sometimes people did not feel heard or appreciated, and that they felt dismissed and/or coerced into taking psychotropic drugs. Nonetheless, I still thought that harmful practices were a product of specific clinicians and not the field as a whole. Early during my graduate studies, I began to realize the full scope of the violations of basic human rights, the lack of informed consent, and the negative and disparaging attitudes that are central to the biomedical system under which psychologists operate and, mostly, actively promote. Albeit, few professionals of any specialty are intentionally depriving people of their rights or causing harm; however, this does not negate the fact that it is happening. There is no room to do justice to these civil rights issues, but suffice it to say that it holds more similarities than differences with other historical violations of human rights. [1]

Despite my reservations about the mental-health field, I was determined to play some role in helping to change bad practices, and this is what keeps me in this field today.

My original interest was not clinical psychology but, rather, research-oriented social psychology. Just before embarking on my doctoral studies, I began graduate school in a terminal master's program at a liberal school that encouraged and rewarded independence and skepticism. In fact, the professor whom I most admired and wished to study with had made his career on examining how and why people question the status quo. I spent the next two years working in a research lab focused on social-justice issues and learning why people legitimize illegitimate authority. The program was compatible with my lack of inhibition in questioning the status quo and willingness to voice unpopular opinions.

Despite my satisfaction with following this line of research, I realized that I had no interest in pursuing an academic career in this specialty. While continuing to work in the research lab, I ventured out of the world of social psychology to explore alternatives. I spent some time doing research for a forensic psychiatrist, wherein I memorized virtually every major diagnostic category that existed in the *Diagnostic and Statistical Manual* (American Psychiatric Association, 2000) and the intricacies of each diagnosis. I realized fairly quickly that categorizing people based on subjective and ever-changing "symptoms" was not nearly as scientific as it was purported to be and appeared to be based more on politics and social control than scientific facts. So, I continued to explore other areas of psychology.

Eventually, I became involved as a volunteer research assistant and clinical interviewer with several major studies (see Amsel, Hunter, Kim, Fodor, and Markowitz, 2012; Chemtob, Griffing, Tullberg, Roberts, and Ellis, 2011; Ford et al., 2013) on trauma and different treatment approaches that were being used. During this period, a passion developed in me, and I ravenously read every book, narrative, and article related to trauma and its complex sequelae that time would allow. Gradually, I learned how much current mental-health practice is predicated on outdated information, rhetoric, and dogmatism. More and more, my awareness was opened to the world of the service user/ex-patient movement, and the harm that comes from many treatment practices. At the same time, I read study after study about trauma-informed treatments that are effective but largely ignored in the treatment of "serious mental illness" (see Fuller, 2010; Grubaugh, Zinzow, Paul, Egede, Frueh, 2011; Read, 2005; Read, van Os, Morrison, and Ross, 2005; Moskowitz, 2011). I presented posters, wrote my master's thesis, and even published a paper on a subject that I soon learned was one that most mental health professionals wanted to ignore: trauma and its relationship to serious mental illness.

FIRST ENCOUNTERS AS A DISSIDENT VOICE

Some may say that when a student enters into studies with professionals who have a clear idea and method about how to treat emotional distress, she should not challenge that approach and tell these professionals that their practices may be harming many people. But the need for justice may trump common sense in such instances. In truth, it never occurred to me that any of my professors were doing anything to harm people or that they would ever take any of my comments personally, as odd as this may sound. Adding to my misunderstanding of how my remarks would be received was my history of being rewarded for independent thinking. Not surprisingly, I had some difficulty during my first year of doctoral studies; I quickly found myself in opposition with, perhaps, half of the faculty and students. It is possible that the process that unfolded has provided me with more education on the psyche than all of my classes combined.

I was genuinely excited when I entered the doctoral program, which was one in which the opportunity existed to continue researching my areas of interest. Moreover, it was the only program in the country that specifically taught a psychosocial approach to treating serious mental illness. I was excited by the prospects this program offered, as well as by the fact that I interviewed completely as myself, not shaping my answers in any way to curry favor with the people who would decide my fate. I assumed incorrectly, however, that open-minded acceptance existed beyond the few faculty members who interviewed and accepted me. Much to my great appreciation, however, these professors stood by me throughout my time in the program.

My enthusiasm for learning and delving into the smallest parts of theory and research outcomes were immense. I was eager to share some of the discoveries I had made during my earlier research experiences and to continue this exploration. My passion did periodically override my better judgment to keep things to myself. The experience I had helping others as a personal trainer was criticized by several faculty members as irrelevant to the field of psychology and doctoral level work. It seemed that personal experiences, in general, were not valued as contributing to the knowledge base of a broader population. While it made sense that graduate school was not a place to dwell on personal anecdotes, it seemed extreme to reject sound and valid research that one simply did not agree with; this is where my struggles began.

The first time discord arose was within the first two weeks of my beginning the program. A professor was lecturing about the "schizophrenia genes," and I visibly became confused and surprised that something that was so completely untrue was being taught as fact.[2] I was called out to explain the look on my face. Quite innocently, at least from my perspective, I explained that it was my understanding there had never been any replicable study showing genes or any other biological marker indicating the presence of "schizophrenia," and that studies actually indicated that most people who develop any type of psychosis (including that categorized under the umbrella label of "schizophrenia") have no family members at all with the disorder (see Fisher, et al., 2014; Joseph, 2012; Ross, 2011; Zammit, et al., 2013). I honestly believed that the professor, and the class for that matter, might find this interesting, since they must not have known that this research existed. Not only was my statement poorly received, but I was belittled, insulted, and told outright, in front of the entire class, that I was a "troublemaker." I was told explicitly that the research I referred to did not even exist. When I offered to bring it in or write a paper about it, I was refused and told that I was being provocative. This type of interaction was soon to become a pattern.

At first I thought this professor and I simply had a clash of personalities. However, this mistaken perception was quickly amended. During the early part of my doctoral studies, I was still heavily involved with one of the previously mentioned studies on developmental trauma, and I was receiving encouragement from multiple sources, including other faculty and students of my program, to continue this work. I continued, for far too long, to believe that the professors with whom I had difficulty simply thought I was young and uneducated, and that if I just had the opportunity to present them with the evidence they would be interested in hearing it.

When we, as a class, were told that discussion and participation were not only welcome but required, I thought this actually meant that people could openly voice viewpoints that might be opposed to the material being presented in the lecture. I believed, if nothing else, that at least the class would be interested in hearing alternative viewpoints that would counter some of what I believed was false and judgmental information, including the idea that people have a "disease" rather than experience normal human suffering. Then, somewhere along the line, I realized that not only were most people uninterested in hearing what I had to say, but that my insistence upon saying it anyway served only to pigeonhole me as an agitator and an outsider.

In numerous interactions with some select professors, my presentation of material that somehow challenged the current dogma was met with insulting personal retorts, rhetoric, and condescending dismissal of extensive research findings. Rarely did a logical or intellectual conversation result in these situations, and most often there was no direct response at all to the material I presented. The message, in the end, was always the same: If I did not agree with the professor, then I was refusing to learn, and my refusal to learn was a clear example of my obstinacy and argumentativeness. This was extremely confusing to me at the time, as I fervently sought every opportunity to learn and did not understand how intellectual criticism was considered argumentative.

MY ROLE AS A SCAPEGOAT

Nevertheless, a pattern was set, and I became the scapegoat by tacit agreement. I certainly played my part in earning this role and brought plenty of the negativity on myself. But much of what I experienced was not a reasonable response to my actual behavior. Looking back I realize that never once did I argue about workload, assignments, caseload, or anything other than the aforementioned theme related to research. I never had a problem with a patient and, in fact, had the highest retention rate of patients compared to most of my peers. Yet, many of the students in my class were able to push the boundaries because I had already drawn the heat as the oppositional black sheep.

Probably the most fascinating interactions between the faculty and me were when professors played out their own discordant dynamics through our relationship. I was not even aware of the triangulation that I was a part of until it was pointed out to me by many classmates on one occasion or another. I had become the unwanted and troublesome child in a dysfunctional family that needed a scapegoat as an outlet for its frustrations and arguments. According to family systems theory, family dynamics exist unconsciously with no one party at fault but with everybody willingly settling in to their respective roles to maintain homogeneity. My role as scapegoat is a familiar one that I clearly found a way to create and perform—and that I knew only too well how to do.

What began to happen within my cohort, however, affected me more profoundly, as disturbing dynamics formed around the issue of me (yes, I had become an "issue"). In my view these dynamics reflected what happens more generally on the macro scale within the mental-health field. A select minority of my peers was particularly well-versed in political correctness and appeasing authority, and they were the most bothered by my dissidence. Content seemed to be less relevant than the fact that I was breaking the social norms that they found safety in. Some took to gossiping and speaking negatively about me to peers and faculty. Fortunately, most people did not pay much attention to these few. The majority of the class, however, simply did not wish to be bothered by the inevitable stress that questions and ambiguity raise; they preferred to "go with the flow" and avoid any type of controversy, thereby inevitably supporting the status quo. At the beginning of training I had few supporters within my cohort, and I became increasingly anxious, insecure, and saddened by the very lonely place I had gotten myself into.

The indifference regarding the issues I raised left me feeling somewhat hopeless about the future direction of the mental-health field and made me question whether this path was the right one for me. A comment made by a fellow student during our first year exemplified the disparity between my view and those of my peers: "You know we are friends, and I really like you.

But nobody wants to hear the hypothetical situations and problems that you talk about. We just want to go to class, be told what to do, and just learn so we can get our degrees and get out of here." This view was not unique to her or to my program. Rather, it is the people who question the status quo, challenge expertise, and hesitate to conform who are in the minority (quite frankly, probably for good reason)—in other words, people like me.

As conflicts continued to occur, the feedback I received from faculty behind closed doors was contradictory and confusing. I did not process their admonishments quickly enough, partly because while I was being chided, these very same people also supported and encouraged me in my viewpoints. I was being told to keep my mouth shut while at the same time to not stop voicing my opinion. I was told in one moment to conform and then in the next encouraged to dissent. These interactions reminded me of the stereotypical scenario where mom forces dad to discipline the child, but when mom is not looking, dad gives the kid a high-five and a wink. This was disorienting to say the least. Politics are not my forte, and I doubt I will ever understand how to navigate this fraught terrain.

Despite these disorienting interactions, the support that I received from particular faculty members was invaluable, and I have nothing but appreciation for these allies. At least one professor went so far as to actively fight for me in faculty meetings, and she never wavered for a moment in defending me and my work. It was this support that eventually motivated me to try to change. In fact, I was not nearly as bothered by the castigation directed toward me from several directions as I was for disappointing those who believed in me. It was clear that on many occasions the feedback that was given to me pained the professor almost as much as me. Perhaps the uncomfortable position in which I put those professors whose views aligned with my own was the reason for the disorienting feedback sessions I experienced. Certainly, there was nothing pleasant for anybody about these critical evaluations of my professional development.

I was informed that not only was I seen as argumentative and oppositional but also as naïve and provocative. I shudder to imagine the labels and other disparaging terms that might have been used about me, when I was not present, in faculty discussions of my behavior. I have sat in on enough case conferences to know what happens when an individual who is considered difficult is being discussed by a group that has spent decades castigating and categorizing others. Every day I contemplated dropping out and finding contentment with the career I already had. As I entered into my second year of studies and my first year of clinical practicum, I was dejected, uninterested, angry, frustrated, confused, and, at the same time, determined to thrive despite the difficulties that I found myself in. Ironically, I also entered into that second year transformed into the type of person that I had been accused of being: defensive, argumentative, angry, provocative, and oppositional. A

self-fulfilling prophecy had come to pass, and my non-compliance was, paradoxically, fulfilling the expectations of my detractors.

This culminated in the ultimate insult toward the end of my second year
when I, as a person, began to be a subject of reproach among the faculty. The
problem no longer was my argumentativeness, passion, or dissent; rather,
it had become who I was fundamentally as a human being. I was told by
different faculty members that my laugh was too loud, I was weird, I annoyed others, and my emotions were irrational and reactionary. This was
particularly interesting in light of the fact that in my life outside of graduate
school I am known as someone who rarely shows emotion or reacts much to
anything. By this time most of my supporters faltered, and the group process
took over. There was doubt about whether I was fit to be a psychologist at all.
I needed to be weaned out, but I was not about to let that happen.

LEARNING TO KEEP A LOW PROFILE

Through observation of my fellow classmates, I learned that behaviors of
studiousness, complacency, stoicism, and conformity were those that were
considered "professional"; interestingly, this resulted in students frequently
not asking questions, not being engaged, telling professors what they wanted
to hear, and rarely expressing any passion or personal opinions if they were
not aligned with the views of the professor. Of course, I am generalizing and
do not mean to suggest that this was the case for every student in every class;
rather, I mean to say that a dynamic of visible conformity did develop. The
values that elicit this behavior are inherent in most of American education
and corporate environments, yet the field of psychology in particular appears
to value compliance above all else. I do not believe for a moment that any
professor was intentionally or mindfully reacting in a manner that reinforced
withdrawal and apathy, nor do I believe that students genuinely did not care
or have opinions of their own. Rather, this was the atmosphere and dynamic
that inherently developed regardless of anybody's intention or desire.

In fact, professors consistently questioned why students rarely participated, rarely attended colloquiums or other opportunities for learning, and why
they appeared so disinterested in many class subjects. The most perplexed
and frustrated were those professors who encouraged dissent, debate, and
critical analyses of material, for they valued something that was not often
reinforced. This is an important dynamic to consider and understand because
these same behaviors are often implicitly reinforced with patients deemed
seriously mentally ill, which sometimes contributes to increased distress.
That is, learning to say what the psychologist wants to hear, suppressing
one's emotions and one's disagreement with the majority viewpoint, and
disengaging beyond a superficial level are exactly the types of behavior that

ex-patients report are necessary to exhibit for the purpose of being released from the hospital or the care of an unhelpful clinician (see Levine, 2012 for an exploration of the socialization of compliance and authoritarianism, particularly within the mental-health field, and its detrimental effects related to so-called "mental illness;" see also Bassman, 2007; Dillon, 2012; Fisher, 1994; Spring, 2014; Thornhill, Clare, and May, 2004). Of course, in light of charged feelings of anger and resentment during this period, my observations may be skewed. Nonetheless, my feedback became considerably better the more I withdrew and stopped caring. This was an unsustainable position, however, because I was unable to tolerate even being around myself at that time.

Fortunately, as I started seeing patients, developing relationships in supervision, and finding ways to sublimate my passion and anger, things started to change. I was actually quite taken aback by the amount of satisfaction I got from my work with patients; these were individuals not unlike myself who just needed a nonjudgmental place to feel safe and heard. To be able to provide that was enormously gratifying, in part because of the supportive relationships I developed in supervision and the safety that I felt during those supervision hours. I cannot emphasize how important it was to have a safe and collaborative relationship with my supervisors. Knowing that I had these individuals in whom I could confide, at least on some level, and who were extremely encouraging despite my unconventional views, were very likely the reasons I did not drop out during that second year.

A CHANGE IN THE ATTITUDE OF MY COHORT

Eventually, a change started to occur within my cohort. Classmates began approaching me in private to apologize for dismissing many of the issues I had brought up and instead thanked me for providing them with information they otherwise would not have received. Fellow students told me that they heard my words when faced with a dilemma in session with severely distraught clients. Other students started to voice opinions that were similar to mine and back me up in class. As we increased our exposure to patients, the amount of support within my cohort grew to about half the group. And as my support grew, my need to voice my opinions or challenge the evidence presented to us in class decreased considerably.

In addition to the increased support within my cohort, I also began receiving more tangible support from several faculty members. For me, the greatest encouragement came when I was asked to teach a graduate-level course in psychopathology. Diagnoses and the assumptions associated with diagnoses along with the etiology of extreme emotional distress are the areas of contention between me and most people in my field. To be trusted to teach a course on this subject, with permission to do so with full autonomy, was probably the greatest show of respect I can recall ever receiving from any professor. In teaching this course my confidence grew, along with my understanding of the level of influence my behaviors and attitude had on others, for better or worse. I received emails from my students telling me I had changed their lives and thanking me for providing them with a different way to view themselves, not just their patients. This brought about the awareness of just how personally faculty and students feel about what they do, which completely shifted my entire perspective and approach to my role as "student."

Unlike the fields of social psychology or religion (my other undergraduate major), the field of clinical psychology draws many people with very personal experiences of the subject matter under study—namely, extreme emotional distress. Many also have extensive experience in the role of "helper." To question or challenge an individual's approach to alleviating another's distress, whether intentional or not, is seen as an attack on that person's identity. It can induce guilt, fear, anger, shame, and many other negative feelings. Additionally, for individuals who have grown up in chaotic, traumatic, and/or emotionally unstable households, as most mental health professionals have, the need for order and definitive answers to life and the problems of humanity can be the greatest defense against mental decompensation. Introducing ambiguity can threaten a person's entire survival system. Never would I interact with a patient in such a manner that attacks his or her defensive structure and worldview, particularly without gradual development of a collaborative relationship. Yet, this is exactly what I did to the faculty and, indirectly, to my fellow students. I believe this was difficult for me to realize because I tend to view authority figures as indestructible; I never imagined that I might affect them on a personal level. As a teacher myself, I came to understand that teachers are vulnerable too.

Subsequent to these realizations, my focus shifted to using fewer personal avenues to create change and voice an alternative view. I collaborated with numerous others, both within and outside my program, on multiple projects. Within six months, I wrote three papers for publication, presented a symposium, presented four posters, and developed the subject for my dissertation. The most rewarding of these projects was when four other students and I traveled to another state to present to a packed room full of discontented ex-patients who despised most mental health professionals. It was there we discovered that our experiences as graduate students were not unlike those of many patients, since, as stated previously, the dynamic of patient and clinician often results in extremes of conformity or oppression, with not a whole lot in between. Our talk was so well received that we were invited back the next year, and an attendee requested one other student and I to present with him at the following year's conference of the American Psychological Association. I recognized that the direction I was taking was the right one but that

I needed to learn how to further tame my passion and direct my resources to more productive avenues.

My passion was difficult to suppress, but when I found alternative outlets I began finding a great deal of success. Fittingly, many of the projects I worked on were related to the exploration of understanding mental health professionals' attitudes toward patients and their own personal experiences with tragedy and emotional distress. These projects served not only to sublimate my frustration but also to help me better understand those very individuals I found myself in conflict with. There may have been many struggles between myself and others, but redirection of the energies that ignited these problems created a niche for my future career. Additionally, the trials and tribulations I experienced during those first two years allowed me to expel much of my opposition just in time for my externship experience.

LEARNING THE ART OF POLITICAL WISDOM

Somehow I managed to get accepted into an extremely conservative community health center, which in many ways was the antithesis of what I was seeking or where I belonged. I was specifically designated to work with those labeled as "seriously mentally ill." The first didactic we ever received as externs was that people with "mental illness" should never have children. Our preceptors remarked how unbelievable it was that patients could not understand that they had a genetic disease that would be transmitted to their children. All who attended found this to be highly amusing, as evidenced by their laughter. I was beyond horrified during these discussions, but I had also grown and learned that nothing positive would come from my voicing dissent. My goal in my career was not to change my classmates, teachers, supervisors, or practicum directors but rather to make a real change in the field and provide alternative experiences for some patients who might not otherwise receive it. Thankfully, I figured this out before experiencing this didactic. Although fury was coursing through every vein in my body, I kept in mind how appreciative I was to be working with the center's population. I further came to realize how lucky I was to have the supervisory experience that came with this particular externship. What happened between a patient and me and what happened in supervision was what mattered most. This didactic was irrelevant.

In classes, too, I learned to be wiser about when to speak and remain silent. Contention still arose periodically, but not with the same level of confrontation that it had previously. The apathetic and withdrawn approach still seemed to work in my favor, but instead of being resentful about this, I learned to use my time to work on projects. My dissertation became like a child to me; the amount of energy and time I invested in it allowed me very little energy for argument or debate with others. The experience of writing my dissertation also allowed me to fully appreciate how fortunate I was to be working with an individual who was open-minded, collaborative, and also of an alternative mindset. Not many would allow a student to write on the subject matter I chose nor to do so from my particular perspective. My relationship with my dissertation chair was one of a few areas in which I could break free from the oppressive atmosphere I experienced elsewhere. This same professor actively fought for me in faculty meetings and was to become an important ally and partner in getting through the remainder of my training.

Aside from my dissertation, I found new collaborations and enterprises to focus on and began to learn how to balance conformity with integrity. Of course, the conformity was only on the surface and did not fool most people, and we settled into a mode of agreeing to disagree. On the other hand, the broader issue of my career and my place within the mental-health field had started to become a more central concern for me.

I realized that the controversial issues I was so invested in were ones that evoked personal emotions, resentment, and discord in many, even those with whom I was very close, and that this discordance would follow me throughout my career. As a result, I greatly expanded my support network to include many professionals who were like-minded and had themselves experienced decades of conflict with the field of psychology. I have heard and read countless stories of professionals who spoke up about many of the things I have touched upon throughout this narrative being fired from multiple positions, losing funding for research and other grant-related projects, being personally attacked for professional views, fearing discrimination, and being ostracized and treated as outsider by mainstream professionals (see, for example, Adame, 2010; Bassman, 2007; Schiff, 2004; Watson, Arcona, Antonuccio, and Healy, 2013; Whitaker, 2010; Whitaker, 2011). These stories reflected my own experience in graduate school, and my knowledge of their similarities with patient experiences allowed me to become a better clinician. I decided, however, that I did not want to continue having negative experiences in my career. It was imperative that I learn to be more constructive with my criticism and to suppress such criticism in environments where it was not welcome. This became easier after discovering that a major paradigm shift was slowly occurring in the field. And the first evidence of this was what I saw start to happen within my cohort.

As stated previously, my cohort was, in many ways, a mirror image of the larger mental health field. More students began to understand how current practices may be oppressive or harmful to many patients and how a trauma-informed, humanistic approach to treating severe emotional states may be beneficial. If nothing else, most of my cohort became open to the possibility that there were other viewpoints than the predominant ones taught in graduate schools. Similar to those students in my class, most professionals do not wish to deal with ambiguity, controversy, conflict, or dissent. But they are also open to change and rational debate. The shift that occurred within my cohort gives me great hope for the field, and, more specifically, for the service user/ex-patient movement and its allies. And, of course, for me.

Most people who enter this field have good intentions and genuinely want to do right by others. They also want to trust that what they are doing is helpful and based on logic and reason. My early challenges were seen as attacks on the basic goodness of others, even though this was inadvertent and unintentional; certainly, I deserved much of the backlash I received. In one way I am thankful for the harsh criticism and personal attacks I received because they prepared me for what I was to face in the real world. This treatment also allowed me to have a glimpse of what patients face every day. My difficult experiences and contentious encounters with faculty and students helped me develop into a stronger, more compassionate, and more tame professional who can work in a variety of environments.

Of course, growth would not have occurred without consistent support from both faculty and other students/friends. It is difficult to accomplish anything worthwhile alone, and my being able to turn my challenges into successes was only because I had people around me who helped me do so. Although many in the faculty were never successful in altering my opinions or getting me to truly conform, I was helped to find a path that allowed me to have less confrontation and more positive interactions with those with whom I disagree.

Most who read this will not be surprised about the problems I encountered. But I am tamer now because of my graduate-school experiences and have learned (and continue to learn) how to navigate the terrain of a field in which I will always be on the outskirts. This would not have happened if I had not been fortunate enough to attend a program in which I generally fit. Certainly, I was trained to be more effective in the real world, and that is a measure of success of any program. My criticism is not targeted at individuals but, rather, at a field that does not tolerate differences, ambiguity, change, or openness. Despite my difficulties, I knew that I was part of a progressive and open-minded program. This fact was brought home to me more clearly when a friend told me of her struggle in the psychology program in which she was enrolled. This friend, who has viewpoints that are similar to mine but also has an entirely different background and personality, learned her lessons in a very different manner: she was held back a year, put on suspension, forbidden to apply for internship, and forced to take on extra responsibilities as punishment for her "behavior." She is a good-natured and even-tempered individual. Nonetheless, she was told that she was unprofessional because she kept advocating for patients (i.e., speaking up against the injustices and inhumane treatment and attitudes prevalent within this field) and refused to learn (i.e., contradicting the status quo).

The conflicts that I experienced are a reflection of the mental-health field, but also of the society in which we live. My program and many of the faculty and students within it encouraged me to develop professionally and, indirectly, personally. I have no doubt that I would have been kicked out of almost any other program. I found a place in my program, despite the contentious interactions I had with some. My headstrong, opinionated, and sometimes aggressive ways of getting information across were molded and shaped into something productive and useful because of people who cared. I needed to change and will still continue to find more acceptable ways to exist within my field as an outsider. This is a struggle that likely will not end any time soon, but at least I am better prepared and more able to keep negative interactions to a minimum. Fortunately, I had a place where people allowed me to go through that transformative period of growth while never losing faith in me.

NOTES

1. A vast amount of literature describes the myriad ways that people are being harmed by standard mental-health care, including pressure and coercion to take dangerous drugs with little clinical benefit and whose negative effects, including permanent brain damage, are actively minimized (Breggin, 2003; Kirsch, 2010; Moncrieff and Leo, 2010; Morrison, Hutton, Shiers, and Turkington, 2012). Other studies cite development of posttraumatic stress disorder as a direct result of "treatment" (Mueser, Lu, Rosenberg, and Wolfe, 2010), lack of informed consent (e.g., Caplan, 2011; Gartner, 2011; Morrison, et al., 2012), and presumption of "illness" with no evidence to support it (Lacasse and Leo, 2005), which often leads to disempowerment, increased stigma, and discrimination (Pescosolido et al., 2010; Magliano, Read, Sagliocchi, Patalano, and Oliviero, 2013; Read, Haslam, Sayce, and Davies, 2006) and an identity wrapped in helplessness (e.g., Delano, 2012; Dillon, 2012). Moreover, unlike any other area of medicine, the mental health field is the only one to which numerous service user groups have arisen to protest these rights violations and advocate for legal ramifications and changes, with some even calling for the complete dismantling of the field as a whole (psychology included). Many of the examples ex-patients give of harmful treatments may actually appear innocuous to some but can be detrimental to those at their most vulnerable. These include treatment from providers who do not show sympathy or do not listen to what patients are saying, as well as treatment that creates stigmatization, oppression, coercion, infantilizing dependency, and decreased self-esteem (Cohen, 2005; Fisher, 1994; Kreyenbuhl, Nossel, and Dixon, 2009; O'Brien, Fahmy, and Singh, 2009; Corrigan, 2004). See also Baker, 2013; Bassman, 2007; Ross, 2011; Saks, 2002; Saugstad, 2005; Stastny and Lehmann, 2007; Szasz, 2003; and Whitaker, 2010, for broad and varied descriptions of many of the rights violations occurring in all specialties of Western mental health and alternatives that result in better outcomes.

It is important to note that the United Nations recently reviewed the report of the Convention on the Rights of Persons with Disabilities and concluded that all countries that have ratified the treaty should prohibit involuntary treatments due to their inhumane nature (Human Rights Council, 2009); the United States has not signed this treaty to date. Additionally, the U.N. Special Rapporteur on Torture and Other Cruel, Inhuman or Degrading Treatment or Punishment specifically called for an immediate ban on forced drugging, shock, restraint, and seclusions and a repeal of laws that allow for non-forensic compulsory mental-health treatment (both in- and outpatient) due to deprivation of liberty and violations of basic human rights (Mendez,

2013). Psychologists are often central figures in the involuntary commitment of their patients. Although many will claim that such "treatments" criticized in the previously cited references are necessary in order to save lives, the evidence, in fact, appears to suggest just the opposite in the aggregate (e.g., Allen and Smith, 2001; Burns, et al., 2013; Crawford, 2004; Deacon, 2013; Harrow, Jobe, and Faull, 2012; Henderson and Hartman, 2004; Kisely and Campbell, 2012; Marks, Breggin, and Braslow, 2008; Qin and Nordentoft, 2005; Whitaker, 2010; Wunderink, Nieboer, Wiersma, Sytema, and Nienhuis, 2013).

2. Although there is a perception that it is common knowledge that such genes and biomarkers exist, the evidence actually does not support such assumptions (see Hunter, 2013, for a detailed analysis describing the distorted information being taught to professionals in training, particularly for such classifications as "schizophrenia," and thereby being disseminated to the public at large). Even the head of the DSM-5 (American Psychiatric Association, 2013) publicly acknowledged that not a single biomarker has been found for any DSM-defined category (Kupfer, 2013). Additionally, the British Psychological Society has publicly called for a paradigm shift due to the lack of validity or reliability of diagnoses, and the lack of any evidence of the causal role that biology plays in human distress (biology is considered, at best, as a mediator of adverse environments rather than causal; British Psychological Society, 2013). Moreover, see Read, Fosse, Moskowitz, and Perry (2014) for a "diathesis-stress" model showing the role that trauma plays in changing the neuronal and genetic structure of an individual, leaving one "predisposed" to developing later psychiatric problems, including "schizophrenia," independent of any purported hereditable factors. Lastly, Kenneth Kendler, MD, a staunch biological psychiatrist who has spent his career researching the genetics of "schizophrenia," recently published a paper (Kendler, 2014) in which he states that "the genetic risk for schizophrenia is widely distributed in human populations so that we all carry some degree of risk."

REFERENCES

Adame, A. L. (2010). *Negotiating discourses: How survivor-therapists construe their dialogical identities* (Doctoral dissertation). Retrieved from OhioLINK Electronic Theses and Dissertations Center, http://rave.ohiolink.edu/etdc/view?acc_num=miami1263579790

Allen, M., and Smith, V. F. (2001). Opening Pandora's box: The practical and legal dangers of involuntary outpatient commitment. *Psychiatric Services, 52*, 342–6.

American Psychiatric Association. (2000). *Diagnostic and statistical manual of mental disorders* (4th ed., text rev.). Washington, DC.

American Psychiatric Association (2013). *Diagnostic and statistical manual of mental disorders* (5th ed.). Washington, DC.

Amsel, L. V., Hunter, N., Kim, S., Fodor, K. E., and Markowitz, J. C. (2012). Does a study focused on trauma encourage patients with psychotic symptoms to seek treatment? *Psychiatric Services, 63*, 386–389.

Baker, D. (2013). *Coercion or care: Involuntary treatment of the mentally ill, a human rights issue.* Urbanfire 13 Publications.

Bassman, R. (2007). *A fight to be: A psychologist's experience from both sides of the locked door.* Albany, NY: Tantamount Press.

Breggin, P. R. (2003). Psychopharmacology and human values. *Journal of Humanistic Psychology, 43*(2), 34–49.

British Psychological Society. (2013). *Division of Clinical Psychology position statement on the classification of behaviour and experience in relation to functional psychiatric diagnoses: Time for a paradigm shift.* Leicester, UK: British Psychological Society. Retrieved from http://dxrevisionwatch.files.wordpress.com/2013/05/position-statement-on-diagnosis-master-doc.pdf

Burns, T., Rugkasa, J., Molodynski, A., Dawson, J., Yeeles, K., Vazquez-Montes, M., . . . Priebe, S. (2013). Community treatment orders for patients with psychosis (OCTET): A randomized controlled trial. *The Lancet, 381*(9878), pp. 1627–33. Retrieved from http://dx.doi.org/10.1016/

Caplan, P. J. (2011, September 4). Full disclosure needed about psychiatric drugs that shorten life. *Psychology Today.* http://www.psychologytoday.com/blog/science-isnt-golden/201109/full-disclosure-needed-about-psychiatric-drugs-shorten-life

Chemtob, C. M., Griffing, S., Tullberg, E., Roberts, E., and Ellis, P. (2011). Screening for trauma exposure, and posttraumatic stress disorder and depression symptoms among mothers receiving child welfare preventive services. *Child Welfare, 90*(6), 109–127.

Cohen, O. (2005). How do we recover? An analysis of psychiatric survivor oral histories. *Journal of Humanistic Psychology, 45*(3), 333–54.

Corrigan, P. (2004). How stigma interferes with mental healthcare. *American Psychologist, 59*(7), 614–25.

Crawford, M. J. (2004). Suicide following discharge from in-patient psychiatric care. *Advances in Psychiatric Treatment, 10*, 434–438.

Deacon, B. J. (2013). The biomedical model of mental disorder: A critical analysis of its validity, utility, and effects on psychotherapy research. *Clinical Psychology Review, 33*. doi: 10.1016/j.cpr.2012.09.007

Delano, L. (2012, October 6). Fighting for our most basic of human rights—the right to be human.   http://www.madinamerica.com/2012/10/fighting-for-our-most-basic-of-human-rights-the-right-to-be-human/

Dillon, J. (2012). Recovery from "psychosis." In J. Geekie, P. Randal, D. Lampshire, and J. Read (Eds.), *Experiencing Psychosis*. New York, NY: Routledge.

Fisher, D. B. (1994). A new vision of healing as constructed by people with psychiatric disabilities working as mental health providers. *Psychosocial Rehabilitation Journal, 17*(3), 67–81.

Fisher, H. L., McGuffin, P., Boydell, J., Fearon, P., Craig, T. K., Dazzan, P., . . . Morgan, C. (2014, January 7). Interplay between childhood physical abuse and familial risk in the onset of psychotic disorders. *Schizophrenia Bulletin.* doi:10.1093/schbul/sbt201.

Ford, J. D., Grasso, D., Greene, C., Levine, J., Spinazzola, J., and van der Kolk, B. (2013). Clinical significance of a proposed developmental trauma disorder diagnosis: Results of an international survey of clinicians. *The Journal of Clinical Psychiatry, 74*(8), 841–9.

Fuller, P. R. (2010). Treatment of trauma: Applications of trauma treatment for schizophrenia. *Journal of Aggression, Maltreatment and Trauma, 19*, 450–63.

Gartner, J. D. (2011, September 15). Has psychiatry been corrupted beyond repair? *Psychology Today.* http://www.psychologytoday.com/blog/the-roving-psychologist/201109/has-psychiatry-been-corrupted-beyond-repair

Grubaugh, A. L., Zinzow, H. M., Paul, L., Egede, L. E., and Frueh, B. C. (2011). Trauma exposure and posttraumatic stress disorder in adults with severe mental illness: A critical review. *Clinical Psychology Review, 31*(6), 883–99.

Harrow, M., Jobe, T. H., and Faull, R. N. (2012). Do all schizophrenia patients need antipsychotic treatment continuously throughout their lifetime? A 20-year longitudinal study. *Psychological Medicine, 42*(10), 2145–55.

Henderson, T. A., and Hartman, K. (2004). Aggression, mania, and hypomania induction associated with atomoxetine. *Pediatrics, 114*(3), 895–6.

Human Rights Council. (2009, December). *Thematic study by the Office of the United Nations High Commissioner for Human Rights on the Structure and Role of National Mechanisms for the Implementation and Monitoring of the Convention on the Rights of Persons with Disabilities* (A-HRC-13-29). Annual report of the United Nations High Commissioner for Human Rights and Reports of the Office of the High Commissioner and the Secretary-General. Retrieved from http://www.ohchr.org/EN/Issues/Disability/Pages/ ThematicStudies.aspx

Hunter, N. (2013). Distortion, bias, and ethical informed consent: Presentations of etiological and treatment factors in abnormal psychology textbooks. *Ethical Human Psychology and Psychiatry, 15*(3), 160–79.

Joseph, J. (2012). The "missing heritability" of psychiatric disorders. Elusive genes or non-existent genes? *Applied Developmental Science, 16*(2), 65–83.

Kendler, K. S. (2014, August 19). A joint history of the nature of genetic variation and the nature of schizophrenia. *Molecular Psychiatry.* doi:10.1038/mp.2014.94

Kirsch, I. (2010). *The emperor's new drugs: Exploding the antidepressant myth.* New York, NY: Basic Books.

Kisely, S. R., and Campbell, L. A. (2012). Compulsory community and involuntary outpatient treatment for people with severe mental disorders. Retrieved from http://summaries. cochrane.org /CD004408/SCHIZ_compulsory-community-and-involuntary-outpatient-treatment-for-people-with-severe-mental-disorders

Kreyenbuhl, J., Nossel, I. R., and Dixon, L. B. (2009). Disengagement from mental health treatment among individuals with schizophrenia and strategies for facilitating connections to care: A review of the literature. *Schizophrenia Bulletin, 35*(4), 696–703.

Kupfer, D. (2013). News release: Chair of DSM-5 task force discusses future of mental health research. *American Psychiatric Association.* Retrieved from http://www.psychiatry.org

Lacasse, J. R., and Leo, J. (2005). Serotonin and depression: A disconnect between the advertisements and the scientific literature. *PLoS Medicine, 2*(12), e393. http://dx.doi.org/ 10.1371/journal.pmed.0020392

Levine, B. (2012). Why anti-authoritarians are diagnosed as mentally ill. http://www. madinamerica.com/2012/02/why-anti-authoritarians-are-diagnosed-as-mentally-ill/

Magliano, L., Read, J., Sagliocchi, A., Patalano, M., and Oliviero, N. (2013). Effect of diagnostic labeling and causal explanations on medical students' views about treatments for psychosis and the need to share information with service users. *Psychiatry Research, 210*(2), 402–7.

Marks, D. H., Breggin, P. R., and Braslow, D. (2008). Homicidal ideation causally related to therapeutic medications. *Ethical Human Psychology and Psychiatry, 10*(3), 134–145.

Mendez, J. E. (2013, February 1). Report of the Special Rapporteur on Torture and Other Cruel, Inhuman or Degrading Treatment or Punishment. 22nd session of the Human Rights Council, United Nations General Assembly, Agenda Item 3. http://www.ohchr.org/ Documents/HRBodies/HRCouncil/RegularSession/Session22/A.HRC.22.53_English.pdf

Moncrieff, J., and Leo, J. (2010). A systematic review of the effects of antipsychotic drugs on brain volume. *Psychological Medicine, 40*(9), 1409–22.

Morrison, A. P., Hutton, P., Shiers, D., and Turkington, D. (2012). Antipsychotics: Is it time to introduce patient choice? *British Journal of Psychiatry, 201*, 83–4.

Moskowitz, A. (2011a). Schizophrenia, trauma, dissociation, and scientific revolutions. [Editorial]. *Journal of Trauma and Dissociation, 12*(4), 347–57.

Mueser, K. T., Lu, W., Rosenberg, S. D., and Wolfe, R. (2010). The trauma of psychosis: Posttraumatic stress disorder and recent onset psychosis. *Schizophrenia Research, 116*, 217–27.

O'Brien, A., Fahmy, R., and Singh, S. (2009). Disengagement from mental health services. *Social Psychiatry and Psychiatric Epidemiology, 44*(7), 558–68.

Pescosolido, B. A., Martin, J. K., Long, J. S., Medina, T. R., Phelan, J. C., and Link, B. G. (2010). "A disease like any other"? A decade of change in public reactions to schizophrenia, depression, and alcohol dependence. *American Journal of Psychiatry, 167*, 1321–30.

Qin, P., and Nordentoft, M. (2005). Suicide risk in relation to psychiatric hospitalization. *Archives of General Psychiatry, 62*(4), 427-32.

Read, J. (2005). The bio-bio-bio model of madness. *The Psychologist, 18*(10), 596–597.

Read, J., Fosse, R., Moskowitz, A., and Perry, B. (2014). The traumagenic neurodevelopmental model of psychosis. *Neuropsychiatry, 4*(1) 65–79.

Read, J., Haslam, N., Sayce, L., and Davies, E. (2006). Prejudice and schizophrenia: A review of the "mental illness is an illness like any other" approach. *Acta Psychiatrica Scandinavica, 114,* 303–18.

Read, J., van Os, J., Morrison, A. P., and Ross, C. A. (2005). Childhood trauma, psychosis, and schizophrenia: A literature review with theoretical and clinical implications. *Acta Psychiatrica Scandinavica, 112*, 330–50.

Ross, C. (2011). *The great psychiatry scam.* Richardson, TX: Manitou Communications, Inc.

Saks, E. R. (2002). *Refusing care: Forced treatment and the rights of the mentally ill.* Chicago, IL: The University of Chicago Press.

Saugstad, J. (2005). *Games therapists play: How punitive diagnoses allow the fracture of patient, civil, and human rights—with impunity.* Boca Raton, FL: Universal Publishers.

Schiff, A. C. (2004). Recovery and mental illness: Analysis and personal reflections. *Psychiatric Rehabilitation Journal, 27*(3), 212–18.

Spring, C. (2014). *Recovery is my best revenge*. Huntingdon, UK: Carolyn Spring Publishing.

Stastny, P., and Lehmann, P. (2007). *Alternatives to psychiatry*. Berlin, Germany: Peter Lehmann Publishing.

Szasz, T. (2003). *Liberation by oppression: A comparative study of slavery and psychiatry.* New Brunswick, NJ: Transaction Publishers.

Thornhill, H., Clare, L., and May, R. (2004). Escape, enlightenment and endurance: Narratives of recovery from psychosis. *Anthropology & Medicine, 11*(2), 181–99.

Watson, G. L., Arcona, A. P., Antonuccio, D. O., Healy, D. (2013). Shooting the messenger: The case of ADHD. *Journal of Contemporary Psychotherapy 44,* pp.43-52. doi: 10.1007/s10879-013-9244-x

Whitaker, R. (2010). *Anatomy of an epidemic: Magic bullets, psychiatric drugs, and the astonishing rise of mental illness in America.* New York, NY: Crown Publishers.

Whitaker, R. (2011, May 25). After 25 posts on this website, Dr. Mark Foster is terminated by his employer. http://www.madinamerica.com/2011/05/%EF%BB%BFafter-25-posts-on-this-website-dr-mark-foster-is-terminated-by-his-employer/

Wunderink, L., Nieboer, R. M., Wiersma, D., Sytema, S., and Nienhuis, F. J. (2013). Recovery in remitted first-episode psychosis at 7 years of follow-up of an early dose reduction/discontinuation or maintenance treatment strategy: Long-term follow-up of a 2-year randomized clinical trial. *JAMA Psychiatry, 70*(9), 913–920.

Zammit, S., Hamshere, M., Dwyer, S., Georgiva, L., Timpson, N., Moskvina, V., . . . O'Donovan, M. C. (2013, October 30). A population-based study of genetic variation and psychotic experiences in adolescents. *Schizophrenia Bulletin.* doi:10.1093/schbul/sbt146

III

Outside the Norm: Effects of Diversity in Training and Treatment

Chapter Nine

A Few Good Men

*The Male Experience of Minority Status
in a Clinical Psychology Doctoral Program*

Ian Rugg

As a new student in a clinical psychology doctoral program (CPDP), I found myself in a sea of women as we read and discussed topics such as sexual assault, sexual harassment, feminism, sexism, empathy, and gender. Suddenly I was one of a handful of men, in the odd position of being a member of a minority group. This chapter describes how male clinical psychology doctoral students cope with their minority status in such a setting. It also discusses my personal experience, as well as the results of my dissertation study on male students' experience of a CPDP (Rugg, 2013). I found that males felt criticized, judged, enriched, marginalized, and special in this setting, all at the same time, simply because of their gender. I drew my observations and conclusions from interviews with seventeen male clinical psychology doctoral students who found themselves members of a small minority, perhaps for the first time in their lives. I will describe what they said when they came together to share their thoughts and feelings. Gender role theory (Bem, 1974, 1975, 1981; Bem and Lenney, 1976; Eagly, 1987; Eagly and Steffen, 1984; Eagly and Wood, 1991; Pleck, 1981, 1995), the "new psychology of men" literature (Levant, 1996), and Watt's model of privileged identity exploration (2007) were used to organize my personal experiences and those of other men.

HOW THE MAKEUP OF PSYCHOLOGY
DOCTORAL PROGRAMS HAS CHANGED

The ratio of men to women in the field of psychology has dramatically changed since the 1950s. According to Ostertag's and McNamara's (1991) seminal article, in 1950 only 14.8 percent of doctoral degrees in psychology were awarded to women, but by the year 1988, this statistic ballooned to 54.8 percent, a trend the authors called "the feminization of psychology." More recently, female dominance in the field of professional psychology has become cemented. In 2009, the APA Center for Workforce Studies showed that in the "Health Service Provider Subfields," 78.1 percent of "New Doctorates," 73.8 percent of "Early Career" psychologists, and 58 percent of the "Doctorate Workforce" in psychology were women (American Psychological Association, 2009). Another study, compiling the results of a National Council of School and Programs of Professional Psychology (NCSPP) self-study, reported that 77 percent of the 13,940 students enrolled in NCSPP programs were female (Frincke, Wicherski, Finno, and Kohout, 2006). According to Long Island University's Office of Institutional Research (2010), in the fall of 2009, 76 percent of ninety-eight students enrolled in the CPDP at the C. W. Post Campus, where I was enrolled, were female. Given the recent shift in gender statistics, it is not surprising that a male student's experience in a CPDP would be colored by his status as a minority student.

THEORETICAL PERSPECTIVE AND RESEARCH FOCUS

Needless to say, my theoretical framework and subjective experience at the time of my doctoral study—of being a thirty-one-year-old, straight, white male attending a female-dominated CPDP—affected my research. Operating from my broadly feminist and psychodynamic perspective, I believed that social, cultural, political, and linguistic forces and their relationship with conscious and unconscious processes of the individual and society/culture at large are paramount to understanding gender identity, gender roles, and gender experience. As a minority male I had a range of experiences in my CPDP, including but not limited to initial surprise at the gender ratio and feeling like my maleness was always on display, even becoming my primary identifying factor. I felt a composite of emotions. For example, I felt special for receiving special treatment as a minority male and more comfortable with women, more well-rounded, and able to access what might be considered stereotypically feminine traits (as parts of myself). Yet, I also felt implicated as a male oppressor or abuser during classroom discussions and in other situations/ settings, and worried whether I was behaving "too male" or, conversely, not male enough.

I regard gender roles as socio-culturally constructed, passed on, and enforced; influenced by the familial and work roles that men and women typically occupy; serving patriarchal purposes; involving the development of gender schemas; impacting self-concept and self-esteem; and ultimately limiting and causing harm to all individuals. My ideas on the unique experience of the male clinical psychology doctoral student are informed by Sandra Bem's work on gender schema theory (1981) and androgyny (Bem, 1974, 1975; Bem and Lenney, 1976), Alice Eagly's approach to role theory (Eagly, 1987; Eagly and Steffen, 1984; Eagly and Wood, 1991), Ronald Levant's work on the "new psychology of men" (1996), Joseph Pleck's writings on the gender role strain paradigm (1981, 1995), and Watt's model of privileged identity exploration (Watt, 2007). My dissertation aimed to explore whether the male student's experience in a CPDP would be affected by the structure of his gender schema(s) and the extent to which it was intertwined within his self-concept or his ability to possess both stereotypically masculine and feminine characteristics. Additionally, I wished to explore if male students in CPDPs saw themselves as less masculine (or more feminine) because the typical clinical psychologist is a woman.

The "new psychology of men" and gender role strain paradigms suggest that traditional male socialization is inherently problematic and potentially traumatic, in part because of the uniquely male problems of "aggression and violence, devaluation of women, fear and hatred of homosexuals, detached fathering, and neglect of health needs" (Levant, 1996, p. 259). Furthermore men experience different types of gender role strain as they compare their actual thoughts, feelings, and behaviors to their internalized masculine ideal. I wondered whether the male student in a CPDP experienced gender role strain and distress: did the new female face of psychology cause him to feel as though he has failed to live up to his internalized masculine ideal?

Watt's (2007) model of privileged identity exploration suggests that when students engage in "difficult dialogues," such as classroom discussions that compel them to reflect on and share their thoughts and feelings about topics of social justice, they often feel attacked and become defensive. This model is based on Festinger's (1962) cognitive dissonance theory, which refers to the distress caused by holding two opposing thoughts or ideas in awareness, and a general psychodynamic view (including Freud, 1937) of defensive "modes" as unconscious and primitive responses to threats to the ego. According to Watt (2007), the discomfort caused by "difficult dialogues" forces individuals to experience cognitive dissonance while also threatening dominant aspects of their identities. This is particularly relevant to the male doctoral student who must contend with classroom topics in which men tend to be the primary beneficiary (i.e., power and privilege) and the primary offenders or oppressors (i.e., sexism, sexual assault, sexual abuse, and domestic violence).

Exploring the experiences of men working in historically female-dominated professions shed some light on the male students' experience in CPDPs and how they respond to these difficult dialogues. According to Lupton (2006) there are two primary lines of research exploring men's entry into female-dominated professions. One explores how men carry their power and privilege with them into the female-dominated setting (Williams, 1995), and the other examines how men's masculinity is especially scrutinized as they enter this arena (Cross and Bagilhole, 2002; Lupton, 2000). The literature inspired the following questions about the male clinical psychology doctoral student experience: Did male students believe they retained their privilege during the training? Were male students impacted by negative perceptions or questions regarding their masculinity?

RESEARCH ON THE MALE EXPERIENCE IN CPDPS

Research and literature regarding the male student's experience in doctoral psychology programs has been restricted mostly to issues related to mentorship in CPDPs (Harden, Clark, Johnson, and Larson, 2009) and sex or sexual intimacy between students and educators in psychology training (Pope, Levenson, and Schover, 1979) in clinical and counseling psychology programs (Hammel and Olkin, 1996). A few studies have examined clinical and academic training as it relates to men's issues, men and masculinity, and the "new psychology of men" (Liu, 2005; Mellinger and Liu, 2006). Using a quantitative methodology, Sbaratta (2011) explored the associations between male psychology doctoral students' gender role conflict and the supervisory working alliance, multicultural competence, and psychological distress. My dissertation study (Rugg, 2013) and this chapter address, among other things, the lack of scholarly attention to the personal and subjective aspects of male students' experiences in CPDPs.

Several articles have covered the more personal aspects of how minority males feel in predominantly female training programs. In an article describing his personal experience of being a male art therapy student, Kim (2007) discussed feeling like a "visitor" at a conference and observed a disproportionate amount of men dropping out of his graduate school program. He witnessed few classroom discussions about gender, and a seeming defensiveness toward such discussions when they did occur, and experienced both exclusion because of his sex and "institutionalized reverse sexism" (p. 37). Willyard (2011) recently described some poignant responses from interviews with male students finding themselves in the minority in different types of psychology doctoral programs. While some described comfort with the gender disparity and even utility in providing opportunities, like receiving an undergraduate internship, others related more negative experiences. One student, discovering he was the only male in a CPDP class of fifteen, noted feeling "shocked . . . embarrassed . . . out of place," and pondered whether he had mistakenly chosen a "girl" profession (p. 41). This student also reported being asked by professors to comment during classroom discussions on sex differences and being anointed the "male voice for a lot of issues," a task he appeared to perceive as a burden (p. 41). Another student, who was one of twelve men in a class of seventy clinical psychology doctoral students, explained that he often felt he wasn't heard, was left out of female-only social events, and considered, along with some of his male classmates, forming a "men's student group" to give voice to their concerns (p. 43).

STRUCTURE OF THE QUALITATIVE STUDY

For my own dissertation study (Rugg, 2013) about the effects of minority status on White men in a CPDP, I used a hypothesis-generating, focus-group mediated, qualitative design based on the methodology of Auerbach and Silverstein (2003). This design emphasized the use of personal narratives to delve into the subjective experience of a previously unexplored population. Briefly, seventeen male students attending CPDPs were recruited to participate in four focus groups. Transcripts of the focus groups were coded and analyzed, and three overarching theoretical constructs were developed:

- The male student experiences minority status: How does it feel to become a "problem"?;
- The confirmation and disconfirmation of traditional male privilege; and
- The professional and personal growth of male students.

What follows is a theoretical narrative, gleaned from my research participants. I also discuss additional, related research, along with my personal experiences as a male in the minority in a CPDP.

THE THEORETICAL NARRATIVE

The concluding step in organizing results using Auerbach and Silverstein's (2003) method of qualitative data analysis is termed the "theoretical narrative" (p. 73). It uses theoretical constructs, themes, and repeating ideas to create a coherent narrative that integrates the subjective experience of participants. In the narrative that follows, themes are denoted in boldface type, and repeating ideas are italicized, with the number of participants who added to each idea identified in parenthesis. Each theoretical construct (described above) will be considered in its turn.

As male students progress through their CPDPs, they encountered a variety of difficulties, struggles, and rewarding experiences. Most striking among these experiences was the perception of minority-group status and becoming a "problem" (**the male student experiences minority status**: how does it feel to become a "problem?"). These men stated, *I feel different and must alter my behavior and the way I perceive things in the CPDP*. Seven participants described having to alter how "masculine" they behaved when socializing inside the CPDP, with comments such as *I have to switch roles/modes in terms of how masculine I behave when socializing inside vs. outside of the CPDP* (7). In a similar vein they stated, *I don't have my normal "dude discussions" or reactions anymore* (7).

Additionally, these men discussed the pressures of conforming to what they perceived to be the qualities and characteristics expected of them in the CPDP, such as sensitivity, empathy, and expressiveness. For example, they said: *the field of clinical psychology attracts and expects a more sensitive/ feminine man* (8); *I feel pressure to be introspective and present as sensitive and empathic in my CPDP* (3); and *I feel pressure to be as talkative and expressive as female students in my CPDP* (3). One participant eloquently described his anxiety regarding becoming more sensitive and introspective:

> I hate thinking about my own emotional life; I'm very male in that way. I do stuff to avoid thinking about it constantly, and ever since I've come here I've felt a lot of pressure to get in touch with it. Because in order to succeed, we're always told that you have to know about yourself, know about your emotions, all that stuff. (Rugg, 2013, p. 36).

Finally, four participants specifically remarked on the difficulty of reconciling men's minority status inside of the CPDP with men's majority status in society, noting that *it is difficult to reconcile being a minority in the CPDP because men are not a minority outside the CPDP* (4).

These men also described experiencing a lack of support from male psychologists in the field of psychology, stating that *I have not been adequately supported/mentored by male psychologists in the field*. Four participants commented, *I did not feel supported/had a negative experience with male professors in my CPDP* (4), and they also remarked, *my CPDP lacks a strong male faculty presence* (5).

Furthermore the men in this study explained the special bond and feelings of safety they felt with each other. They spoke specifically to this special bond, saying, *male students have a special connection/bond with each other* (6). One participant stated: "But there was something special about having the guys. There were only six of us, I think, in my class of fifteen. But there was a special bond that I had with the guys and a certain pact. That we were men or something like that" (Rugg, 2013, p. 37). Four participants described creating a safe location for men only *(men created a safe male place/space in the CPDP [4])*. They also experienced a feeling of "safety in numbers," remarking, *there were enough men in my cohort so I didn't feel outnumbered or marginalized* (5). Finally, four participants detailed, *I had a better relationship/connection with my male clinical supervisors than my female clinical supervisors during my training* (4).

These men also reflected on the stress created by being perceived as persons sexually attracted to and interested in their female counterparts in the CPDP (the burden of heteronormativity). Some men commented on the increase in potential romantic partners: *I perceived being surrounded by so many women in my CPDP as an increase in romantic options* (7). However, the primary focus was on the anxiety and fear associated with being perceived as motivated by sexual interest, with statements such as: *there is safety in being in a committed relationship because I am not perceived as being "on the prowl"* (2), and *there is an awareness/expectation that male and female students in the CPDP will be sexually interested in each other* (6).

The predominant theme within this theoretical construct was men's descriptions of their experience as defensive and conflicted. Some men detailed playing different roles or parts within CPDP, expressing ideas such as: *male students take on a comedic role in the CPDP* (3); *sometimes I behave like a provocateur in my CPDP* (3); and *there is a spectrum of machismo/masculinity among the male cohort in my CPDP* (3). Six participants cited the need *to represent maleness* (6), while others explained behaving *more masculine/male . . . to overcompensate* (10). Finally, some men described wanting to avoid being masculine or male when they were in the therapist role, saying, *I don't want to be male when I am conducting therapy* (2).

Some men's defensive and conflicted experiences were depicted as fear of being perceived as aggressive: *I am reluctant to be more active or involved in my CPDP because I would be perceived as domineering or aggressive* (7); *men's aggressiveness is less accepted in my CPDP than women's aggressiveness* (4); or *I fear being accused of being a misogynist/chauvinist* (3). One participant explained his frustration and anger over being accused of male chauvinism by virtue of being male: "[They] just [call] you a chauvinist and you happen to be male, so by definition they're right. It's like what are you supposed to say to that?" (Rugg, 2013, p. 38).

The men also expressed their belief that feminist or feminine viewpoints and behaviors were dominant in the CPDP, stating, *feminist and liberal viewpoints dominate* (5), and *feminine activities/skills are taught as therapeutic coping skills in my CPDP* (4), while *the male student opinion is often ignored or not sought after in the CPDP* (3). In addition, six participants identified feeling *defensive when the topic of gender/gender differences comes up* (6). Furthermore, although five participants explained that they *have a higher bar to clear in terms of proving awareness/sensitivity* (5), others remarked that *female students/faculty are overwhelmed by too much male introspection* (3). This highlights a particularly difficult double bind for male students.

Another way in which the participants conveyed their defensive and conflicted experience was in their depiction of male students as more effective communicators and as having a more calm and rational approach to academic and clinical training when compared to female students. Six participants remarked, *male students speak in a more concise and careful manner than female students in the CPDP* (6). Additionally, some participants commented on *male students' . . . laid-back/low-anxiety approach toward academic training [compared] to female students* (7). Others explained the benefits of their level-headed approach and demeanor, saying that *behaving more rationally/unemotionally helps me to present as more professional* (3).

These men discussed feeling outnumbered and paying special attention to the gender ratio of both students and clinical supervisors: *I am aware of the gender ratio/feel outnumbered by women in my CPDP* (7) and *the ratio of male-to-female clinical supervisors is important in my training* (6). While some men commented on problems with the perception and definition of maleness, saying, *there is a need for a more comprehensive view/definition of maleness* (2), others remarked on the derogatory manner in which maleness is discussed in their CPDP, noting that *maleness is pathologized in my CPDP* (8). One participant poignantly stated: "A lot of elements of traditional masculinity that I've grown up with and really think have been positive character traits have been pathologized within this program" (Rugg, 2013, p. 40). Other participants highlighted more dramatic and troubling experiences within the CPDP such as: *professors pit male students against each other* (2), and *my CPDP expects me to apologize/feel guilty for being male* (3). Finally, six participants identified feeling *discriminated against for being male in [their] CPDP* (6).

These men described a variety of social factors that complicate the male student experience (male students have different reactions to/ways of coping with social aspects of the CPDP). Two participants stated *that it is more difficult being a male student in the beginning of the CPDP* (2). Some discussed the social exclusion they faced because of being male, where *female students develop cliques and exclude male students in my CPDP* (5). These men also explained that they *focus on the practical/tangible aspects of being male in [the] CPDP to cope with the social difficulties in [the] CPDP* (4).

These participants also alluded to a series of emasculating, shameful, and embarrassing emotions within this theoretical construct (male sensitivity to humiliation: adding fuel to the fire). Two participants described a disconnect between the process and end-goal of clinical psychology doctoral training, explaining that *the doctorate degree is masculine but the process is not* (2). Some participants explained *feel[ing] emasculated and as if [they] have to tone down [their] masculinity* (4). Four participants cited how their student status and lack of money negatively impacted their ego (4). Other men detailed that it is disgraceful for men to show intense emotions, expressing that *it is unacceptable/shameful for men to show affection/extreme emotions* (7). One participant detailed the efforts to suppress emotions while in the classroom (Rugg, 2013):

> I wanted to be upset, but I didn't [allow myself to be]. I completely shut it down right away, and looking back on it now, it was because there was some level of shame I would feel if I did something like that. Whereas, I've heard so many stories of people crying at internships, people crying at their externships, and I [said to myself] I would never do that. If I was upset, I would probably go home and have a beer. I would do something very manly. I would never cry because that's not professional. (p. 41)

These men also expressed a variety of viewpoints about how traditional male privilege translates to the CPDP (the **confirmation and disconfirmation of traditional male privilege**). Their acceptance and denial of male privilege was reflected in the theme of *perceptions of male privilege*. Some participants cited differential treatment as integral to their recognition of male privilege, with statements such as: *male students are listened to differently in the CPDP* (4) and *male students have an easier time in my CPDP because less is expected of them* (2). One participant detailed his experience that men's classroom comments were considered more seriously than women's: "I have the sense that we're listened to in a different way in class, but I may be wrong. I feel when we speak as males we're definitely listened to in every situation, whereas in some cases when someone speaks up that's female, once in a while there won't necessarily be that type of attentiveness" (Rugg, 2013, p. 41).

These participants also pointed to success in securing practicum positions and anticipated career benefits as evidence for male privilege: *It is/was easier for me to get training placements because I am male* (5); *I have a competitive advantage in this field because I am male* (9); and *it is comforting to think men have a competitive advantage in the field* (4). Some men pinpointed *particular clinical settings/situations, with clients and other professionals, in which it was especially helpful to be male* (5). Finally, three participants alluded to their general *recognition of male privilege during [their] training* (3).

Other participants denied or questioned whether they experienced the benefits of male privilege in the CPDP. This included three participants who described that they *wrongly assumed being a male student would help [them] get an externship or internship* (3). Some men highlighted the limitations of their training experiences as a result of being male, stating *I am less well-rounded/my clinical experiences have been limited because I am male* (6).

Some had pervasive *belief[s] that women are better suited to work with certain sensitive populations* (9). One participant explained how being male prevented him from working with specific sensitive populations, such as sexually abused and exploited adolescent girls, at an externship practicum: "I'm not allowed to see those cases at all. It was said from the very beginning, 'You cannot be a part of this program because you're a male and that would complicate transference and they don't want to see men'" (Rugg, 2013, p. 42).

In their rejection of male privilege, three participants detailed *misconceptions about how male therapists help clients* (3). In addition, some men stated that male privilege was not something they discussed or considered and that it was primarily a focus of female students (*mostly female students speak about the male privilege in my CPDP* (5)). Finally, five participants plainly denied experiencing any male privilege in their CPDP, saying, *I did not experience any male privilege during my training* (5).

Another primary focus for the participants was on their personal and professional development in their CPDP (the **professional and personal growth of male students**). This included discussions of the benefits of their training experiences (positive consequences for men resulting from training experiences), with statements such as: *it was an enriching experience being male in my CPDP* (4), and *it was a new/exciting experience to be interacting/ studying with women* (5). These men felt they could be authentic and different (*non-traditional* (6)), and both *learned to be more aware and accepting of [their] emotions* (3) and *aware of more parts of [their] maleness* (4) in their CPDP. One participant succinctly said: "It means I'm not locked into typical male stereotypes because I have another way of being" (Rugg, 2013, p. 43). Ten participants even found the process of the focus group beneficial, admitting that *I found this focus group helpful or interesting* (10).

These men also detailed professional growth, explaining how understanding maleness affected their clinical work (understanding the impact of my maleness on my clinical encounters). Some participants commented on differences in their approach with male versus female clients: for example, being *more competitive . . . with men* (4) and *more sensitive/careful with female clients* (3). This caring and compassionate approach in their interactions with female clients was exemplified by the following statement from one participant: "I find that as a therapist I'm much more supportive and protective and empathic with women almost no matter what. And with men my mannerisms and my way of being with them could vary drastically" (Rugg, 2013, p. 43).

In their clinical encounters these men also identified taking on a *more dominant/ authoritative* role (5) and being *more direct or active* (4) when co-leading with a female therapist and in the group or family-therapy situation, respectively. Other participants described having to adjust to their different experience of male versus female clients with statements such as *I had to adjust to my experience that female clients discuss more relational/emotional issues than male clients* (2). Finally, two additional participants detailed recognition of how their *maleness impacts the transference/countertransference with female clients* (2).

A FURTHER EXAMINATION OF THREE THEORETICAL CONSTRUCTS

This next section illustrates how my personal experiences mirrored that of the study participants. In addition, two vignettes and other personal anecdotes are used to illuminate the theoretical constructs already discussed. This section will also examine how other social groups as well as individuals, including male students in CPDPs, experience being or becoming a "problem." Finally, I will revisit the relevant research to examine how white men experience minority status in female-dominated professions and discuss the importance of developing masculinity as multicultural competency (Liu, 2005; Mellinger and Liu, 2006).

Vignette 1: The Male Student Experiences Minority Status; How Does It Feel to Become a "Problem?"

During my second year of clinical psychology doctoral training, I headed off to practicum interviews, eager for a rewarding and challenging training experience. Drawn to the universality of trauma in psychopathology, I sought training with a focus on trauma work and was thrilled to find a hospital that offered training on an inpatient psychiatric female trauma unit. To my surprise and chagrin, the psychologists interviewing me, one man and one woman, were apparently not as thrilled to take on this eager and enthusiastic graduate student. They were more curious and ostensibly suspicious of a young male therapist's interest in working with traumatized women. The interviewers asked me: "And why do you want to work with this population? A lot of these women have been severely traumatized by the men in their lives—fathers, uncles, brothers, husbands, boyfriends—I'm not sure these women could tolerate the presence of a man, let alone therapy with a man . . . And why do you want to work with these women again?"

I became defensive. Reeling, I tried unsuccessfully to explain myself: "Well, trauma is central to most psychopathology. . . . Women with a trauma history make up a large percentage of the patients who seek treatment." My efforts were feeble, primarily because my explanations became the ramblings of a man who felt he was being judged as a potential abuser and perpetrator of violence against women—vulnerable women. I began to feel nauseous and enraged. I believed I was being perceived not as a trainee hoping for experience with a troubled and sensitive population but as a man with ulterior motives of the worst order. How am I to understand this interaction, the questions of the interviewers, and my response? Were the interviewers more curious than suspicious? Did I overreact or misinterpret this interaction?

Men Experience Minority Oppression

The findings that were uncovered in exploring the first theoretical construct were striking and surprising. It is difficult to imagine how men who reap the rewards of Western patriarchal society can experience the same oppression and discrimination felt by other minority groups. My contention is not that we men actually had comparable experiences to minority groups, but that the unique context of the CPDP had us experiencing, possibly for the first time in our lives, what it was like to be a "problem."

The concept of being a "problem" is borrowed from W. E. B. Du Bois, who described the experience of Black Americans in the late 1800s. This group of people was made to feel as if it was a "problem" for dominant White society, in that Blacks were largely blamed for their inability to progress despite oppression, prejudice, discrimination, hatred, and fear (Du Bois, 1903/2004, pp. 696-697). The concept of being a "problem" can be applied to any social group that has been historically oppressed, because there is an integral connection between systems of oppression and discrimination and blame, attack and feelings of hatred, and fear among the dominant class. Examples include discrimination against the LGBTQ (lesbian, gay, bisexual, transgender, queer) community (Hudson and Ricketts, 1980), Muslims and Arabs, especially after the attacks of September 11 (Patel, 2012) and Jews in many periods throughout history, and especially during the rise of Nazism (Engel, 1999).

Most examples of becoming a "problem" depict loss of privilege or status, fear of attack, blame, or rejection, and shame and humiliation. Male clinical psychology doctoral students encounter academic and clinical training in which they are confronted with issues of sexism, sexual assault, abuse and spousal abuse. Undeniably, the primary perpetrators of these societal ills are men, and the victims are overwhelmingly female. It is my contention that men feel blamed or attacked as representing, defending, or belonging to this class of perpetrators and abusers, and thus feel as though they have become a "problem." This sentiment was detailed by several participants in my dissertation study (Rugg, 2013), represented in the repeating idea that *maleness is pathologized in my CPDP*. I also experienced these feelings in the above vignette, in which my response to perhaps harmless curiosity or necessary vigilance about my intentions was rage and concern that I was being grouped with perpetrators of abuse and violence. One participant from my dissertation study described his belief that the majority of classroom discussion was spent detailing all the harm straight White men have perpetrated on society.

Struggles with Male Identity

Research on men in female-dominated fields suggests that men often experience feeling scrutinized as feminine or not masculine and are questioned about their sexual identity (Cognard-Black, 2004), are perceived as strange or unsuccessful (Allan, 1993; Benton DeCorse, and Vogtle, 1997; Carmichael, 1995; Heickes, 1991; Morgan, 1992; Williams, 1995; Lupton, 2006), and receive poor treatment from female colleagues (Allan, 1993; Cognard-Black, 2004). Such sentiments were relayed by the participants in my dissertation study (Rugg, 2013), especially in the repeating ideas such as *I feel emasculated/like I have to tone down my masculinity,* and *it is detrimental to my ego that I am a student and not financially successful.* Additionally, in comparison to male-dominated professions, men in female-dominated professions suffer financial and status penalties (Cognard-Black, 2004; England and Herbert, 1993; Powell and Jacobs, 1984).

Despite these challenges, the same research posits that men in female-dominated fields retain their privilege and advantage over women in terms of their progression to higher ranking, specialized, and better paying positions. Thus, there still exists pervasive institutional sexism that favors men and discriminates against women in these fields (Allan, 1993; Benton DeCorse and Vogtle, 1997; Lupton, 2006; Williams, 1993, 1995; Wingfield, 2009). This suggests that at least some of the difficulty for men is related to how the work environment makes them struggle with their masculinity, rather than their experiencing systemic discrimination, because men are the benefactors of institutional sexism. Perhaps men in female-dominated fields perceive themselves as less masculine because they are occupying roles typically held by women (Eagly,1987; Eagly and Steffen, 1984; Eagly and Wood, 1991) or are experiencing gender role strain because being part of a female-dominated profession makes them feel as if they have failed to live up to their internalized masculine ideal (Levant, 1996; Pleck, 1981, 1995).

As noted earlier, emotions of shame and humiliation are an integral part of the experiences of both being a "problem" and becoming a "problem." The theme of how male sensitivity to humiliation adds fuel to the fire encapsulates men's emasculated and disgraced feelings in the CPDP and reveals how these feelings intensify men's experience of becoming a "problem." Feelings of shame and humiliation were involved in the above vignette and fueled my defensive reactions. Chodorow (2012) follows Greenson (1968) in describing the "fault lines of masculinity," first saying that the male sense of self and gender is developed "in relation to women and femininity," first shaped in the infant-mother dyad (p. 130). She asserts that one primary aspect of masculinity is the need to define itself as not-mother, not-feminine, and, thus, not-other, whereas the female sense of self does not appear to develop in opposition to the father, masculinity, or the other. This makes men foundationally more primitive in their defensive needs to protect their self-hood and fearful of "dependency, abandonment, . . . loss of self, . . . and fear of women's sexuality" because of the potentially humiliating omnipotence of the mother (Chodorow, 2012, p. 130). Surrounded by female classmates, professors, supervisors, and clients, some men feel extremely threatened by this overwhelming number of women (seen in the repeating idea that *I am aware of the gender ratio/feel outnumbered by women in my CPDP*).

Even more crucial, according to Chodorow (2012), is men's sensitivity to humiliation as determined by their relationship to other men. As much as it is not-mother, not-feminine and not-other, masculinity is also not-boy and not-child. The second part of this defining is, of course, determined by the boy's relationship with his father and how he navigates his Oedipal development without inspiring paternal retribution or shaming. We see here it is for men to "not being subordinate to, shamed by or humiliated by other men" (Chodorow, 2012, p.131). This might explain the participants' perceived negative interactions with and lack of support from male psychologists in the field as relayed in the theme **I have not been adequately supported/mentored by male psychologists in the field.**

Vignette 2: The Confirmation and Disconfirmation of Traditional Male Privilege

In my experience, it was not uncommon to observe male clinical psychology doctoral students, especially early in their training, making statements fraught with sexist or misogynistic undertones and subsequently being quickly shot down and silenced by a large number of female classmates. I never imagined I would find myself in this situation. During my first semester in my CPDP, classroom discussion in one course turned toward aspects of the infant-caretaker dyad. I expressed an opinion I thought to be fact: "I think we can all agree that women are better caretakers than men." Surprised by the level of disagreement and intensity of upheaval this comment caused, I argued my point more intensely: "Breast feeding enables the mother to foster a stronger relationship with the infant. . . . Women are inherently more nurturing." At the time I was unaware of the implications of my statement or the power and privilege it denoted. Yet I quickly learned that one of the most insidious and problematic aspects of privilege is the tendency of the privileged to be unaware of the benefits they have been granted (Black and Stone, 2005). After all, prevailing gender ideology largely determines which gender is the primary caretaker of children in a given society or culture. In addition, opinions purported as fact, such as the one shared above, have been used to serve patriarchal purposes, limit and subjugate women for centuries, and roll back the gains of the women's movement (Levant, 1996).

The Professional and Personal Growth of Male Students

My early missteps notwithstanding, I have grown professionally and personally in countless ways during doctoral training. Many of my experiences of personal growth reflect those of the participants in my dissertation study (Rugg, 2013), which included feeling enriched, authentic, unique, and more aware and accepting of my emotions and parts of my masculinity. An understanding of how my unique masculinity impacted my clinical work also mirrors the experiences of the participants in my dissertation study. I have generally found myself contending with feelings of competition with male clients while feeling the need to support and protect female clients. Most profound and problematic for me, especially early in my training, were my interactions co-leading groups and families with female therapists. In one such clinical situation, compelled to be authoritative and "take charge," I made a crucial and impetuous clinical decision without conferring with my female co-leader. Surprised by the impulsivity of my choice, I not only had to mend the relationship with my female co-leader but also reflect on and work to change this aspect of my own problematic masculinity. In another clinical situation, I co-led an inpatient therapy group with a licensed female psychologist who was my clinical supervisor. Despite the fact that she was more clinically refined and experienced than I, and responsible for my clinical work, I consistently struggled with feeling the need to protect her, especially from confrontations with male clients.

Admittedly, the previous vignettes and theoretical constructs paint a largely negative picture of the male student experience in the clinical psychology doctoral program. However, the participants in my dissertation study (Rugg, 2013) additionally detailed various positive experiences related to professional and personal development, which I also experienced. This was reflected in the third theoretical construct (professional and personal growth of male students). These experiences of personal growth included becoming more aware, accepting, fulfilled, and emotionally complex as a man.

Men's Masculinity as a Multicultural Competency

The participants in my dissertation study (Rugg, 2013) and I also detailed professional growth in terms of an enhanced recognition of how gender affected our work as clinicians (as depicted by the theme of understanding the impact of my maleness on my clinical encounters). Despite the years of research and study that resulted in the development of the "new psychology of men," only recently has there been a call to integrate men and masculinity into multiculturalism and multicultural competence (Liu, 2005; Sbaratta, 2011). According to the knowledge, skills, and awareness model (Sue, Arredondo, and McDavis, 1992; Sue and Sue, 2003), best practice for working with diverse groups (in this case men) includes skills and knowledge about the particular difficulties and problems that men bring to the therapy situation through male gender-role socialization (Sbaratta, 2011). Additionally, one must become aware of how one's own beliefs, attitudes, emotions, and stereotypes about male clients, along with clients' unique gender dynamics, affect the therapy milieu. Of course such self-awareness is particularly relevant for male clinicians in light of crucial issues of oppression, power, and privilege.

Given traditional gender role norms (Pleck, 1981, 1995; Levant, 1996), which champion competition among men, it is not surprising that many participants in my dissertation study described a competitive therapeutic stance towards their male clients. Furthermore, male students' careful and protective approach to female clients exhibited commonly held stereotypes about women and reflected a type of benevolent sexism observed in "complementary gender stereotypes" (Jost and Kay, 2005, p. 499). Women are generally viewed as communal and stereotyped as passive, emotional, interpersonally warm, and relationship focused. The delicate approach to female clients demonstrates that these women are both loathed and respected, since the exclusive view of women as caring and kind also subverts their competence (i.e., they require sensitive approach because they are delicate and fragile; Jost and Kay, 2005; Langford and MacKinnon, 2000).

The male clinical psychology doctoral students' experiences as therapists and co-therapists of groups and families involved a particularly interesting finding. Those in my study (Rugg, 2013) relayed comfort in being more direct and dominant in group and family therapy and when co-leading with a female therapist. These results can be understood as clinical situations that inspire a more hegemonic form of masculinity, such that male therapists experience threats to their masculinity and feel compelled to take an authoritative role with a group of people and a dominant role over a female co-therapist (Connell, 1995; LoMascolo, 2008). The male students in my dissertation study described being particularly surprised by their female co-leaders' deference to them in the co-therapy situation. This can be viewed as an enactment of traditional gender role norms, in which men distance themselves from the threats of gender equality or assuming a secondary role to women. Simultaneously, women, trained to be passive and deferential to men, yield power and control to men in this situation.

FINAL THOUGHTS

The experience of male clinical psychology doctoral students is singular, difficult, and rewarding. In many ways male students represent a privileged minority and reap the benefits of institutionalized sexism (Evans, 1997; Sbaratta, 2011). At the same time, they face challenging and threatening aspects of being male in a female-dominated program and may have to contend with their perceived kinship with other males who act out abuse and oppression in relationships, especially with females. It is my assertion that this makes male students feel they have become a "problem," and this can lead to a myriad of defensive responses. If these students are to grow and thrive during this important time in their lives and careers, they must confront their own defensive responses and personal involvement in systems of abuse and oppression and become agents of change. For me, this journey of reflection, insight, and acceptance has helped to set me free from a problematic and limiting aspect of my masculinity.

REFERENCES

Allan, J. (1993). Male elementary teachers: Experiences and perspectives. In Williams, C.L. (Ed.), *Doing "women's work": Men in nontraditional occupations* (pp. 113–27). Newbury Park, CA: Sage Publications.

American Psychological Association, American Psychological Association Center for Workforce Studies. (2009). Washington, DC.

Auerbach, C. F., and Silverstein L. B. (2003). *Qualitative data.* New York, NY: NYU Press.

Bem, S. L. (1974). The measurement of psychological androgyny. *Journal of Consulting and Clinical Psychology, 42*(2), 155–62.

Bem, S. L. (1975). Sex role adaptability: One consequence of psychological androgyny. *Journal of Personality and Social Psychology, 31*(4), 634–43.

Bem, S. L. (1981). Gender schema theory: A cognitive account of sex typing. *Psychological Review, 88*(4), 354–64.

Bem, S. L., and Lenney, E. (1976). Sex typing and avoidance of cross-sex behavior. *Journal of Personality and Social Psychology, 33*(1), 48–54.

Benton DeCorse, C. J., and Vogtle, S. P. (1997). In a complex voice: the contradictions of male elementary teachers' career choice and professional identity. *Journal of Teacher Education, 48*(1), 37–46.

Black, L. L., and Stone, D. (2005). Expanding the definition of privilege: The concept of social privilege. *Journal of Multicultural Counseling and Development, 33*(4), 243–55.

Carmichael, J. V. (1995). The gay librarian: a comparative analysis of attitudes towards professional gender issues. *Journal of Homosexuality, 30*(2), 11–57.

Chodorow, N. J. (2012). Hate, humiliation and masculinity. In *Individualizing gender and sexuality: Theory and practice* (pp. 121–136). New York, NY: Routledge.

Cognard-Black, A. J. (2004). Will they stay or will they go? Sex atypical work among token men who teach. *The Sociological Quarterly, 45*(1), 113–39.

Connell, R. W. (1995). *Masculinities.* Berkeley, CA: University of California Press.

Cross, S. , and Bagilhole, B. (2002). Girls' jobs for the boys? Men, masculinity and nontraditional occupations. *Gender, Work and Organization, 9*(2), 204–226.

Du Bois, W. E. B (2004). The souls of Black folk. In H. L. Gates Jr. and N. Y. McKay (Eds.), *The Norton anthology of African American Literature* (2nd ed., pp. 692–784). New York, NY: W. W. Norton & Company, Inc.

Eagly, A. H. (1987). *Sex differences in social behavior: A social-role interpretation.* Hillsdale, NJ: Lawrence Erlbaum.

Eagly, A. H., and Steffen, V. J. (1984). Gender stereotypes stem from the distribution of women and men into social roles. *Journal of Personality and Social Psychology, 46*(4), 735–54.

Eagly, A. H. and Wood, W. (1991). Explaining sex differences in social behavior: A meta-analytic perspective. *Journal of Personality and Social Psychology 17*(3), 306–15.

Engel, D. (1999). The concept of anti-Semitism in the historical scholarship of Amos Funkenstein. *Jewish Social Studies, 6*(1), 111.

England, P., and Herbert, M. S. (1993). The pay of men in "female" occupations: Is comparable worth only for women? In Williams, C. L. (Ed.), *Doing "women's work": Men in nontraditional occupations* (pp. 28–48). Newbury Park, CA: Sage Publications.

Evans, J. (1997). Men in nursing: Issues of gender segregation and hidden advantage. *Journal of Advanced Nursing, 26*(2), 226–231.

Festinger, L. (1962). *A theory of cognitive dissonance.* Stanford, CA: Stanford University Press.

Freud, S. (1937). *The ego and the mechanism of defense.* London, England: Hogarth Press.

Frincke, J., Wicherski, M., Finno, A., and Kohout, J. (2006). *2005 NCSPP self study: Final results.* Washington, DC: Retrieved from NCSPP www.ncspp.info/2005%20NCSPP%20Self%20Study%20Final%20Report.pdf

Greenson, R. R. (1968). Dis-identifying from mother: Its special importance for the boy. *The International Journal of Psycho-Analysis, 49*(2-3), 370–4.

Hammel, G. A., and Olkin, R. (1996). Student–educator sex in clinical and counseling psychology doctoral training. *Professional Psychology: Research and Practice, 27*(1), 93–7.

Harden, S. L., Clark, R. A., Johnson, B. W., and Larson, J. (2009). Cross-gender mentorship in clinical psychology doctoral programs: An exploratory survey study. *Mentoring & Tutoring: Partnership in Learning, 17*(3), 277–90.

Heickes, E. J. (1991). When men are the minority: The case of men in nursing. *The Sociological Quarterly, 32*(3), 389–401.

Hudson, W. W., and Ricketts, W. A. (1980). A strategy for the measurement of homophobia. *Journal of Homosexuality, 5*(4), 352–357.

Jost, J. T., and Kay, A. C. (2005). Exposure to benevolent sexism and complementary gender stereotypes: Consequences for specific and diffuse forms of system justification. *Journal of Personality and Social Psychology, 88*(3), 498–509.

Kim, S. (2007). A reflection on inclusion. *Art Therapy: Journal of the American Art Therapy Association, 24*(1), 37–38.

Langford, T., and MacKinnon, N. J. (2000). The affective bases for the gendering of traits: Comparing the United States and Canada. *Social Psychology Quarterly, 63*(1), 34–48.

Levant, R. (1996). The new psychology of men. *Professional Psychology 27*(3), 259–65.

Liu, W. M. (2005). The study of men and masculinity as an important multicultural consideration. *Journal of Clinical Psychology, 61* (6), 685–97.

LoMascolo, A. F. (2008). *Do you want excitement? Don't join the army, be nurse!: Identity work and advantage among men in training for the female professions.* (Doctoral dissertation). Retrieved from ProQuest Dissertations and Theses. (DP19385)

Long Island University, Office of Institutional Research. (2010). Enrolled Students by Gender, Clinical Psychology Program: C.W. Post Campus, Fall 1999–Fall 2009.

Lupton, B. (2000). Maintaining masculinity: Men who do 'women's work.' *British Journal of Management, 11*(S1), 33–48.

Lupton, B. (2006). Explaining men's entry into female-concentrated occupations: Issues of masculinity and social class. *Gender, Work and Organization, 13*(2), 103–128.

Mellinger, T. N., and Liu, W. M. (2006). Men's issues in doctoral training; A survey of counseling psychology programs. *Professional Psychology: Research and Practice, 37*(2), 196–294.

Morgan, D. H. J. (1992). *Discovering Men.* London, UK: Routledge.

Ostertag, P. A., and McNamara, R. J. (1991). "Feminization" of psychology: The changing sex ratio and its implications for the profession. *Psychology of Women Quarterly, 15,* 349–369.

Patel, T. G. (2012). Surveillance, suspicion and stigma: Brown bodies in a terror-panic climate. *Surveillance & Society, 10* (3/4), 215–234.

Pleck, J. H. (1981). *The myth of masculinity*. Cambridge, MA: MIT Press.

Pleck, J. H. (1995). The gender role strain paradigm: An update. In R. F. Levant and W. S. Pollack (Eds.). *A new psychology of men* (pp. 11–32). New York: Basic Books.

Pope, K. S., Levenson, H., and Schover, L. R. (1979). Sexual intimacy in psychology training: Results and implications of a national survey. *American Psychologist, 34* (8), 682–9.

Powell, B., and. Jacobs, J. A. (1984). Gender differences in the evaluation of prestige. *The Sociological Quarterly, 25*(2), 173–90.

Rugg, I. (2013). *The male student's experience in a clinical psychology doctoral program: A qualitative study* (Unpublished doctoral dissertation). Long Island University (LIU Post Campus), Brookville, NY.

Sbaratta, C. A. T. (2011). *Male psychology doctoral students: The influence of GRC on training*. (Doctoral dissertation). Retrieved from ProQuest Dissertation and Theses. (3472702)

Sue, D. W., Arredondo, P., and McDavis, R. J. (1992). Multicultural counseling competencies and standards: A call to the profession. *Journal of Counseling and Development, 20*, 644–88.

Sue, D. W., and Sue, D. (2003). *Counseling the culturally diverse: Theory and practice* (4th ed.). New York: John Wiley.

Watt, S. K. (2007). Difficult dialogues, privilege and social justice: Uses of the Privileged Identity Exploration (PIE) model in student affairs practice. *College Student Affairs Journal, 26*(2), 114–26.

Williams, C. L. (Ed.). (1993). *Doing "women's work": Men in nontraditional occupations*. London, UK: Sage.

Williams, C. L. (1995). *Still a man's world: Men who do women's work*. Oakland: University of California Press.

Willyard, C. (2011, January). Men: A growing minority? *gradPYSCH, 9*, 41–44.

Wingfield, A.H. (2009). Racializing the glass escalator: Reconsidering men's experiences with women's work. *Gender and Society, 23*(1), 5–26.

Chapter Ten

Notes from a Queer Student's Graduate Training

Kathleen Kallstrom-Schreckengost[1]

Getting through graduate school in psychology is all about balancing an overwhelming number of varying and often conflicting identities. Within the course of one day, my classmates and I were expected to be students, academics, clinicians, supervisees, teachers, and supervisors. We looked to our professors for guidance, mentorship, and evaluation while also paying for their services. We attempted to help our clients understand themselves as people while trying to figure out who *we* were as therapists (knowing the whole time that our clients offered us at least as much in trust and experience gained as we were able to offer them in therapeutic help). As a bisexual graduate therapist, my status as a sexual minority added another layer of complication to this matrix of identities. My sexual identity had an impact on my clinical experiences, my relationships with my peers, professors, and supervisors, and my identity as a therapist and psychologist.

This chapter describes some of my personal experiences working with professors, peers, supervisors, and clients during my five years as a graduate student in psychology. Part memoir and part guidebook, it can be read as both a case study and something more generalizable. By reflecting on these events, I hope to provide a unique, queer perspective on the experience of earning a doctorate in psychology and also to share some of the knowledge I've gained through this process with individuals just beginning their graduate school careers.

QUEER EXPERIENCE IN GRADUATE TRAINING

I write with the recognition that my experience is *one* experience and certainly does not represent the perspective of all or even most sexual-minority graduate students. The question of how much sexual identity comes into one's life as a graduate student is complex and personal and looks different for each person (sexual minority or not). My experience has been defined not only by my identities as queer and bisexual but also by my gender, gender presentation, ethnicity, socioeconomic status, religion, region of origin, previous education, ability status, body size, personality traits, defensive style, and innumerable other attributes. For instance, I have a tendency to take responsibility for the comfort of others in one-on-one situations and to avoid direct conflict. This is a pattern that has often affected how and when I come out (and whether I challenge my mentors regarding sexual minority issues) and is directly connected to my background as a woman and a Midwesterner, not to mention my anxious/obsessive personality style. In contrast, I sometimes rely on an "offense is the best defense" kind of performativity when feeling threatened or insulted. The juxtaposition of these particular defenses means that I was much more likely to speak up on sexual minority issues in my graduate school classes than in individual supervision. These aspects of my personality and background are intertwined in my experiences as a queer graduate student, and they have had as much of an effect on my experiences as my sexual identity. All of this goes to say that another queer student with a different matrix of personal traits would likely perceive the experiences of going through a doctoral program in psychology very differently than I.

One aspect of my identity that has had a significant effect on my experience as a graduate psychologist is my relative invisibility as a sexual minority. Since college (when I went through a radical and purposefully visible period in sexual-identity development), I've settled into a more conventional (and for me, more comfortable) gender presentation. Throughout my time as a graduate student, I dressed in traditionally feminine clothing, wore my hair long, and was generally "read straight" by strangers. In many ways, conforming to a traditional gender presentation has served as a powerful form of privilege for me. If I don't come out, no unfavorable judgments are made about me based on an assumed sexual-minority status, because most people assume that I am part of the sexual majority. However, this status as an invisible minority also comes with a set of considerations that can complicate professional and clinical interactions. In particular, my concerns regarding identity disclosure would have been quite different if my sexual identity were more noticeable to others.

This relative invisibility, along with myriad other aspects of my gender presentation, sexuality, personality, and defensive style, have impacted my experience as a queer woman in a graduate psychology program. Of course, sexual minority students who are men and those who are more visibly gender-deviant would have different experiences than mine, as would those more private than I, more or less political than I, or those of a different ethnicity, religion, ability status and so forth. However, I hope that the sharing of my experiences will provide a jumping-off point for graduate psychologists of all sexual identities to begin to consider the complex ways each of our identities (sexual and otherwise) impact our work as students, supervisees, and clinicians.

STUDENT-SUPERVISEE INTERACTIONS

I have found myself in many situations throughout graduate school in which my mentors (professors, supervisors, and bosses) in psychology were not able to guide me in the area of my developing identity as a bisexual psychologist, and even required some educating themselves. When faced with situations in which authority figures expressed ignorant, unfounded, or even offensive views on sexual minorities, I always felt a conflict between my role as a student/trainee (and I am a student who really wants my professors and supervisors to like me) and my role as a queer person who feels a responsibility to combat homophobia and ignorance.

Despite my attempts to respond thoughtfully and with integrity, I've rarely felt at peace with my reactions to situations in which I was faced with a choice between speaking up to a mentor about a sexual-minority issue and keeping quiet. When I have let things go, I have felt complicit with heterosexism and the subtle, seemingly benign assumptions that people make about sexuality and sexual orientation. On the other hand, when I've made a point of correcting a supervisor or "making an issue" of a comment made in class, I usually felt as if I was "overreacting," being "too sensitive," or drawing unnecessary attention to myself (thus internalizing homophobia).

Because of my own personality, political beliefs, defenses, and so forth, I tend to come out quickly to people with whom I expect to have a long-term relationship. Therefore, my cohort and professors knew of my sexual identity and relationship status within about an hour of meeting me on the first day of orientation. However, because of the goal-directed, uber-professional, and often isolated nature of supervisory relationships (i.e., meeting a community supervisor in his or her office for exactly fifty minutes, once a week), I have rarely come out to a clinical supervisor who was not otherwise involved in my professional life (as a professor or training director). This caused some uncomfortable situations in the midst of the supervisory relationship, which is why I avoid such awkward scenarios by "coming out hard and fast" in other relationships that I expect to be more enduring.

For example, early in my clinical training, I worked with an assessment supervisor over four sessions. During our second session, as we discussed my intake of the client I was testing, my supervisor asked me if I had the sense that this client "had gender-identity issues." Confused, I asked her to clarify. "You know," she said, "is this girl going to come out?" It took me the rest of our supervisory session just to process what had happened (in the moment, I think I said something like "Ohhh . . . no, she expressed interest in dating men, but I didn't ask her about her sexual identity." Later, I contemplated explaining the (very important) difference between gender identity and sexual orientation to my supervisor, a very competent, popular child and adolescent psychologist. But in the end I dropped the idea, feeling that it would be too awkward to bring up the issue, apropos of nothing, at a later session. Years later, I still feel a bit guilty for giving up the chance to help someone who works with kids and adolescents every day (many of whom, no doubt, are struggling to develop their own gender and sexual identities, and who are looking for guidance from the adults in their lives) to be more informed and accurate regarding sexual orientation, gender identity, and coming out.

Another instance in which I considered correcting an authority figure but stayed quiet instead involved the attending psychiatrist on an inpatient unit. During the team meeting one morning, he discussed his initial session with a young patient who felt he was suffering from post-traumatic stress syndrome (PTSD) as a result of bullying at school. During his consultation, the patient stated that he had been bullied for being gay, and the psychiatrist challenged this assumption, insisting that it was the patient's non-confirmative clothing that caused the bullying and not his sexual orientation. "Maybe if you stopped dressing like that, the other kids would leave you alone," the psychiatrist reported telling the patient. While I found the doctor's perspective and interventions appalling, I did not feel that I could discuss his comments with him without seriously ruffling some professional feathers.

At other times (and in some ways as a result of these unsatisfying situations early in my training), I made a conscious choice to correct a mentor or speak up about my understanding of a situation having to do with my identity. Another community supervisor with whom I became fairly close over a year of working together once assumed in passing that I was married to a man. She said, "Your patients can see your wedding ring; they know you have a husband." Immediately I felt the familiar and terribly uncomfortable feeling of being perceived inaccurately, which reminds me of the often squeamish experience of listening to oneself on tape ("Is *that* how people hear me?"). The comment came at the end of our supervision session, and I mulled over the experience for the rest of the week, finally deciding that I would steel myself to correct my supervisor in the following session. When I did, I felt awkward and out of place, as if I had traded the discomfort of being perceived as straight with the discomfort of taking on the role of evaluator. My supervisor gracefully apologized for her assumption and we continued on with no detrimental effects, but I was left feeling guilty for pointing out my mentor's error without the sense that our interaction had benefited our relationship in any real way.

Part of my difficulty in managing the situations discussed above was the conflict between feeling that what had happened wasn't that big of a deal and simultaneously feeling that I had an absolute responsibility to respond appropriately. Did it really matter that my supervisor knew I was married to a woman and not a man? And if it didn't matter, then why hadn't I just corrected her on the spot, without hesitation? Who was I to correct a supervisor or psychiatrist? Certainly I held so little power as a student that I had better keep my mouth shut. This conflict was central not only to my experience as a sexual minority in graduate school but to my experience as a student in training to be a psychologist. There are peculiarities in training for a position of authority. In some cases graduate students are expected to take charge and display competence, while in other areas, they are expected to follow "the party line" and quietly take in the expertise of others. Especially in situations in which a student has prior knowledge, these conflicting roles can feel confusing and burdensome.

DEALING WITH INSTITUTIONAL MARGINALIZATION

The complexity of this quandary was demonstrated by the following experience that I had in graduate school. Several years into my clinical training, my program invited US military recruiters to speak to students about psychological careers. Our department was buzzing with controversy on the day of the presentation, with several professors speaking out against the questionable ethics of the military and, by proxy, the ethicality of our program in inviting them to recruit our students. At the time, "Don't Ask, Don't Tell (DADT)" was in force as military policy, and army psychologists were "consulting" on cases at Guantanamo. No surprise that this visit was a hot topic.

I attended the presentation of the military recruiters (who all refused to speak about DADT and its effect on recruitment of psychologists) before leaving early to join a protest presentation in which several professors were discussing the various evils of the U.S. military. The discussion was engaging and academic, and many students participated. But I felt a strange shift during the conversation with regard to my role in the room. I loved conversations like these—thoughtful, multifaceted, academically rigorous, and altogether hypothetical. But this issue wasn't hypothetical for me. DADT *actually* existed and would *actually* prevent me from entering the military if I applied for the jobs the recruiters were advertising.

Several people were discussing the potential merits of working within an imperfect system: you couldn't solve all the problems of the military, but there were still soldiers who needed mental-health care. I remember feeling patently left out, a sensation that was very unusual for me in my academic life (and I don't like feeling left out at all). I interrupted the conversation, saying, "That's all well and good, but some of us don't get to choose whether we work within the flawed system or not. If there was an employer who didn't accept black applicants or Jewish applicants, they never would have been invited here."

As I was talking, I felt a wave of emotion overcome me (an uncomfortable feeling in a room full of classmates and mentors). The meeting stopped just minutes later, and two of my professors apologized to me for not taking into account the personal impact that the invitation to the army would have on us queer students (which left me with another weird and uncomfortable feeling). I had dealt with this situation of the military visit differently than I had handled similar past events. I had met ignorance with a reasonable and clear perspective, and yet, I still did not feel good afterward. I felt vulnerable and out of place, forced into a sense of not belonging. For a brief moment, I felt that my sexual orientation defined me in a way that was completely out of my control. My pride, my performativity, and my defenses had failed me, and I felt like an outsider.

It may strike some readers that I write too dramatically, from a privileged perspective, about a relatively benign incident. I have certainly lived a life of privilege, both as a sexual minority and otherwise. I have experienced conflict over writing about this particular incident, which I believe sheds light on the difficulty and delicacy of feelings of differentness and separateness. Among other things, I felt shame that day, for being the topic of conversation and enjoying that attention, while also feeling strangely displaced by it, for calling out my valued mentors in front of everyone, for being the kind of person who is not wanted or acknowledged by the institutions of our country, and for being the kind of person who can ignore that kind of discrimination most all of the time.

ISSUES OF DISCLOSURE IN CLINICAL WORK

In learning to do clinical work, one thing I have struggled with most is the discomfort of maintaining a "neutral" demeanor with clients when sexual identity is raised as an issue. Issues of disclosure are always a challenging aspect of clinical work, especially as new clinicians attempt to navigate the strictures and suggestions of different supervisors as well as various theoretical orientations. As a psychoanalytically oriented graduate psychologist, I have been trained to limit my personal disclosures to clients in favor of exploring their fantasies and allowing their experience of transference to take precedence. While I wholeheartedly believe in this professional reticence, it is sometimes very difficult to contain the transference assumptions a client makes. There's a natural twinge and a compulsion to shout, "But that's not true!" especially when a client's fantasy about one's age/ethnicity/identity/lifestyle/feelings is unfavorable (either in the therapist's or the client's opinion). I have often felt an internal squeamishness at having a label (i.e., critical, young, athletic, New Yorker, and so forth) placed on me by a client but never such a strong reaction as when a client assumes that I am straight.

This reaction in part has signaled my need for more self-analysis in this area of my identity. My sexuality is an aspect of my identity that has had less time to become stable and comfortable in my personal narrative (after all, I've had nearly two decades more of experience being white, a woman, a Midwesterner, and an American than I have had identifying as bisexual/queer), and my discomfort at being assumed straight represents an area that needs more thought and reflection. While recognizing that the need for more internal work is paramount in coping with the demands of clinical graduate training, I also know that it is important to take cultural influences into account as one learns to be a therapist. Issues of sexual identity and other kinds of status that put people in the minority are strong cultural components that warrant attention and reflection. In other words, it's always good to look inward with curiosity when experiencing strong feelings as a therapist, but it can also be important to look at external (and often quite subtle) factors to better understand one's emotions and to guide clinical decision-making. In my ongoing exploration of issues of disclosure of sexual orientation, the historical oppression of LGBQ individuals is a crucial part of that curiosity.

POLITICAL ACTIVISM AND ISSUES OF NONDISCLOSURE

One of the most subtle and yet extremely powerful aspects of homophobia is the erasure of LGBQ experience through heterosexist language, media, and the like. The many examples of personal, institutional, and physical oppression of LGBQ individuals have silenced and restricted queer people, as has the unrelenting heterosexism of our culture. For example, I can't remember the last time I saw a film that was a romantic comedy in which the couple was anything but straight. It is the inexorable heterosexist presumption of straightness, the implicit societal pressure to be "normal," that leads sexual minorities to stay in the closet. More precisely, the assumption of heterosexuality creates the closet from which sexual minorities must consciously exit, since, without the assumptions of straightness, there would be nothing for queer people to come out about.

Putting aside heterosexist assumptions is fundamental to the advancement of gay rights. The changing tide in public opinion regarding same-sex marriage is in large part a result of more straight people becoming aware of LGBQ individuals in their lives; the more openly gay people one knows, the more supportive one tends to be of gay rights. This means that, in some small yet profound way, queer individuals can improve the status of sexual minorities at large simply by being out in their personal and professional lives. This principle has guided my personal disclosures regarding my sexual identity: I come out in most personal and professional situations that last longer than a few minutes. When I don't come out, or when I fail to correct someone's assumptions about my sexual orientation, I usually feel guilty. I see it as my responsibility as a well-supported, highly educated, and otherwise privileged person to do what many queer individuals cannot (for fear of family rejection, job loss, harassment, or physical harm), which is to inform others of the LGBQ presence in their lives and communities by being purposefully and vehemently out. But in the clinical realm, this responsibility in combination with the prescription of limited self-disclosure has resulted in quite a conflict for me in deciding whether or not to disclose my sexual identity in my role as a therapist.

Of course, individuals in the field deal with this issue in many different ways. Some psychologists advertise themselves as having a specialization with LGBQ clients. Others disclose their sexual orientation along with other professional and demographic information during initial sessions with clients. Other clinicians never disclose personal information about themselves, whether it is sexual identity, age, nationality, or any number of other demographic identifiers. This is a personal choice that every clinician makes for himself or herself, and one that psychotherapists (queer and otherwise) will need to make over and over again throughout their careers.

In my own clinical experience thus far, I have not yet disclosed my sexual orientation to a patient (a repeated decision that illustrates my reliance on and true belief in the psychoanalytic principles of careful thought over action). I *have* disclosed my openness to sexual diversity to clients through indirect methods, such as asking questions about sexual orientation and desire or posting a "Safe Zone" sign on my office door. However, for all this rigorous "neutrality," I have often questioned my decision to stay "in the closet" (or to remain a "blank screen," depending on how you look at it) to clients and have devoted several hours of therapy, supervision, and peer discussion to grappling with this issue. On several occasions I have experienced intense conflict about whether to disclose my sexual orientation in therapy. Oftentimes, these were situations in which the topic of sexual orientation was of particular importance to the patient with whom I was working. At other times, however, my conflict over disclosure had more to do with my overall connection with the client, and my sense that by allowing him or her to assume my heterosexuality, I was at worst lying to that person and at best remaining complicit with the heterosexism that allows for discrimination against sexual minorities.

One example of this discomfort occurred during my internship at a college counseling center where I co-led a process group of several female students. One of these young women, R, had come to the clinic in the midst of her coming-out process. From case conferences I knew that her individual treatment focused on her relationship with her emotionally manipulative girlfriend, her coming-out process with her family and friends, and her attempts to find her place at college as a lesbian. R was not out to the group, however, and never spoke of her girlfriend or sexual identity, focusing instead on her symptoms of anxiety in group sessions.

As the group continued and R became more comfortable participating, I found myself more and more uncomfortable with this situation. I felt stuck in my role as a group therapist, unable to acknowledge what seemed an obvious omission on R's part, and of course, on my own. For several weeks, I pondered over the group situation—R clearly did not feel comfortable sharing her sexual identity with the group, and it certainly wasn't my job to force her. But in knowing about her identity and still not sharing my own, I felt that I was doing more than "nothing." By staying silent on the subject, I was allowing the unspoken assumption of the group (that all the group members were straight) to go unchallenged. When other group members nonchalantly referred to "meeting guys" or feeling anxious "when guys are around," it seemed that R's silence, combined with my own, not only failed to inform the group of our presence as sexual minorities but also actively confirmed the other group members' assumptions that we were all straight. I couldn't help but feel that I was doing a disservice to R by neglecting to offer an alternative perspective to those presented by other group members. Additionally, what disservice might I have been doing to other clients in the group with nonnormative sexual identities or with questions about their attractions and desires?

Particularly frustrating was my feeling that I could not even acknowledge R's reticence on the subject of her sexual identity. Because I was not her individual therapist and her individual therapist did not see her in group, R's experience of individual and group treatment was completely separated, allowing her to handily split her experience (and identity) between the two. I never felt that a direct disclosure of my identity would have been appropriate, and yet, I felt obligated to do something and was uneasy with my lack of action. At the same time, this particular group had proved extremely challenging in other ways. Our membership was quite small and, although consistent attendance was an agreed-upon requirement in our group contract, we often had only two or three people show up for sessions. Building rapport had been a challenge, and many of the group members had difficulty over-coming their social anxiety and shyness in order to share anything at all.

Perhaps with a more talkative and close-knit group, I would have been able to find an intervention that would have opened up the conversation and allowed R the space to come out. Or perhaps an attuned and thoughtful intervention of this kind would have increased the group members' feelings of safety and facilitated more open communication in general. Whether it was my own inexperience, my relationship with my co-leader and supervisor, or the dynamics among the group members, I was never able to find an appropriate intervention to acknowledge the issue of sexual identity. As I struggled with this issue, I discussed it in supervision, didactic seminars, peer supervision, and therapy but never felt that I got satisfactory answers about how to deal with the situation. In the midst of my strongest feelings about the group, I found myself choosing a particular rainbow bracelet one morning while getting ready for work. In my feeling of impotence, I acted out my desire to connect with R and intervene, to show her that I recognized her and to be recognized in return. (This idea of "wearing your sexuality on your sleeve" is something I've found many queer individuals do in everyday per-sonal settings in order to be recognized by and included in their commu-nities.) I don't know if R or any of the other group members noticed my "acting out through accessories," but I do have a fantasy (or memory, I'm not sure which) of R's eyes lingering briefly on my wrist.

In our last group session, R brought up an issue with her "best friend" for the first time. She described a recent argument with her friend, and her concern that her friend had not spoken to her for nearly a week. It was clear to me that R's friend was actually her girlfriend, but I did not know what to do with this information in the context of the group. As the other group members advised R that if her friend did not come around the relationship was "probably not worth it," I managed a supportive comment or two, but ultimately felt unsatisfied as we ended the session and terminated for the year.

Another instance of conflict for me regarding identity disclosure occurred in my penultimate session with a thirty-five-year-old male patient, A, who'd been in twice-weekly treatment for about eighteen months. I was leaving my externship placement the next week, and we had spent several sessions pro-cessing termination. This man was one of my first long-term clients, and he worked hard in session, making steady gains throughout his treatment. Per-haps because of this, and because of our similar ages, I had many strong feelings for A and was feeling sad and overwhelmed by our upcoming termi-nation. A often tested boundaries with me by asking me personal questions and attempting to break the therapeutic frame (i.e., by asking to meet outside of therapy or to record our sessions, etc.).

As we discussed termination, he mentioned his frustration with never getting the chance to know "what [I] really thought about [him]" and wondered what I told my husband about him. I felt at once the tension that came along with A's sporadic boundary pushing, but there was something else as well. After all this time, after all the work we had done and the intimate rapport we'd established, A's assumption was a reminder that he really didn't know me, at least not at all in the way I had grown to know him. The comment brought the finality of our upcoming termination into sharp focus, making it clear that, as meaningful as our relationship had been and as much good as it had done us both, it remained a very specific, restricted kind of relationship, one in which I wouldn't be known in this fundamental aspect of my identity. Obviously, this is one of the realities of our work, and it would not have been appropriate for me to look for reciprocation in learning about me from A, but this is a lesson I've found is more difficult to learn in practice than in theory. This moment in particular helped me develop as a professional by giving me the very important experience of containing the weirdness of the therapeutic relationship.

In this instance, as with R in group, I didn't question whether to correct A about his assumption of my spouse's gender. I had taken a fairly strict, classical psychodynamic approach (through the tutelage of my supervisor) to his case, and a disclosure at that point in our relationship would not only have been unwarranted but also likely jarring to A, given the rest of our treatment. But I did feel ambiguous about it. My responsibilities as a psychologist had been fulfilled: I contained A's fantasies about me, facilitated his exploration of those fantasies, and helped to synthesize them with his understanding of himself and his important relationships. *But what of my ethical responsibilities to further social justice in my work as a psychologist (not to mention my personal dedication to these issues as an often "invisible" minority)?* As I terminated with A, I knew that he would be leaving with positive feelings about our work and about therapy, but I also knew that he wouldn't attribute those feelings to his relationship with a sexual minority. In the language of psychoanalysis, I had remained neutral, played close to the "blank screen," and prioritized the internal life of my patient over my own needs. But in the language of queer theory or gay rights, "staying in the closet" had made me complicit with the heterosexist assumption that everyone is straight and had denied the client an opportunity of experiencing a helping professional as someone who also happens to be queer.

Throughout my clinical training, I have tried to explain my conflict over this issue to several supervisors, classmates, and queer friends and have felt at a loss to express the importance of both sides of the issue, clinical and political. One important thing for sexual minorities (and other minorities) to remember while navigating graduate school is that your heterosexual (or white, abled, Christian, male, liberal, etc.) supervisors may not have the answers to your questions about the role of your minority status in clinical work. I have found that supervisors often find the intensity of my feelings about my sexual orientation difficult to understand, while queer friends without a psychology background find it tough to grasp the caution with which psychotherapists approach disclosures to clients. This isn't to say that I have not gained appropriate insight and support from my supervisors, but my experience of coping with these issues in my clinical training has been marked by an overall feeling of aloneness and separateness.

Whether to disclose one's sexual orientation (or any other identifying information) to clients is a complex, personal decision with no single "right" answer. Rather, choice points like this offer an opportunity for new (and experienced) therapists to explore their own emotions, defenses, theoretical beliefs, countertransferences, and conflicts on a deeper level that is closely linked with actual clinical decision-making. In other words, it is much less important what the clinician decides to disclose or not disclose than it is to think deeply, openly, and critically about these questions over time. In discussing my own struggles and thought processes in deciding whether and how to integrate my sexual identity into the therapy I provide, I offer one example of how to open oneself up to these questions and how to contain the inconclusiveness of the process. I expect to become more comfortable with my sexual identity vis-à-vis my clinical work as I gain more clinical experience, but I also know (and gladly welcome) that these are questions that will never be fully answered, and that will need to be returned to time and time again, like a good book that offers new insights with each read.

DEALING WITH IGNORANCE AND
HOMOPHOBIA FROM CLIENTS

One aspect of LGBQ clinical experience that most sexual-minority students expect, but which is worth mentioning anyway, is the inevitable eventuality of homophobic and/or ignorant comments made by clients. I have experienced a continuum of these comments throughout my training and expect to hear many more in the coming years. One client I met just last week indicated that she wasn't interested in attending Smith because "I'm just, I'm not a lesbian." She paused for a beat and chuckled to herself, saying, "It would just have been *too* much for me." In a different setting, another client, O, was attempting to explain his disgust with his girlfriend's desire to get a body piercing and commented, "It's like the gay rights thing. I mean, I have no problem with people doing . . . whatever they're into (with a tone that said, "And people are into some *disgusting* stuff!"), but don't look at me to—I mean, *I'm* not going to go be with a guy."

A particularly intense example of homophobic comments made by patients occurred during an anger-management group I led as part of an externship on an adolescent inpatient unit. One young man joked that every time someone has gay sex, "an angel dies." When my group co-leader reminded the patient of the unit policy about respectful language toward all groups of people, he responded that he "wasn't joking," and went on to express his understanding that gay men were criminals and child molesters. Working with adolescent clients comes with its particular challenges, of course, including taking a good helping of rude or hurtful comments in stride. However, learning a young person's terribly misinformed and hurtful beliefs about a minority group and feeling little ability to do anything about it can be distressing.

Because I know that homophobic and/or heterosexist comments are more likely to rile me than other topics my clients might discuss, I make careful note of my reactions to negative comments and try to remain curious about what these reactions might say about me *and* my patient. For instance, while I doubted that O consciously suspected that I was queer, I did have a sense that he was throwing several unattractive and judgmental ideas at me with the (unconscious) goal of testing my reactions. In previous sessions, O had described his annoyance with his girlfriend's parents, who would demean his interests and accomplishments and intrusively assert their own opinions. Perhaps, I thought, he had gleaned that I was liberal and open to diversity and wanted to see if I would try to force my beliefs on him, like his girlfriend's parents did.

O often felt insulted and belittled, and he defended against feelings of vulnerability with a rigid masculine gender presentation (he was a power lifter who struggled with bouts of road rage). I suspected that his assumption that gay-rights activists expected him to "get with a guy" represented another form of this vulnerability, as if he had so little control over his own sexuality that someone else could force him to be interested in having sex with men. (For O, as for many straight men, this type of reaction to gay individuals also likely represents a fear of his own repressed homosexual desires.) Given this understanding, I contained my own annoyance at my client's ignorant commentary and instead approached his comments with curiosity (they were curious, after all), encouraging him to explore the emotions that went along with his thoughts about body piercings and gay rights. Of course, "containing my annoyance" was a little more involved than this short phrase may imply. I also had to acknowledge my own biases and hateful thoughts regarding his comment. I watched myself writing my patient off as a low-class, ignorant, misogynist man for whom there was no hope. I struggled with my annoyance and assumptions about him for several weeks and spoke with my supervisor about my reactions. I made a conscious effort to allow space for O to grow and broaden, not only in reality but also in my perception of him. Several weeks into treatment, I began to see a thoughtful and surprisingly insightful side to O. He commented once, "I know that women have to deal with a lot, but men are expected to be strong and rational all the time, and it's tiring."

No less important in my clinical work were comments in support of LGBQ issues, such as, "I just don't get how the gay marriage thing is even an issue; love is love." Just like homophobic comments, I found that these comments struck a chord within me in a way that many others did not. I found myself liking clients who share my views and interests. But even these all-good feelings deserved acknowledgment and observation; a client's beliefs on any topic deserved exploration. If nothing else, my patients' comments regarding homosexuality, gay rights, or anything else reminded me to check in with my own feelings and countertransference about this particular person and our relationship.

WORKING WITH LGBQ INDIVIDUALS AS AN LGBQ THERAPIST

When working with LGBQ clients, I often felt a strong desire to join with them by disclosing my sexual identity. There can also be a pull to over-identify with queer clients as a queer therapist, equating their experiences of coming out, dating, developing their identities, and so forth, with one's own. For me, decisions about how and what to explore felt much more fraught with sexual-minority clients. My first experience with an out sexual-minority client was in therapy with a young bisexual woman whom I saw briefly on an inpatient unit. She mentioned coming out to her mother as bisexual very briefly during our first session and then never brought it up again. I remember feeling surprised and anxious about addressing the subject with her. I very much wanted to talk about her bisexuality, but how could I know that it would be a solid clinical decision to do so? I felt overwhelmed by the situation, when the decision about whether to bring up this issue with her again was probably relatively minor either way. I did bring it up with her again, which led to an exploration of her relationship with her mother and her understanding of her burgeoning sexual identity.

With other sexual-minority clients I have felt a sense of camaraderie and have often found that their reported experiences bring up memories and feelings related to my own sexual identity. For instance, one young queer-identified woman often discussed her community of LGBTQ friends at college, and I found myself nostalgic for my collegiate queer community and jealous of her connections to a world that was years in the past for me. It has been an important part of my experience of working with LGBQ individuals to monitor my feelings of identification with a client and to actively allow for LGBQ clients to have different experiences, beliefs, and identities than my own. However, I have also found that speaking with queer clients about their sexual-identity development, coming out, or experiences with discrimination is often particularly moving for me, because hearing these stories stirs up my own similar experiences. I have often felt privileged to work with LGBQ clients (though this is true of straight clients as well), in that I truly enjoy getting to know other individuals in my community and having the unique opportunity to learn from them by bearing witness to their lives and their resilience.

All in all, my experience as a queer woman and psychologist in training was one marked by curiosity, exploration, and a sharp learning curve. Coming into graduate school, I assumed I would be spending several years learning about how other people's minds functioned when actually I learned at least as much about my own mind. This is one of the best kept secrets about graduate psychology and about psychotherapy in general. Because we use ourselves as the instruments of our craft, much of the work we do as psychologists is work on ourselves. The experiences discussed within this chapter illustrate some of the work I have done to build a better understanding of myself as a sexual minority. Graduate school offers a time to explore your many beliefs, values, traits, quirks, and identities—a time to get to know yourself. It is hard work without a clear conclusion, even as you gain letters after your name and a license to hang up in your office. But learning to reflect on your emotions, reactions, biases, and beliefs is also rewarding; it leads to a life of choices and of meaning, to an existence in which you can connect more fully with others because you are connected with yourself.

NOTES

Names and identifying data were changed to disguise the identity of the persons involved.

1. Throughout this chapter, I use the terms queer and LGBQ (lesbian, gay, bisexual, and queer) somewhat interchangeably to describe my own identity and the sexual minority population in general. While this term has carried a negative connotation historically, it is currently accepted language within the academic and LGBQ community. Of course, many individuals in the LGBQ community do not identify as queer (or as L,G, or B, for that matter), and my use of these terms mostly amounts to linguistic shorthand. However, my usage does represent my own beliefs and identifications, since the term "queer" tends to invoke a social constructionist understanding of sexual attraction and desire and emphasize the "umbrella" community that includes many types of sexual minorities. I have also not included the "T" (for transgender) traditionally found in the "LGBTQ" acronym, since this chapter focuses on sexual orientation/identity and does not include a discussion of gender-identity issues.

Chapter Eleven

Finding My Place in Psychoanalysis as a Black, Female Student

Adjoa Osei

My White therapist lunged at me, moving quickly toward me with out-stretched arms. Naturally, I felt the need to protect myself. I pressed back into the rigid, hard-backed chair and instinctively hugged myself tightly. She hovered dangerously over me and leered. I felt like she was daring me to fight. I was helpless. I tried to yell, but only a weak whimper escaped my lips.

"You need to face the truth," she snarled.

"But . . . but, I don't know," I stammered.

I looked around the room for an escape. My heart was running a marathon in my chest, and I could barely breathe. The gray walls were closing in, and the pea-colored furniture blankly stared back at me. I was trapped in this prison of a room. My therapist leaned in closer. Her face was only a few inches from my mine, and her white skin glowed against my brown skin.

"You do know," she said in a softer tone.

I awoke with a jolt, covered in a thin layer of sweat. My eyes wildly scanned the room as I tried to determine my location. My dog peacefully slept in her bed. "Thank goodness, I'm home and not in that dreadful office," I thought. It was my therapist's first office, a cold, bland, and uninviting place that contrasted with my therapist's kind and animated nature. I was so pleased when she stopped using the shared offices at her postgraduate center and started renting her own place. Her new office was decorated with art-work and painted in orange and red tones, which was more reflective of her bubbly personality. Glancing at the clock, I realized I had only ten minutes to get ready for therapy. I dreaded being late, mainly because I did not want to waste precious therapy minutes analyzing my resistance and reasons for being late. Or at least that is what I consciously thought.

I began analytic therapy about a month after starting my academic program. At the start of my first semester, I began looking for a therapist, knowing that I would need support as I progressed through the program. I thought of asking a professor for recommendations but was concerned that it might not be appropriate to do so and was too scared to disclose that I needed help. I had not specifically sought to be in psychoanalysis. It was purely accidental and seemed like the most appealing option after speaking to several psychologists over the phone and experiencing unsuccessful first sessions with a few therapists. Another reason I pursued this course of treatment was so that I could be a training case for a low-cost fee. I reluctantly agreed over the phone to meet with a therapist three times a week for eighteen dollars per session, which I knew was a steal after contacting many therapists and being dismayed by fees that I could not afford.

My therapy sessions always started in the car. On the drive to the therapist's office, I practiced my opening line and reflected on how I would introduce my dream into the session. At this point I was in analytic therapy for a few months but was still uncomfortable with the idea of free association. I learned all my life to self-censor and to be cautious with my words. How could I possibly embrace the technique of saying whatever came to mind, especially when it was a disturbing thought like the one that occurred in my dream? It was in direct contrast to my desire to be polite and not offend others. Therefore, I was reluctant to spend forty-five minutes discussing how and why my therapist was portrayed in such an unflattering light, and I was also fearful of what the dream would say about me.

I envisioned Woody Allen and the ease with which he could descend into a neurotic rant. To me he was the poster child of psychoanalysis and the client I tried to emulate in therapy sessions. I put pressure on myself to be the good patient and felt like I needed to prepare subject matter and jokes for my therapy sessions. I wanted to be able to lie comfortably on the couch and fill the room with deep and profound thoughts that reflected a pathway to my unconscious. I wanted to be my therapist's favorite intellectual patient who had an insightful response to each interpretation.

As I entered her office, I felt my usual hesitancy about why I was in analytic therapy in the first place. How could I justify seeing a therapist three times a week when I was not in acute distress and was able to function fairly well, day-to-day? Was I one of the elite "worried well" that I secretly despised? As a Black woman, was psychoanalysis really for me? All these questions, wrapped in a blanket of guilt, swirled around in my mind. On one hand, my biases about the field of psychoanalysis were rooted in my own discomfort and beliefs that I held before entering the doctoral program and analytic therapy. On the other hand, my misconceptions were also grounded in the perceived elitism of the psychoanalytic tradition.

THE TYPICAL ANALYSAND:
WHITE, WEALTHY, EDUCATED

In its history and practice, psychoanalysis has often been viewed as a therapeutic method only for members of the elite. The analyzable and ideal client is often visualized as an individual who is White, wealthy, and educated. To a certain extent, the psychoanalytic tradition has reinforced this myth (Altman, 2004). While tending to and favoring the issues of the elite and privileged, the psychoanalytic tradition has largely been indifferent to people suffering from problems of poverty, oppression, and discrimination (Altman, 2004). This history of ambivalence with regard to classism, racism, and other forms of social oppression has implications for training future therapists and is important for understanding how psychoanalysis might appear inaccessible to students from minority groups. This perceived indifference might lead to therapists in training and who are not White to feel excluded from, and they may question their role within the analytic community. Through her work with graduate students in clinical psychology, McWilliams (2000) has found that graduate students often have little knowledge about psychoanalysis and hold common misconceptions about the analytic field.

As a Black woman and doctoral student, I had my own biases about the psychoanalytic tradition, doubted its accessibility, and questioned its relevance. The rest of this chapter will explore how psychoanalysis came to be perceived as an elitist enterprise, and I will present personal reflections as a student of color, including my ambivalence about joining a profession that is often perceived as "White" and my own early misconceptions about the analytic field. I will trace part of my journey through analysis and how it played a crucial role in broadening my perspective. I will further examine how dynamically oriented classes and personal analysis challenged my misconceptions and biases. In addition, this chapter will identify innovative and creative methods that were utilized in dynamically oriented classes. Through this personal account, I hope to provide hints for how to engage minority students who might feel isolated and marginalized within their academic programs.

PSYCHOANALYSIS AS A "WHITE THING"

Altman (2004) explored how psychoanalysis within the United States sought to define itself as a White privilege and how this movement was reflective of the influence of racism within this country. This formed association in the

United States between psychoanalysis and White privilege is significant considering the presence of anti-Semitic activity during Freud's lifetime. As noted by Gilman (1993), being Jewish meant being marked as different and the Jewish and African males were often considered threats to the White race. At times, Freud had even been labeled a Black Jew (Gilman, 1993). So what did psychoanalysis stand to gain in the United States by defining itself as a White privilege and as an elite practice? Was there a conscious or an unconscious wish to use psychoanalysis to move up the social ladder and symbolically make it a "White thing" to reap the perceived benefits of whiteness?

Ponder (2007) suggested that the perception of psychoanalysis as elitist and exclusionary in the United States is rooted in defending against feelings of marginalization and inadequacy, stemming from Freud and European psychoanalysts' experiences with prejudice, loss, and exclusion. Freud grew up in a culture that was patriarchal with prejudicial attitudes and behaviors toward women and Jews and Freud along with many other European psychoanalysts were forced to flee their homeland to escape the Holocaust. It is hypothesized that within the establishment of psychoanalysis there was an institutional and multigenerational transmission of these cumulative traumas (Ponder, 2007). Essentially, psychoanalytic institutes symbolized an enclave from these traumas and allowed for the development of theories, the transmission of knowledge, and provided support for pursuing a career within the field. In the United States, psychoanalysis was generally well received after Freud published his works and gave a series of lectures at Clark University. Psychoanalysis evolved into an elite specialty by aligning with the medical profession and many refugee analysts who immigrated to the United States assumed leadership roles in American psychoanalysis and supported high standards of training (Ponder, 2007). Considering the transmission of past traumas and the sense of safety provided by psychoanalytic institutions, a historical narrative of preserving the sanctity of psychoanalytic institutions might have been passed down in the development of American psychoanalysis. It is possible by continuing to brand psychoanalysis as elitist and being exclusionary with standards served as a way to protect identity and group membership, to reduce the possibility of experiencing prejudice, to reduce feelings of marginalization, and to defend against losses by achieving success.

Furthermore, Altman (2004) highlighted several factors that contributed to what he termed a blind spot in which race, class, and culture were avoided or excluded from clinical work and the psychoanalytic tradition. First, psychoanalysis in the United States adopted the principles and values of ego psychology, which emphasized individualism, tolerance for frustration, and abstaining from gratification. Therefore, psychotherapy became appealing and meaningful for those who accepted this Northern European and Calvinist value system. Second, psychoanalysts aligned themselves with the medical establishment and predominantly went into private practice. This resulted in psychoanalysis becoming a high-priced medical specialty, which meant that it was accessible mostly to White America and the privileged. In addition, with an individualistic and intrapsychic focus, psychoanalysts tended to ignore the social context, such as factors like poverty, discrimination, and oppression that could play a significant role in people's lives (Altman, 2004).

This bias toward privilege is reflected in the concept of analyzability. The term suggests that patients are being scanned for membership into an exclusive club and that in order to be successful in this form of treatment, they should possess certain qualities at the start of treatment. In addition to patient characteristics, certain syndromes might seem more suitable for psychoanalysis than others, which further contribute to a sense of elitism (Spiegel, 1970). In addition, the establishment of criteria for analyzability, based on Western values, such as verbal skills, emotional self-control, and psychological-mindedness often correspond to the degree of a person's enculturation into the Western ideal of selfhood (Walls, 2004). So where does that leave the person who does not fully embrace such Western values? Are they not analyzable?

WILL I HAVE TO WHITEWASH MYSELF AGAIN?

The aforementioned view of psychoanalysis as an elitist field and practice was firmly imprinted on my mind when I entered my doctoral program and began analytic therapy. As a Ghanaian-American, I have spent my life walking the line between adopting Western values and embracing an Afrocentric perspective. In the world of academe, I learned that I had to either mute my "blackness" or leave it outside of the classroom to fly under the radar and avoid ruffling feathers. For most of my academic career, I was in the minority as a Black woman and often felt isolated socially and estranged from the curriculum. Gay (2004) said that marginalization is a major issue for graduate students of color and highlighted three aspects of marginalization that occur within doctoral programs: isolation, benign neglect, and problematic popularity. Graduate students of color are often physically, culturally, and intellectually isolated due to their minority status within the program. The majority of their academic peers do not share their racial and ethnic backgrounds, and few professors of color are present within their academic departments. In addition, students of color are usually exposed to a curriculum with a Eurocentric, male bias and are often unintentionally excluded from intellectual discussion. Benign neglect occurs when faculty question or invalidate research focused on ethnic and cultural differences and avoid giving constructive feedback to minority students due to a fear of being perceived as prejudiced. Problematic popularity reflects how graduate students of color are often placed in a position to promote diversity within the academic program and considered to be representative of their racial, ethnic, or cultural group. For example, students of color are asked to represent diversity on committees and called to make guest appearances in classrooms. Oftentimes, consideration is not given to whether students have the competencies to complete these tasks and students may feel that they are placed within in a position in which they cannot turn down these invitations due to potential negative consequences (Gay, 2004).

Throughout my academic career, I experienced these different aspects of marginality that Gay (2004) described. I became accustomed to not having my perspective represented, to hearing lectures and discussions that overlooked issues related to people of African descent, and to being designated as the token for the entire Black community. To not further alienate myself, I was cautious in my classroom participation, avoided using slang, and tried not to speak too passionately about issues related to race so that I would not be labeled as angry. For example, I vividly remember an incident from my master's program: an awkward silence ensued after I presented a paper on the lack of diversity in research on evidence-based treatments, followed by dismissive comments from my classmates. They minimized the findings of my research and suggested that studies were already including diverse groups of participants, despite my research reflecting that this was not necessarily true. I noticed that my other classmates' presentations went unchallenged and did not bring about the same type of reactions and comments. While I do not believe my classmates were purposefully trying to be malicious, I was taken aback by their resistance and the ease with which they dismissed my presentation, partly because it was an uncomfortable topic. I expected my classmates, who consisted of master's-level and doctoral students, to be more open-minded and willing to discuss issues related to race and ethnicity, since we were being encouraged to take into account the influence of society and culture. Subsequently, I found that I withdrew from classroom discussions and avoided bringing up topics related to race. Not surprisingly, upon entering the doctoral program, I wondered about the racial climate and inclusiveness of the curriculum. Would I have to whitewash my academic self again in order to fit in? I wondered whether I would be seen as a psychologist in training or a Black psychologist in training and how would I define and label myself. It was with this apprehension that I entered into my first dynamically oriented class and delved into a complicated relationship with psychoanalysis.

DIFFICULTIES WITH FREUD

Through teaching, McWilliams (2000) found that graduate students often have little knowledge about psychoanalysis and hold common misconceptions about the analytic field. Some common misconceptions were:

• Analysts are cold and narcissistic.
• Analysts are arrogant and regard other orientations with disdain.
• Analysts are White, upper-middle class, and male and are insensitive to ethnic, cultural, racial, and social diversity.
• Analysts idolize Freud.
• Psychoanalysis has been empirically discredited.

She suggested that due to this current anti-analytic climate, psychoanalysts need to adapt their training and supervisory practices to make the field more accessible (McWilliams, 2000).

Prior to starting my classes and training, I did not have any knowledge about the differences among theoretical orientations, but I did hold several misconceptions about psychoanalysis. My beliefs were primarily based on Freudian references in pop culture and my exposure to Woody Allen movies. I thought psychoanalysis was a luxury for the elite and that the field consisted primarily of White analysts and patients. I also thought that there was a lack of empirical support for psychoanalytic theories. In my master's program in general psychology, I had not taken a class that was primarily taught from a dynamic perspective, so I felt wholly unprepared for the journey of my first dynamically oriented course in adult psychopathology. Prior to this class, I remember talking with a fellow classmate about her graduate program, which was primarily analytic. She named theorists I had never heard of, and I felt ashamed about my lack of knowledge so I pretended to know them.

Each week as I read and prepared for this class, I felt like an imposter and questioned whether I was competent enough to be in the program. While I found the class to be intriguing and engaging, I was having difficulty keeping up. I assumed that my colleagues readily grasped and understood the material and that I always two steps behind them. A classmate would make an insightful comment, and I would wonder why I had not thought of that idea. I read and re-read articles, highlighted every other sentence, and filled the margins with question marks. I dreaded being called on and frequently rehearsed preplanned comments in my mind during classroom discussions. As we further explored classical psychoanalytic literature, I felt more and more distanced from the material and questioned the universality of the theories being presented for people of color. Would my voice and experience be represented in this class? Based on past academic experiences, I was hesitant to bring up issues of cultural diversity and debated the relevance of these theories in silence. I shrugged off psychoanalysis as being a "White thing."

My feelings of inferiority and isolation were challenged the day we did a group reading of a paper by Freud. As usual, my professor asked a question about the assigned reading and I patiently waited for one of my classmates to make an insightful comment before I would respond with my thoughts and try to join the majority opinion. However, this time an awkward silence developed in the room. I looked around and saw blank faces that matched my facial expression. Was it possible that I was not the only one who did not understand Freud? Sensing our discomfort, the professor suggested that we read the article aloud as a group. As we stumbled through the reading, I felt like I bonded with my classmates, and the group activity reduced my feelings of isolation and distancing that I experienced when I read alone. By working together to understand the assigned material, we were given the opportunity to question line by line, challenge, and place Freud's theories within a social context. This approach also allowed me to observe that all of us were struggling to a certain extent with some form of imposture syndrome. We were all questioning our competency and faking it till we made it. In addition, I recognized that each of us came in with our own beliefs and biases and that I was not the only one trying to establish and clarify my viewpoint through a dynamic lens.

Another significant event that initially broadened my perspective and reflected McWilliams's (2000) argument that the teaching techniques of psychoanalytic literature need to be more diverse was my experience with the midterm and final exams assigned by my adult psychopathology professor. When I heard that the midterm would consist of essays, I expected that I would need to regurgitate concepts from the assigned readings and prove my understanding of them. However, I was pleasantly surprised by creative questions that allowed for the dissecting of assigned readings and for the creation of fictional characters diagnosed with mental illnesses through journal entries and role-plays. The assignment brought the literature alive, took away the pressure to conform to a certain school of thought, and allowed me to transform the clinical material into a medium that helped me to better understand it. Who wouldn't want to jump at the chance to write a short story about perversions as a graded assignment? I still chuckle when I think about creating the character "Brian Wellington," a former childhood-reality star who roamed the streets with his video camera, and how this exercise helped me to understand how trauma could relate to voyeurism.

A SURPRISE FROM MY ANALYST

Things were also improving in my therapist's office. After being in therapy for a few months, I was slightly more comfortable with letting my thoughts roam freely around my analyst's room. However, I was still hesitant to criticize or express negative feelings toward my therapist. I kept ruminating about the transference dream I described earlier in which my therapist appeared so threatening. Although, I believed that we had successfully analyzed the dream and come up with several themes that were relevant to my presenting problem, there was another level to the dream that I sensed needed exploration. I could not find the words to describe what was still puzzling me about the dream, so I kept my thoughts to myself. However, I noticed that as my therapist became more friendly and talkative and deviated from my expectations that she act cold and distant, the more irritated I became with her. Each session, the questions, "Who are you?" and "Why are you so friendly?" danced around in my head. Even her laughter struck an uncomfortable chord within me. It was as if I wanted her to serve as an object within the room and not engage me beyond a superficial level. I only wanted to talk at her and exchange brief pleasantries.

One day, I arrived to my session with the usual discomfort weighing heavily on my mind. I heard two voices speaking Spanish in the hallway. One voice I recognized as belonging to a member of the male housekeeping staff, who always greeted me warmly when I entered the building. The other voice was a recognizable woman's voice that I, nevertheless, did not recognize. As I turned the corner, I briefly froze as I saw that it was my therapist engaging in conversation in the hallway. Wait a minute! She is fluent in Spanish? I gave a half-hearted smile and quickly scurried into the waiting room. How did she learn to speak Spanish so well? I avoided bringing it up in session and came to the conclusion that she must have done a study-abroad program.

The next session, I arrived with a cup of coffee, which was unusual for me. I explained to my therapist that I was sensitive to caffeine, but was drinking the coffee to stay awake for an assignment that I needed to complete that night. She remarked how growing up in Argentina, she had been drinking coffee since she was a child and was practically immune to its effects. ARGENTINA! The word did leap in my mind. My White therapist was not so white! Why did I assume she was White? She saw the shocked expression on my face and inquired about it. I started to free-associate about what occurred last week when I witnessed her speaking Spanish and recalled my transference dream. The image of her glowing white skin came to mind, and I connected it to my fear that her whiteness would contaminate me and that I had to whitewash myself to fit into analysis and my academic program. I also discussed cross-racial therapy and my desire to keep her at distance. She reflected my concerns about how someone from a different racial group might not be able to understand my experience as a Black woman and for that reason I might have a tendency to avoid the topic of race during our sessions. This dialogue was significant in that it gave words to my feelings of "otherness" and allowed me to connect on a deeper level with my therapist through the disclosure of her ethnicity. It revealed that the analytic space had room for me as a Black woman, and I no longer viewed psychoanalysis as just a "White thing."

BLACK PSYCHOANALYSTS EXIST

As I entered into my clinical psychology in the public interest course, I found that I was more ready to acknowledge that analytic therapy could be beneficial for minority groups and underserved populations. I had successfully completed my first semester and was gaining some confidence in making my thoughts and opinions known during classroom discussions. Therefore, I was excited as I looked over the syllabus for this course and saw a range of readings focusing on social justice, White privilege, and marginalized groups. I had no idea what I was in for, however, and my excitement waned as our classroom discussions became more emotionally charged and difficult.

I believe the course was taught through a critical psychology and psychoanalytic lens, and this professor made it clear that we had to go further than reciting what we learned from the readings. He wanted us to think and then think about our thinking. It was refreshing and scary at the same time. We were expected to make our opinions explicitly known and apply the readings to current social issues. While this class was demanding, and I squirmed in my seat each week, I greatly appreciated being exposed to current psychoanalytic literature and to hearing diverse voices represented in the room. I craved to hear about multicultural issues and from authors who were not White and male, and that need was often gratified in this class. By the end of this course, I had moved past the idea of psychoanalysis as a luxury and began to critically examine its application to people of color and underserved populations. It was in this course that I developed my research interests in racial-identity development and recruitment and retention of minority doctoral students.

My embrace of the psychoanalytic world was strengthened by my first year of dynamic supervision in the training clinic. Despite having only a few dynamic sessions with clients throughout the year, I had many enriching discussions with my community supervisor. In particular, I appreciated how he brought up the topic of cross-racial therapy and acknowledged my concerns about being a therapist of color. This discussion signaled to me that it was safe to talk about race in this supervisory relationship. In addition, I found it helpful to do case conceptualizations with my dynamic supervisor on other clients whom I was working with in different treatment modalities. The additional viewpoint allowed me to reflect on transference and counter-transference reactions, and this level of processing allowed me to better tailor therapeutic interventions, regardless of orientation. I grew to treasure our weekly meetings.

Along with dynamic supervision, an event sponsored by the Institute for Psychoanalytic Training and Research (IPTAR) cemented my belief that I could find some space in the analytic world. One Saturday morning, I received two separate emails from my professors. At first, I felt the initial panic that I missed an assignment, but then I realized that they were merely forwarding me information about an event labeled, "Black Psychoanalysts Speak." Obviously, I was thrilled to hear of a panel of Black psychoanalysts reflect on their training and clinical experience. There is such a thing as a Black psychoanalyst! As I imagined, the event was a validating experience as I listened to panel members discuss positive aspects of their analytic training, but also describe the challenges and discrimination they faced within their training institutions. I met two of my classmates at the event and was also pleasantly surprised to see one of my professors there. Her presence reflected to me she had a genuine interest and was committed to exploring issues and topics related to cultural diversity. I truly felt like I had arrived, and my foot was firmly planted in the dynamic world.

THE POWER OF AN INTERPRETATION

Two years into analytic therapy, I was comfortably settled into my role as an analysand. I perfected a relaxed posture on the couch, angled the pillows in the right position, and learned how to let my feet slightly dangle off of the couch. My eyes easily closed as soon as I sank into my therapist's couch, and I happily descended into my unconscious. I was under the impression I had become a pro at this free-association thing. I filled the room with thoughts and theories at a rapid pace and reflected on my behavior. I grew more comfortable with discussing transference and how it played out in our therapeutic relationship.

But still, I was bothered by my need to engage in an unnecessary daily ritual of counting to four in anxiety-provoking situations without fully understanding its purpose. It was a ritual that caused as much as anxiety as it did relief and I had a strong desire to rid myself of it. Despite the annoyance, it provided such comfort that I was ambivalent about giving it up. I talked at length with my therapist about it in our latest session, but I rarely heard her responses through my ruminating thoughts.

"In some ways, you need it to protect you," she said when I paused to take a breath.

"So I just . . . wait, what . . ." I responded.

"In some ways, you need it to protect you," she repeated.

Her interpretation punched through my monologue and I found that I was unable to continue my original train of thought. Had she said this before? Protection? Protection from what? What did it mean? "You need it to protect you." The words chipped away at my exterior and sunk deeply into my body. They resonated with me, and I struggled to describe how and why. We discussed the themes of safety and protection for the rest of the session. It was not until I get home that I realized I had taken her words home with me. "You need it to protect you." Weeks later, I realized that I had stopped performing the ritual with ease. I did not experience any anxiety, and there was no struggle. Instead, I remarked to myself that I did not need this form of protection anymore. I had created my desired safe place within my therapist's room.

While I have done numerous readings on psychoanalytic techniques and the power of interpretations, I now had a deeper level of understanding when I experienced the benefits of analysis for myself. The ability to confront a symptom through insight and understanding and to use interpretation to change a maladaptive behavior was two things I grew to treasure.

I AM A BLACK PSYCHOLOGIST IN TRAINING

So where do I stand today? Have I found my place within psychoanalysis? I cannot say that I have fully unpacked and settled in. Instead, I feel like a visitor who is allowed to come and go as she pleases with a loaned key. However, I do dream of pursuing analytic training in the future but struggle with whether I would be fully accepted as a Black woman. Will I have to leave part of my identity outside of the training institution? Will my voice truly be heard and represented? Recently, I attended the annual convention of the Association of Black Psychologists (ABPsi). I felt empowered by presentations that centered on people of African descent and on research and clinical work conducted through an Afrocentric perspective. I wondered why I had to go outside of my academic program to gain more insight into Black psychology, and I felt slightly bitter about the dearth of diversity within my program. However, the experience did cause me to reflect on my theoretical orientation and return back to my initial struggle about whether I was a psychologist in training or a Black psychologist in training. Currently, I see myself as a Black psychologist in training who embraces a dynamic orientation, yet views her work through a psychoanalytic and Afrocentric lens. I am working toward building a safe space within my academic institution, but I have also anchored myself in an outside organization, ABPsi, that I believe represents and advocates for my interests as a Black woman and trainee. Despite my continued reservations and criticisms, my love affair with psychoanalysis continues, and I hope one day to be able to label myself as a Black psychoanalyst.

REFERENCES

Altman, N. (2004). History repeats itself in transference-countertransference. *Psychoanalytic Dialogues, 14*(6), 807–15. doi:10.1080/10481881409348807

Gay, G. (2004). Navigating marginality en route to the professoriate: Graduate students of color learning and living in academia. *International Journal of Qualitative Studies in Education, 17*(2), 265–88. doi:10.1080/09518390310001653907

Gilman, S. L. (1993). *Freud, race, and gender.* Princeton, NJ: Princeton University Press.

McWilliams, N. (2000). On teaching psychoanalysis in antianalytic times: A polemic. *The American Journal of Psychoanalysis, 60*(4), 371–390. doi: 10.1023/A:1002046915249

Ponder, J. (2007). Elitism in psychoanalysis in the USA: Narcissistic defense against cumulative traumas of prejudice and exclusion. *International Journal of Applied Psychoanalytic Studies, 4*(1), 15-30. doi: 10.1002/aps.119

Spiegel, R. (1970). Psychoanalysis: For an elite? *Contemporary Psychoanalysis, 7*(1), 48–63. doi: 10.1080/00107530.1970.10745189

Walls, G. B. (2004). Toward a critical global psychoanalysis. *Psychoanalytic Dialogues, 14*(5). 605–34. doi: 10.1080/10481880409353129

Chapter Twelve

From the Closet to the Clinic

An Orthodox Jewish Man
Comes Out in Training

Jeremy Novich

"You will leave this program different from the way you are now," warned one of the faculty members on my first day of orientation to graduate school for clinical psychology. Psychologists almost never guarantee outcomes and are hesitant to predict the future, but this strong assertion was made with a calm grounded in unwavering confidence. She had seen students enter and exit the program for almost twenty years and knew that change was inevitable.

She was right. My journey through graduate school was professionally stimulating and personally transformative. I entered as a young, bright, handsome, Orthodox Jewish man with traditional values and a conservative perspective—an eligible bachelor for some sprightly, Orthodox woman. By the time the internship application process rolled around in my fourth year, however, the picture had changed. I believe my positive physical and character attributes remained intact after three years of stressful doctoral training, but I was no longer a typical, Jewish bachelor; rather, I had become an openly gay, Orthodox Jew.

As I gain life experience and engage in personal reflection, I find that I have no single, comprehensive story of coming out of the closet. Instead, my story unfolds across multiple contexts and time periods and can be understood from various perspectives. However, in the pages that follow I will focus on the segment of my coming out process that occurred during my first three years of doctoral training.

EARLY DEVELOPMENT AND RELIGIOUS TRAINING

My first inklings that I was a gay occurred when I was fourteen, but I swiftly swept these feelings under the rug because they had no name that I knew. I questioned my sexual orientation again at around sixteen. At the time I was seeing a mental health professional, and he explained that having attraction to men at my age did not necessarily indicate that I was gay. He noted that experiencing attraction to people of both sexes was somewhat common for straight people, adding that sexuality is still in flux until the early twenties. This provided me some relief. I realize now that at the time of that early therapy, the idea of being gay terrified me. My therapist sensed my anxiety and offered me welcome respite from that doom.

After graduating high school, I took up religious studies for a year and a half in an all-male institution in Israel. Though I experienced attraction to various peers during that period, I was mostly consumed by the enormous tension I felt as a result of the religious values inculcated by the school. However, my behavior did evidence my gay identity. For example, I once attended a question-and-answer session with a rabbi at the school during which students submitted questions anonymously on index cards. The rabbi read each question and answered it. Although questions could be asked on any topic, this session traditionally served as a time during which students could ask the details about the Jewish laws concerning sex. Are there preferred positions for the man and woman? Can one have intercourse more than one time per night? Must the lights be out? Anonymity gave this exercise a certain entertainment value—we were a bunch of eighteen- and nineteen-year-olds—so I decided to submit the following unusual question: Can two men make out, provided there is no penetration? There was a loud uproar from the audience, and the question was never answered. It certainly shocked people. At the time, I thought I submitted the question as an act of rebellion against the institution. However, I now realize that the content of my question was anything but random. In addition to expressing general contempt for the school's religious philosophy, I was also specifically interested in Orthodoxy's view of same-sex intimacy. There was seriousness to my question of which I was unaware.

COLLEGE DAYS IN THE CLOSET

During college, I was immersed in the Orthodox Jewish community, even taking a high-level leadership position in a campus organization. I remained closeted to myself and dated a few women for short stints. My attraction to them felt forced, but something about being in a relationship with a woman seemed exciting. During this time, I was still attracted to men, both physically and emotionally. My friendships had a romantic feeling to me, though I did not recognize what this meant until later.

My roommate in my senior year, who remains today one of my best friends, helped open my eyes. Following one of our daily fights, he said, "Jeremy, I love being your friend, but this is starting to feel like a romantic relationship." His words pierced me. I was terrified, disgusted, angry, and also relieved—finally, here were the words that perfectly described how I related to my roommate, albeit unconsciously. For me, it *was* romantic. My roommate, a kind, thoughtful, patient, and extraordinarily accepting person, told me that to him it did not matter whether I was gay or straight. On that spring evening in 2008, I began a conscious effort to do something with my sexuality other than ignore it. My roommate was one of two people I spoke to about my dilemma before I began graduate school.

PERMISSION TO EXPLORE THE LGBT LIFESTYLE

By July 2009 I was enrolled in my graduate program but still living with my parents. One day, while sitting at the computer in my home office, I received an email from a co-leader of Safe Zone, a required, year-long, student-run, LGBT (Lesbian, Gay, Bisexual, Transgender) sensitivity training program for first-year students. We were instructed to choose a movie to watch from a list provided by Safe Zone, in preparation for the first meeting on September 9. I was puzzled by my excitement about this activity. I chose the movie *Shelter* and asked my father to order the film for me from Netflix for school.

After the movie arrived, my father asked me,

"Jeremy, are you ready to watch *Shelter*?"

"Um . . . I don't think you want to watch that with me, Abba. It's gay cinema."

Although I was slightly anxious during this exchange, given the personal meaning of the film, I also felt calm because I knew that I was watching the movie for school. In essence, I had a free pass to watch a gay film. I watched the movie twice and identified with the main character while simultaneously falling in love with him. I was strongly impacted by the film—less isolated and more hopeful—but to others it looked like I was simply doing my home-work.

TENTATIVE EXPLORATIONS OF A NEW IDENTITY

On Wednesday morning, September 9, 2009, I sat in my first class of gradu-ate school. Approximately twenty peers arranged themselves around a long table in a conference room for a course in developmental psychology. The instructor went around the room and asked us to share an important moment in our development. One of the first few students stated with bold confidence: "Coming out to my parents." A visceral reaction to this student and his disclosure left me feeling anxious, annoyed, resentful, and, perhaps most of all, jealous. Part of me wished I could be where he was.

Nevertheless, I began exploring my gay identity in that first semester, in my choice of paper topics for my child psychopathology course. We were asked to examine a contemporary social issue from a theoretical perspective and then present it to the class. I enthusiastically took on the issue of suicide among gay youth and argued that in the mix of causative factors are religion and government policies. In presenting my paper to the class, I wondered if anyone suspected that my topic was cathected with personal meaning. My second assignment for this course was a research proposal for a study design to test a hypothesis. The title was "The Benefits of Online Communities for Religious and Secular Gay Youth." While working on this paper, I joined an online listserv for Orthodox and formerly Orthodox Jewish gay youth. I used an academic cloak to hide my contemplation of my emerging gay identity.

In the spring semester of that first year, I was enrolled in "Clinical Psychology in the Public Interest: Social Justice/Human Rights." This class discussed, among other things, the rights of women and sexual minorities. I raised my hand and somewhat nervously threw out this question: "What about gay people in religious communities? Those people suffer tremendously." I was removing my academic cloak, leaving myself open to ridicule. As I sat there feeling very vulnerable, my teacher remarked, "*those* people," pointing out how I had distanced myself from those "others."

This made me angry. His critique of my language and presumption of my judgment of gay "others" overlooked the content of what I had said. At the very least, my statement should have been seen as an expression of empathy for a marginalized group and could also have been understood as an enormous personal disclosure. My professor's reaction was both infuriating and enlightening. I learned that as a yarmulke-wearing Orthodox Jew, I was presumed to hold certain beliefs and to be straight. Although these assumptions were not all that different from those held by members of the Orthodox community, they were helpful in the Orthodox world because they protected me from suspicion. In my liberal graduate program that focused on social justice, however, these assumptions about my viewpoint and orientation were stigmatizing and painful. The place that I expected to be open to and supportive of complicated identities was not giving me sufficient space to grow. These assumptions about my beliefs and orientation became problematic as I was misunderstood and seen as "the enemy."

In the summer of 2010 tension related to my gay identity arose again, when a group of students met with a faculty member to plan a combined research and clinical project. Each student therapist had to fill out a demographic questionnaire, which included an item asking about sexual orientation. I was outraged that a program that touted sensitivity toward sexual minorities would ask such a question. I raised my hand and gently requested that the question be removed. My openly gay classmate, however, took the opposite viewpoint, arguing that to not measure sexual orientation was to delete "his data." My objection sounded purely theoretical because it was not clear to others that anything personal was at stake. In truth, the inclusion of this item was inconsequential to the other students, except for me and the other gay man. Without hearing a convincing argument from me, the group and faculty member decided to let the item stand with the option for students to omit items to which they objected. This left me furious and disappointed. I was unable to fully speak my mind and did not feel that others were trying to understand me. I felt unsupported and misunderstood.

As the summer wore on, I felt more stifled by the strictly online nature of my gay identity. I was using a pseudonym and separate email account that could be deleted with a few clicks of the mouse. Nonetheless, I increasingly felt the need to meet other gay, Jewish men from the Orthodox community. The organization operating the listserv offered small coffee meetings to new members before they attend the larger monthly meetings. The idea of joining a small meeting was both attractive and terrifying. Thinking about meeting a group of gay, Jewish men made me sweat and have trouble swallowing. What if I met somebody I knew? What if word got out? What if my parents found out? Somehow I mustered the courage to go to a meeting and survived it. In fact, I felt amazingly triumphant afterward, because I was on my way to overcoming what no longer seemed like an insurmountable obstacle.

In the fall of 2010, I came out to one of my classmates, another Orthodox man. His response was remarkable and helpful. A close friend and an even closer friend after, he did not shun me, criticize me, or distance himself. Instead, he asked with utmost openness and sincerity, "What's it like?" After we spoke for a while, I felt, without a doubt, that he was on my side. A few months later, I paced back and forth in our training clinic unable to decide whether to attend a community-wide LGBT Chanukah party that evening. This was a large event, and my fear of being discovered and outed was powerful and paralyzing. The back of my head was literally in painful knots. Still closeted, I could not talk to most of my classmates. I called my Orthodox classmate, and he said, "If you go, you might have a good time, or you might regret it, but if you don't go, you will definitely regret it." His advice was immensely helpful, and I attended the party, feeling proud of my accomplishment and thankful for my friend.

In the second year of the doctoral program, it was time for me to follow the almost universal recommendation for psychologists in training—which is to begin one's own therapy. In my first session I said: "I'm coming here under the guise of being a second-year doctoral student who is supposed to be in therapy once he is seeing patients, but really I am Orthodox, gay, and in the closet." I spent a lot of time in therapy obsessing and mourning. I felt like a commuter inside a subway station, standing at the turnstile and pondering whether to exit. If I owned my gay identity, there would be no turning back. If I left the closet, I could not return and would be forever exposed. Over the next few years, therapy helped me own my identity, join the Orthodox Jewish and larger LGBT community, and come out to the world and my parents.

IDENTITY AND THE THERAPIST-PATIENT DYAD

I was not only a patient, however; I also began to be a therapist. One of my first patients, a man in his early-forties, came to therapy complaining of intractable, chronic depression. He lived with his disabled father whose needs had to be met, no matter the consequence. He took care of others while neglecting himself and putting up with ungratefulness from his father and absorbing teasing from co-workers. This patient forgave everybody to suppress his anger. Our relationship took on a complexity that could not be attributed to the patient's clinical presentation or my therapeutic style. During our first session, this devout Mormon said, honestly and matter-of-factly, "I'm gay, and I've always hated that about myself." I both appreciated his honesty and detested his attitude toward our shared sexual identity. He reported being celibate and discussed the religious reasons for not acting according to his nature and making physical love with other men. He contrasted his religious observance with that of his younger cousin, who was also gay and had a lot of "promiscuous gay sex." He spoke with true condemnation about being gay and living as such.

During the treatment period, I was on my own journey of exploring and coming to terms with my sexuality and slowly sharing this part of myself with trusted others. Hating myself for being gay, committing to celibacy and labeling same-sex relations as promiscuous was the place I was trying to escape from. My relationship with religion had been strained for a number of years because of my experience in the religious institution mentioned earlier and because I was at odds with other aspects of Orthodox Judaism. As a result, I saw my patient as indoctrinated and contaminated by the harmful aspects of religion. Of course, we barely discussed his sexuality in therapy. Exploration and open examination of his gay identity was not on his to-do list. To him, the fact of being gay was an unfortunate reality of his life.

Every week during this brief treatment, I was required to meet with my supervisor, the instructor who earlier on highlighted my "otherizing" language when I spoke of gay, religious people. My awareness of his commitment to equality for LGBT people and his strongly held negative views of religion as the source of LGBT oppression made supervision anxiety-inducing for me, a yarmulke-wearing, publicly Orthodox Jew. Yet another part of me was comforted by the yet-unrealized safety of supervision—as this supervisor was an LGBT ally. I had a desperate desire to say, "Look, I am gay, too. And not all religion is bad." Unfortunately, I did not feel free to talk about my sexual orientation and how that impacted the treatment.

INCHING OUT OF THE CLOSET

Meanwhile, my involvement in the Orthodox gay community was increasing. After some gentle pushing from an Orthodox LGBT community organizer at the aforementioned Chanukah party, I hesitantly agreed to come to the first-ever retreat for Orthodox LGBT Jews. My anxiety increased as the retreat approached, and I was plagued by doubt. Would they like me? Would I fit in? Was this really me? If not, who was I? I knew that the best way to tackle my fears was to go to the retreat and tolerate the anxiety. So much seemed to be at stake, and I still feared being outed. But I went through with my plan, and during that weekend in January I spoke with a number of people at meals, in group discussions, and during activities. I heard about their journeys and was impressed by their resilience, strength, and integrity. The diversity of stories comforted and calmed me, and I realized that I had to write my own story of being gay and following traditional Judaism.

On Saturday night, after Shabbat (Sabbath) had ended, the retreat participants enjoyed a talent show. With sweaty palms, racing thoughts, and a dry throat, I found myself debating whether to try the stage. I had done standup comedy before, but this venue was different—a talent show at the first LGBT retreat for Orthodox Jews. Though my attendance at the event was a milestone in my identity development, I felt out of place. My courage won out, however, and I got on stage. Sans microphone and in front of a packed room, I belted out at the top of my lungs, "My name is Jeremy Novich, and I am from the closet!" The audience laughed, and I had connected. Days after I returned from the retreat, I still walked with a new sense of freedom, pride, and comfort in my selfhood. I knew I had a community behind me and friends to call on for support. The anxiety, worry, and fear that occupied a significant part of my life before the retreat had been replaced with peace, security, and newfound meaning. Like a pivot in a martial arts routine, the retreat helped me change direction, opening up a whole new vantage point and set of options.

Two weeks after the retreat, I was back in my supervisor's apartment on the Upper West Side. We did not discuss my patient during the meeting because no therapy session had taken place. But I desperately wanted to tell my supervisor about my weekend. "Okay, we have to stop," remarked my supervisor, which was his typical way of ending our meetings.

"May I make one doorknob statement on my way out?"

He answered in the affirmative.

"I just wanted to say that two weeks ago I went to a retreat for gay Orthodox Jews."

"Okay. Thank you for sharing," responded my supervisor.

I got up from my chair, walked across the apartment, and grabbed the doorknob to leave. That's when my supervisor said,

"Uh . . . Jeremy, that's the closet." A brief analytic pause ensued, and he added, "Why would you want to go back in there?"

We both laughed hysterically. Finally, my gay-self, psychologist-self, and religious-self were becoming one.

As time wore on, the assumptions that I was straight hurt me more and more. My aforementioned gay classmate and I agreed to run an LGBT support group for college students during our second-year externship, but I was still closeted to him, most of my class, and all of the faculty except for the supervisor already mentioned. My classmate and I met with our group supervisor, and she said, "I'm not going to beat around the bush: your yarmulke." I appreciated her pointing to the elephant in the room and indirectly asking why a visibly Orthodox Jewish man should co-lead an LGBT support group. I explained that I might provide a corrective emotional experience to the group as someone who was religious and an LGBT ally. Nevertheless, the supervisor, concerned about the possibility that my yarmulke would be an obstacle to recruitment, decided that she wanted "a different face" for the group. I graciously respected her viewpoint during our meeting. However, inside I was boiling with anger as I was marginalized by my supervisor. I was viewed as straight and threatening to LGBT people because I was an Orthodox Jew. Most infuriating to me was that being openly Orthodox and privately gay was beginning to cost me meaningful professional opportunities. After this meeting, I came out to my openly gay classmate. It was calming to finally speak with a gay man with whom I shared a friendship prior to coming out to him.

My vacillating feelings about coming out continued into the spring semester of 2011, when it was time to pick a dissertation topic. The teacher in my research methods course advised us that we could benefit the most from the course if our research proposal, which we would work on all semester, was the same as our dissertation proposal. Since writing had already proved to be a meaningful way for me to express my gay self without formally coming out, I chose to write about the experiences of LGBT people in the Orthodox Jewish community. Over the course of the semester, my teacher read between the lines of my outlines and drafts. I finally told her that I was gay, which accounted for my interest in the topic. She offered me her unwavering support, both academically and personally. She warned me that although my topic could initially remain private, dissertation topics become very public later on in the process through program-wide presentations. I decided to continue with the project in the hope that my coming-out process and research project might inform each other.

With encouragement from a mentor, I signed up to participate in an Orthodox LGBT speakers' training in May 2011, whose purpose was to prepare people to tell their stories in Orthodox spaces. Although I had not yet come out to my parents and was not quite ready to speak publicly, I still attended the training. In a sharing circle at the end of the training, I broke down in tears, feeling terrible, freakish, and underdeveloped. I didn't feel like I belonged with this seasoned group of LGBT Orthodox Jews who were comfortable with themselves and with others knowing who they were, since I was still working on those issues. The fact that I was considering speaking in public without yet telling my parents that I was gay made me feel tremendously guilty, and I realized I had a long way to go.

A few weeks after this training, I informed my dissertation chair—the supportive supervisor mentioned earlier—that I did not feel ready to write about my gay identity and endure the public exposure and possible scrutiny that I would be subject to when the dissertation topic became public. He supported my decision, and thus I started from scratch with a new topic, writing a literature review for a dissertation in which I planned to create a psychoanalytic conceptualization of ADHD. This proved to be a difficult task, however, since my motivation really lay elsewhere.

By the end of the summer I had moved out of my parents' home and was immersed in a new routine involving an externship and classes. But the transition was painful, as evidenced by panic attacks and an inability to relax. I was in a new living space with a new roommate and doing a new commute to a new externship with a new supervisor. In therapy, I spent a few sessions crying intensely out of sheer panic and then getting angry, saying that I left the previous session feeling like my therapist had cut me open and left my guts hanging out. Every minor stressor seemed like the end of the world during this period. I called my mother in tears almost nightly and, following attachment theory, went back to my parents' home frequently to make contact with my secure base. I knew that I had moved out so that I could take on more of my gay identity. I wanted to attend events and socialize with other gay people without worrying about what my parents might suspect or, God forbid, find out. Nonetheless, I did not feel free.

FREE AT LAST

On one of my visits home in the fall, as we were talking at the kitchen table, my mother astutely remarked, "I'm missing something here. I'm missing the key to the whole thing," referring to my difficult adjustment from having moved out and frequent panicked calls to her.

"You are missing something," I acknowledged. "I wouldn't say that it is the key, but, yes, you are missing something."

The next day in therapy I said that I was thinking of coming out to my mother. I was careful to tell my therapist not to give his opinion because I wanted to make the decision on my own. I went home immediately after the session and sat down with my mom again.

"Mom, there is something I haven't told you because I was afraid of your reaction." I said. "I wanted to let you know that I'm gay."

She paused. "I still love you," she assured me.

A long, meaningful conversation followed, and I felt relieved and hopeful and stayed over that night.

Two days later in therapy I decided to put my father in the loop. Once again in my parents' house, I sat next to my father in the family room and told him the same thing.

"I'm still proud of you," my father replied, and a pleasant conversation followed. Before going to sleep in my own apartment that night, I told the one remaining brother who also offered a similarly positive response. As I put my head on the pillow that night I no longer feared my parents' finding out my secret from somebody other than me. There was no more secret. I went to sleep knowing that I was still loved.

The next day I had a meeting with my dissertation advisor.

"I came out to my parents last night," I said. "I think I would like to go back to my original topic."

"Wow!" he remarked, "How did that go?"

"It went well. It could not have gone better."

"Great!" he said. "Still, it's too soon to make this big decision. Please think about it and let me know."

I thought about it and reached the same conclusion. I decided to pursue my original dissertation topic.

MY CLASS AND MY PROGRAM

In October 2011, I wrote a required paper, which I presented to my class, about how cultural differences and similarities between myself and a client impacted treatment. I decided to finally own my identity and come out to my class. The paper was about the treatment of the Mormon client discussed earlier. I had grown very close to many of my peers in almost three years of training. About half of them already knew I was gay. Nonetheless, I had never come out to a predominantly straight audience. In front of the class, my muscles tensed and I developed a lump in my throat. I presented the case and then, as I moved on to discuss the similarity/difference component of the treatment, I uttered the words, "I am gay." Apparently, at least one classmate teared up, and I got loads of support after, including many hugs. With each coming-out experience I felt more complete, accepted, and hopeful.

In March 2012, my classmates presented their dissertation proposals to the faculty and student bodies. I prepared my slides in advance, and I was ready to present my topic and myself in the allotted five minutes. Although I was close with my class and some of the faculty, the audience encompassed many people who did not know me at all. When I came to the slide about personal biases and theoretical framework, I said, "As a gay Orthodox Jew, I come to this project with a range of unique perspectives." After my presentation, I received many compliments and much support from students and faculty alike.

OBSERVATIONS AND ANALYSIS

Gay people come out of the closet, both to themselves and others, at different ages. The trend, however, is to come out at increasingly younger ages (Pew Research Center, 2013). As is the case in the clinical and personal domains, timing is a major factor that influences outcome. I attended religious institutions most of my life. I studied in Orthodox Jewish day school from nursery through high school. After graduating high school, I spent a year and a half in the Old City of Jerusalem studying in a religious institution. Even when I went to a liberal, Jewish university, I involved myself in Orthodox Jewish life and became the president of the Orthodox organization on campus, limiting my opportunities for personal growth in the area of sexuality. My acceptance to the clinical psychology doctoral program at LIU Post, which has an orientation toward public interest and social justice, was fortuitous. For the first time in my life, I was part of a community that strove to respect individual differences and foster personal growth in the ways I needed. Although I cannot speak about other programs, the program at LIU Post viewed students' openness about themselves and their countertransference as valuable opportunities for professional growth.

Still, this process was hardly comfortable for me. Specifically, my perception was that openness and acceptance had its limitations. If a student's struggle was more in the past than the present, then it was welcome. For example, a student who had recovered from a gambling addiction might be invited to speak about how her past informed her work as a budding clinician. However, a student who disclosed his current obsessive-compulsive behaviors was viewed with more concern and judgment. Although being gay is neither a disorder nor a behavioral problem, coming out of the closet is a developmental task increasingly completed during adolescence. My perception was that coming out was something that I should have completed before graduate school. Thus, I felt immature, delayed, and behind my peers. The challenge of coming out in graduate school was partially due to the fact that I was wrestling through a piece of my identity development that I felt should have been completed before I was helping patients. It would be helpful for doctoral faculty and supervisors to promote openness and reflection on program cultural norms so that students are encouraged to share their current personal challenges. The personal difficulties of students should not be equated with professional impairment.

Nonetheless, some components of my experience were unnecessarily uncomfortable. First, it is important to discuss the place of religion in clinical psychology training programs. In my view, religion is insufficiently and inadequately discussed. Nancy McWilliams (2004) was concerned about her use of the word "faith" to describe a "gut level confidence" in the psychoanalytic process for "fear of offending readers who are uncomfortable with a term so rooted in religious and theological discourse" (p. 42). McWilliams's fear of causing discomfort by speaking about religion is shared by many psychologists. For instance, Lew Aron (2004) saw religion and God as taboo in the psychoanalytic community. Omitting conversation about religion and God from professional training prevents students from gaining competency in this important area of cultural diversity.

As mentioned earlier, I believe that faculty members, and perhaps students as well, saw me for the yarmulke I wore to the exclusion of other possible parts of my identity. Most people assumed I was straight and antigay based on my religious attire. This was probably the most frustrating aspect of my experience. Psychologists should know better than to hold such assumptions without checking and programs should do better at looking for the complex identities of their students, as this will certainly model good clinical work.

It is important to note that all of the faculty and peers mentioned in this chapter are individuals with whom I share strong, positive relationships—both personal and professional. I do not believe any of them ever intended to make me feel marginalized or hurt. Still, whether it was pointing out otherizing in defense of LGBT people or trying to create a welcoming presence for an LGBT therapy group, well-intended comments were hurtful. Having said that, it is unfair to paint these interactions as purely harmful. Each instance of marginalization motivated me to consciously explore my identity and eventually share it with others. Regarding the interactions I have described, it is hard to assess to what extent they provided a motivating discomfort and to what extent they caused unnecessary pain.

As it turns out, what we were told at orientation was true. I have changed—and grown by leaps and bounds. The young man who entered graduate school as a closeted, politically conservative, and religiously orthodox person graduated as an openly gay, politically complex, and still religiously committed man. My personal journey informs my views of politics, social justice, ethics, and religion. My process also continues to enhance my academic and clinical work. Most important, however, my world view has evolved, along with my sensitivity to those who are different or do not fit in.

During graduate school, I came to assist with admissions interviews. Over the course of the day, I answered applicants' questions between their interviews with faculty members. One of my favorite selling points for my program was the culture. I would say: "There is a palpable family feel here. We're like one big family." And I believe that to be the case. Like any family, relationships and interactions are not always perfect, but they are unavoidably intimate. I am grateful to have had the opportunity to be a part of my training program, which supported me throughout my unique coming-out process.

NOTE

Names and identifying data were changed to disguise the identity of the persons involved.

REFERENCES

Aron, L. (2004). God's influence on my psychoanalytic vision and values. *Psychoanalytic Psychology, 21*(3), 442-451.

McWilliams, N. (2004). *Psychoanalytic psychotherapy: A practitioner's guide.* New York, NY: Guilford Press.

Pew Research Center. (2013). *A survey of LGBT Americans: Attitudes, experiences and values in changing times.* Retrieved from http://www.pewsocialtrends.org/2013/06/13/a-survey-of-lgbt-americans/

Index

Index

About the Contributors

Adi Avivi is originally from Israel. Since earning her PsyD from Long Island University, C. W. Post, in 2013, she has been completing her postdoctoral training at Long Island Jewish Hospital in Glen Oaks, New York. She lives with her partner in Brooklyn, New York.

Brianna Blake is a fifth-year clinical psychology doctoral student at Long Island University,C. W. Post Campus, with training in the treatment of serious mental illness. Prior to entering the doctoral program, Brianna assisted with research on obsessive-compulsive and eating disorders while completing her master's degree at Boston University. She has researched and professionally presented on the topics of post-traumatic stress disorder, traumatic loss, and eating disorders and plans to specialize in the treatment of eating disorders.

Silvia Fiammenghi is originally from Pavia, Italy, where she became licensed as a psychologist in 2006. She earned her PsyD from Long Island University, C. W. Post Campus, in 2012, after completing her internship at Bronx Psychiatric Center. She is currently working as the staff psychologist for New York University in Florence, Italy, where she lives with her husband and three cats. She is the author of a short novel in Italian (*O come Obesa*) and peer-reviewed papers. Her clinical interests include cross-cultural psychology, the treatment of severe mental illness, and study-abroad college counseling.

Benjamin Gottesman, originally from New Jersey, earned his doctorate from Long Island University, C. W. Post Campus, in 2014 and completed his clinical internship at Woodhull Medical Center in Brooklyn. Since graduating, he has been working as a psychologist at the Clear View School, a special education school and day-treatment program in Westchester, New York. He and his wife Rachael live in Manhattan and enjoy playing Ultimate Frisbee.

Noel Hunter is a clinical psychology doctoral student at Long Island University, C. W. Post Campus. She has published and presented papers on the link between trauma and various anomalous states, stigma and negative attitudes toward patients as they relate to therapists' personal experiences of extreme emotional difficulties, and the need for recognition of states of extreme distress as meaningful responses to overwhelming life experiences. Currently, Noel is working with a group of dedicated individuals to expand the Hearing Voices Network in New York City and is also beginning her dissertation— for which she is interviewing individuals who have experienced severe dissociative phenomena.

Dustin Kahoud is originally from Garden City, New York, and received his PsyD from Long Island University, C. W. Post Campus, in September, 2014. He is also a credentialed alcoholism and substance abuse counselor (CA-SAC) and teaches courses on addictions in undergraduate and graduate programs at Adelphi University. Dustin has a background in creative writing and continues to write about the relationship between creativity and substance abuse. He currently specializes in the treatment of addictions at Nassau Alternative Counseling Center and lives with his wife and son in Roslyn Heights, New York.

Kathleen Kallstrom-Schreckengost earned her PsyD from Long Island University, C. W. Post Campus, in 2013 and completed her internship and postdoctoral fellowship at Fordham University and Montclair State University Counseling and Psychological Services, respectively. She currently works at Arbor Family Counseling Services, a group practice in her hometown of Omaha, Nebraska, where she lives with her wife, son, and three destructive yet lovable cats.

Robert Keisner has been a practicing psychologist and psychoanalyst for many years. He is the founder and former director of the clinical psychology doctoral program at Long Island University, C. W. Post Campus, whose central mission is to train professional psychologists to promote social justice by providing services to underserved populations. As founder of the clinical psychology program, he received the American Psychological Association Presidential Citation award for promoting psychology in the public interest. Professor Keisner served as chairperson of the New York State Board of Psychology, teaches ethics and public interest psychology and serves as a clinical supervisor in the program. He has been involved in the asylum process, conducting interviews for Healthright International for over seven years.

Danielle Knafo is a professor in the clinical psychology doctoral program at Long Island University, C. W. Post Campus, where she chairs a concentration on Serious Mental Illness (SMI). She is also an adjunct clinical professor and supervisor in New York University's program for psychotherapy and psychoanalysis. She is a practicing clinical psychologist, psychoanalyst, and author of five books and dozens of articles. She has written and lectured extensively on psychoanalysis, creativity, trauma, and gender. Her latest book is *Dancing with the Unconscious: The Art of Psychoanalysis and the Psychoanalysis of Art*. She maintains a private practice in Great Neck and New York City.

Shoshana Lawrence is originally from Long Island, New York. She earned her PsyD from Long Island University, C. W. Post Campus, in 2008, after which she completed a two-year postdoctoral fellowship at the William Alanson White Institute in New York City. She is currently in private practice in Hewlett, New York, and serves as an adjunct faculty member at C. W. Post. Shoshana resides in Long Island with her husband and children.

Matthew Liebman is originally from Fair Lawn, New Jersey. He is a fifth-year doctoral candidate completing his pre-doctoral internship at Montefiore Medical Center in the Bronx, New York, and intends to continue serving the New York/New Jersey communities after graduating. He currently lives in New Jersey with his wife and works full-time as a professional musician. Matthew's doctoral research was a clinical trial examining the impact of fast-paced television on children with ADHD. He intends to continue his research as he expands his specialization in child and adolescent treatment.

Jeremy Novich is currently a postdoctoral fellow in Student Counseling and Disability Services at Stevens Institute of Technology in Hoboken, New Jersey. He earned his doctorate from Long Island University, C. W. Post Campus, in 2014. Jeremy's clinical interests include psychodynamic and group therapy with a focus on college students and LGBT individuals.

Adjoa Osei obtained her PsyD from the clinical psychology program at Long Island University, C. W. Post Campus, in 2014. She completed her internship at Woodhull Medical Center and hopes to continue working with underserved populations. She is an active member of the New York chapter of the Association of Black Psychologists and continues to participate in analytic psychotherapy. She considers both of these activities to be an integral part of her ongoing professional development.

Ian Rugg is originally from New York, New York. Since earning his PsyD from Long Island University, C. W. Post Campus, in 2013, he has been working as a psychologist for the New York City Police Department. He will soon be licensed in New York State and hopes to work in a hospital setting and develop a part-time private practice. He lives in Brooklyn, New York, with his fiancée.